The Vietnam Experience

The North

by Edward Doyle, Samuel Lipsman, Terrence Maitland,
and the editors of Boston Publishing Company

Boston Publishing Company/Boston, MA

Boston Publishing Company

President and Publisher: Robert J. George
Vice President: Richard S. Perkins, Jr.
Editor-in-Chief: Robert Manning
Managing Editor: Paul Dreyfus
Marketing Director: Jeanne Gibson

Senior Writers:
Clark Dougan, Edward Doyle, David Fulghum, Samuel Lipsman, Terrence Maitland, Stephen Weiss
Senior Picture Editor: Julene Fischer
Senior Editor: Gordon Hardy

Staff Writer: Denis Kennedy
Researchers:
Richard J. Burke, Steven W. Lipari, Anthony Maybury-Lewis, Nicholas Philipson, Janice Sue Wang, Robert Yarbrough

Picture Editors:
Wendy Johnson, Kathleen A. Reidy, Lanng Tamura
Picture Researchers:
Lauren Chapin, Robert Ebbs, Tracey Rogers, Nana Elisabeth Stern, Shirley L. Green (Washington, D.C.), Kate Lewin (Paris)
Archivist: Kathryn J. Steeves
Picture Department Assistant: Rebecca Black

Production Editor: Patricia Leal Welch
Editorial Production:
Dalia Lipkin, Elizabeth Campbell Peters, Theresa M. Slomkowski

Design: Designworks, Sally Bindari
Design Assistant: Diana Maloney

Business Staff: Amy Pelletier, Amy P. Wilson

About the editors and authors

Editor-in-Chief *Robert Manning*, a long-time journalist, has previously been editor-in-chief of the *Atlantic Monthly* magazine and its press. He served as assistant secretary of state for public affairs under Presidents John F. Kennedy and Lyndon B. Johnson. He has also been a fellow at the Institute of Politics at the John F. Kennedy School of Government at Harvard University.

Authors: *Edward Doyle*, a historian, received his masters degree at the University of Notre Dame and his Ph.D. at Harvard University. *Samuel Lipsman*, a former Fulbright Scholar, received his M.A. and M.Phil. in history at Yale. *Terrence Maitland* has written for several publications, including *Newsweek* magazine and the *Boston Globe*. He is a graduate of Holy Cross College and has an M.S. from Boston University. Messrs. Doyle, Lipsman, and Maitland have coauthored other volumes in *The Vietnam Experience*.

Historical Consultants: Nayan Chanda served as Indochina correspondent for the *Far Eastern Economic Review* between 1974 and 1980. Currently, he is Washington correspondent for the *Review*. His book, *Brother Enemy*, covers Vietnam's post-1975 war. *Lee Ewing*, editor of *Army Times*, served two years in Vietnam as a combat intelligence officer with the U.S. Military Assistance Command, Vietnam (MACV) and the 101st Airborne Division.

Picture Consultant: Ngo Vinh Long is a social historian specializing in China and Vietnam. Born in Vietnam, he returned there most recently in 1980. His books include *Before the Revolution: The Vietnamese Peasants Under the French* and *Report From a Vietnamese Village*.

Cover Photo:

Tet 1968. With a heavy machine gun team offering covering fire, Communist soldiers press an attack in South Vietnam. The surprise offensive of Tet Mau Than (the Year of the Monkey) was a major turning point in the war.

Library of Congress Catalog Card Number: 86-70769

ISBN: 0-939526-21-2

10 9 8 7 6
5 4 3 2 1

Contents

Chapter 1/The Brink of War   14

Chapter 2/A Race Against Time   38

Chapter 3/Fortress North Vietnam   68

Chapter 4/Mobilizing the Home Front   94

Chapter 5/The North Takes Over   118

Chapter 6/The Road to Saigon   146

Chapter 7/The Fruits of Victory   162

Chronology   188

Names, Acronyms, Terms   192

Picture Essays
The Long Revolution   6
Ho Chi Minh Trail   62
Easter Offensive   138
A Restive Peace   178

Sidebars
The People's Intelligence   26
Watching Hanoi   30
Modernizing PAVN   54
Vietnam's Veterans   100
The Other Psywar   108
Truong Chinh: Hanoi's Hard-Liner   126

Maps
North Vietnam   4
Infiltration Routes   5
Political/Military Command Structure   44

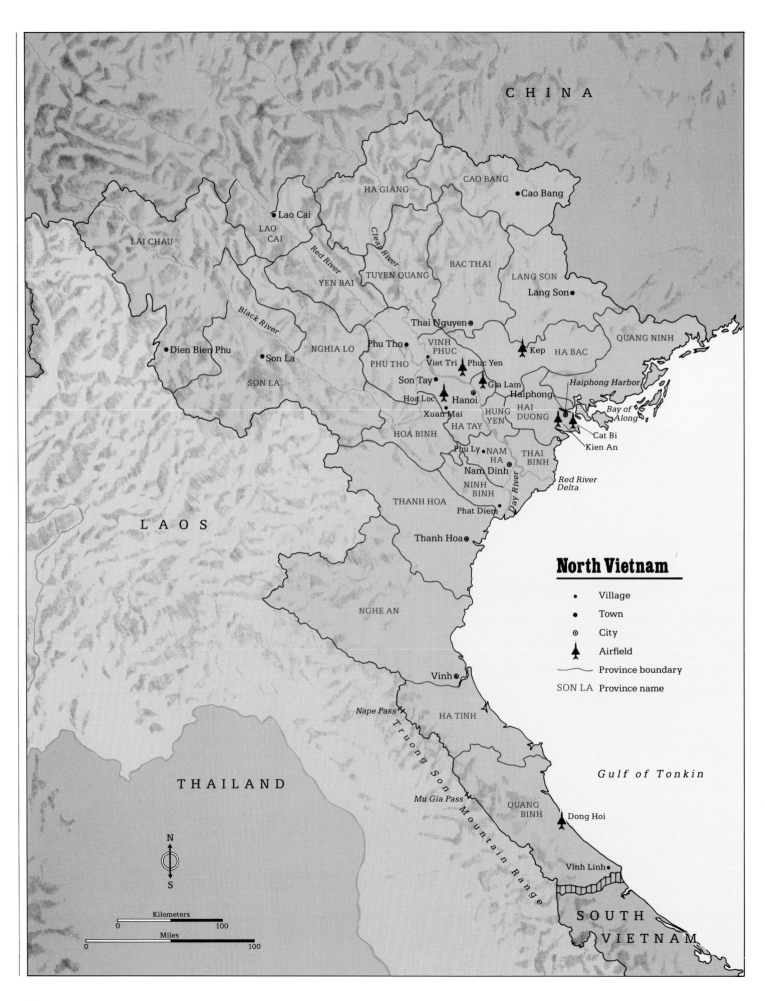

C H I N A

CAO BANG

HA GIANG

• Cao Bang

• Lao Cai

LAO
CAI

LAI CHAU

Clear River

BAC THAI

LANG SON

Red River

TUYEN QUANG

YEN BAI

Lang Son •

Black River

NGHIA LO

Thai Nguyen ◉

QUANG NINH

• Dien Bien Phu

• Son La

Phu Tho •

VINH
PHUC

Kep

HA BAC

SON LA

PHU THO

Viet Tri •

Phuc Yen

Haiphong Harbor

Son Tay •

Gia Lam

Haiphong

*Bay of
Along*

Hoa Loc

Hanoi ◉

HAI
DUONG

HUNG
YEN

Cat Bi

Xuan Mai •

Kien An

HA TAY

Phu Ly •

NAM
HA

THAI
BINH

HOA BINH

• Nam Dinh ◉

NINH
BINH

*Red River
Delta*

Day River

THANH HOA

Phat Diem •

Thanh Hoa ◉

North Vietnam

- •   Village
- •   Town
- ◉   City
- ♠   Airfield
- ⌇   Province boundary
- SON LA   Province name

L A O S

NGHE AN

Vinh ◉

Nape Pass

HA TINH

Gulf of Tonkin

T H A I L A N D

Mu Gia Pass

Truong Son Mountain Range

QUANG
BINH

Dong Hoi

N

S

Vinh Linh •

Kilometers

0   100

Miles

0   100

S O U T H

V I E T N A M

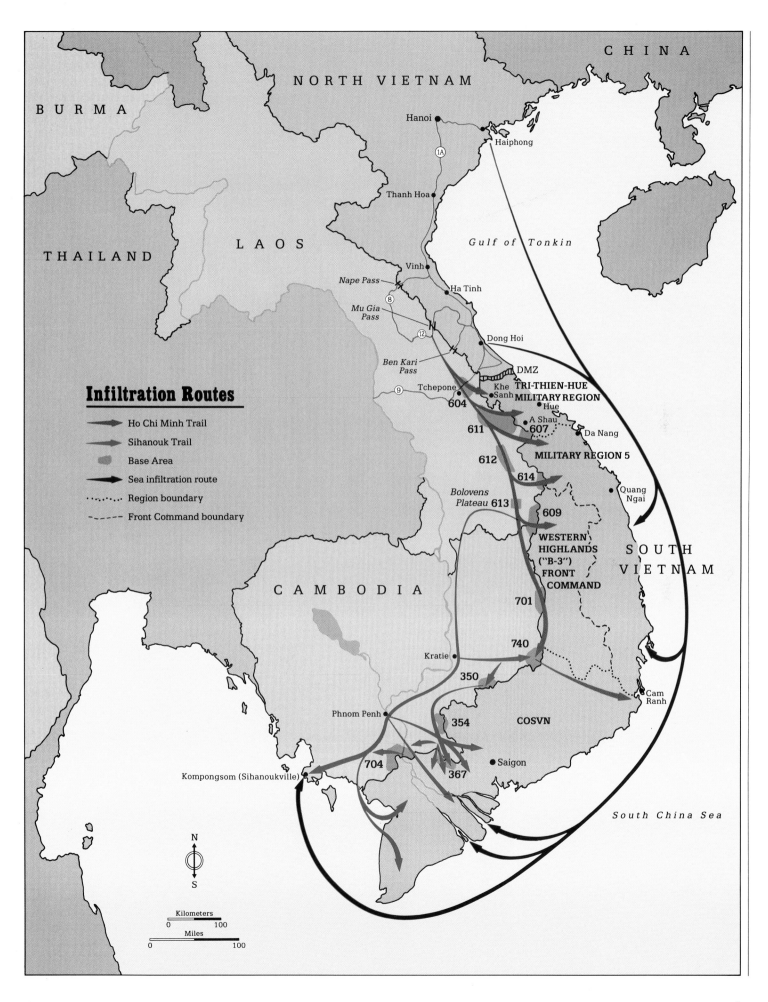

CHINA

NORTH VIETNAM

Hanoi

Haiphong

1A

Thanh Hoa

LAOS

Gulf of Tonkin

THAILAND

BURMA

Vinh

Nape Pass

Ha Tinh

8

Mu Gia
Pass

12

Dong Hoi

Ben Kari
Pass

DMZ

9

Tchepone

Khe
Sanh

TRI-THIEN-HUE
MILITARY REGION

604

Hue

611

A Shau

607

Da Nang

612

MILITARY REGION 5

614

Bolovens
Plateau

613

609

Quang
Ngai

WESTERN
HIGHLANDS
("B-3")
FRONT
COMMAND

SOUTH
VIETNAM

701

740

Kratie

350

Cam
Ranh

CAMBODIA

354

COSVN

704

Phnom Penh

367

Saigon

Kompongsom (Sihanoukville)

South China Sea

Infiltration Routes

- Ho Chi Minh Trail
- Sihanouk Trail
- Base Area
- Sea infiltration route
- ⋯⋯ Region boundary
- ----- Front Command boundary

N
S

Kilometers
0   100

Miles
0   100

5

The Long Revolution

In the service of their revolution the Vietnamese Communists employed some of the world's most modern political techniques as well as some of Vietnam's oldest. Lacquer painting is a traditional Vietnamese art form with a distinguished history spanning almost two millennia. It experienced a renaissance in the North after 1954 as the Communists applied this craft to political propaganda. On the following pages, striking contemporary examples of this age-old medium document the history of a modern guerrilla war.

When the Communist party of Vietnam initiated a well-organized insurgency against the Southern government of Ngo Dinh Diem in the late 1950s, its leaders knew that the villages of the lowlands would be the critical battleground. Communists made the Mekong Delta region a major target of their efforts. As portrayed here, guerrillas moved with relative safety during the darkness of night in order to summon new recruits and plan their next ambush.

"Night March" by Nguyen Hiem (1958).

Special War

Within a few years the guerrillas had gained political momentum and military victories. The United States responded by substantially increasing the number of advisers operating with South Vietnamese military units. The National Liberation Front, the political arm of the insurgency, developed a new propaganda theme. Calling the U.S. involvement "imperialist aggression," the NLF labeled it a "special war" because South Vietnamese troops still did most of the fighting. The NLF sought to organize popular opinion against the new foreign foe. As depicted here in highly romanticized fashion, the Communists saw the South Vietnamese population confronting and destroying the American-led South Vietnamese troops.

"The Heart and the Gun" by Huynh Van Gam (1963).

The PAVN Offensive

In the aftermath of the Communist Easter offensive of 1972 launched by conventional North Vietnamese forces in three areas of South Vietnam, it was no longer possible for the North to maintain that its own troops from the People's Army of Vietnam (PAVN) were not engaged in South Vietnam. Instead, as portrayed here, they considered PAVN to be the "liberator" of the Southern population. Backed by modern Soviet and Chinese armored tanks and heavy artillery, the products of a rapid modernization, the North Vietnamese troops were every bit the match for the heavily U.S.-supplied South Vietnamese army.

"Meeting" by Duong Vien (1973).

To Rebuild a Nation

The ten-year war against the Americans and South Vietnamese left Vietnam a ravaged nation. In the North, U.S. bombing heavily damaged six industrial cities and thirty-two towns and obliterated the transportation network—roads, bridges, railways, and ports. The 1976-1980 five-year economic plan set ambitious and, as it turned out, unrealistic goals for postwar reconstruction. Before increases in food production or industry could be achieved, Vietnam had to rebuild its ruined infrastructure, including bombed-out roads, pipelines, and ports. Reconstruction of the shipping industry was also critical. The Bach Dang shipyard near Haiphong was heavily damaged during the 1972 U.S. Christmas bombing but is portrayed here as fully operational just three years later.

"Bach Dang Shipyard" by Nguyen Van Chu (1975).

The Brink of War

It was mid-1955 when the last of almost 90,000 former Vietminh soldiers in the South boarded a boat for regroupment in North Vietnam as required by the Geneva accords of 1954. They were joined by a handful of leading civilians—political leaders Communist party officials believed would be more usefully employed in the North. One of them was the man known to his Southern compatriots as Anh Ba, Brother Ba. Anh Ba boarded the ship, and tears filled his eyes as he bid good-bye to the Southerners whom he had led throughout most of the war of resistance against French rule. But Anh Ba never sailed to North Vietnam. Once on board, he waited for the cover of midnight's darkness to slip into a sampan waiting for him at the boat's side. He eventually made his way to the Cau Mau Peninsula, at the southernmost tip of Vietnam, where he could find safety and anonymity in the Communist redoubt in the U Minh Forest. Anh Ba, the code name for the Communist leader Le Duan, had

been ordered by the party to remain in the South and lead the Southern Communists through the most difficult period of their existence.

The life of a revolutionary

Le Duan had come a long way since his birth in 1908 in Quang Tri, which in 1954 became the northernmost province of South Vietnam. Little is known of the early years of his life, but Le Duan maintains that as a youth he was moved by the condition of his countrymen. "This is why I joined the Communists," he later told a journalist.

One day my poor mother was cracking rice to separate the bran from it. She was surrounded by other poor people who were so hungry that whenever she had separated enough bran from the rice they would reach out, grab the bran, and eat it dry on the spot. Hungry as they were, they were still honest enough not to touch her meager rice ration. It is the system that was wrong, not the people.

Le Duan's parents, like most Vietnamese peasants at that time, lived in poverty, but they provided their son with some advanced education. When young Le Duan migrated to Hanoi in his late teens, he gained employment as a clerk in the national railway, a position that required some literacy. In Hanoi he came into contact with the most radical nationalist thought of the day. He became an early recruit of Ho Chi Minh's Revolutionary Youth League, the first Marxist organization in Vietnam, and in 1930 a charter member of the Indochinese Communist party.

Le Duan was arrested in 1931 for revolutionary agitation and spent five years in the infamous Poulo Condore prison, where he earned the respect and friendship of high-ranking party officials such as Pham Van Dong. He faced fifteen more years of prison when the French government declared a general amnesty in 1936. In the more liberal atmosphere of the years just prior to World War II, Le Duan opened a bookstore in Hue to disseminate party propaganda. A year later the party recalled him to his home province, where he rose to province party secretary.

When war in Europe erupted in 1939, the French government outlawed the Communist party, and Le Duan began a new underground existence as a member of the Central Committee for Nam Bo, as the Communists called the Mekong Delta region. When France surrendered to Nazi Germany in early 1940, the Nam Bo committee, effectively cut off from communication with the party headquarters in the North, decided to strike on its own. A badly mangled coup in Saigon led to the decimation of the Southern Communists, a blow from which they never entirely recovered, and another prison sentence for Le Duan, who was then thirty-two.

Released from prison after the Communist August revolution of 1945, Le Duan quickly assumed a leading role in the organization resisting the recently restored French rule in the South. When the Lao Dong, the Communist party of Vietnam, established the first Central Office for South Vietnam (COSVN), Le Duan assumed command of all Vietminh forces in the South. Among his lieutenants were two men who were to become lifelong allies and colleagues on the Communist Political Bureau, Pham Hung and Le Duc Tho. Pham, like Le Duan, was a native Southerner, born in the Mekong Delta. Tho, although a native of the North, gained his primary revolutionary experience serving in the South. The trio would become the staunchest advocates of the Southern cause in the party Political Bureau—the party's executive committee also known as the Politburo.

All three were deeply disappointed by the results of the Geneva conference in 1954, which ended the French-Indochina War and provisionally divided the country at the seventeenth parallel. Le Duan went so far as to castigate the party leadership in public for its "betrayal of the Southern cause."

"Our darkest hour"

When the peace of Geneva arrived in Vietnam in July 1954, neither Ho Chi Minh nor the other leaders of the Lao Dong party in the North believed that they had betrayed the South. In fact, they were certain that it would be only a short time before they would reach their long-sought goal: the reunification of their country. The Geneva accords called for elections throughout Indochina by July 1956. Some Western observers have since suggested that Ho Chi Minh never believed that those elections would be held. There is evidence to support that conjecture because the Communists never believed that the newly installed government of Ngo Dinh Diem in the South would survive those two years. Rather, they expected the collapse of Diem's rule and political chaos leading to, at worst, a coalition government and eventual reunification. Whether by electoral success or by taking advantage of the South's chaotic political environment, as the *Pentagon Papers* later analyzed Lao Dong strategy, reunification would be inevitable and achievable by peaceful means.

In accordance with these scenarios, the party instructed its members in the South to struggle for "personal rights, freedom and negotiations concerning general elections ... so that the country could be peacefully reunited." The Sixth Plenum of the party's Central Committee advised the Southerners in July 1954 to be "as self-contained and self-supporting as possible so as not to drain away vital northern resources."

In executing these instructions as well as the requirements of the Geneva accords, most of the approximately 87,000 armed Vietminh loyalists in the South regrouped to

Preceding page. "Regroupees," Vietminh sent North after the Geneva accords of 1954, prepare to disembark from a ship that carried them to North Vietnam from the South.

North Vietnam along with a small number of civilians. The regroupees, as they became known, totaled 90,000.

Not all of the regroupees came North with their weapons. Many left them buried in the South in order to rearm small detachments of former resistance fighters. These armed guerrillas—probably not exceeding 3,000 or 4,000—reopened five ex-Vietminh base areas deep in the Mekong Delta and near the Cambodian border. The rest of the party members were told to go about their normal business and to conduct what Americans might call precinct-level political organizing. The majority conducted their political propagandizing in Saigon and other urban centers, the key areas in any elections or to a peaceful reunification of the country.

Le Duan, meanwhile, had reportedly "lost faith in political struggle" and wanted the Diem regime "forcibly overthrown." His sentiment was widely shared by the Southerners, and Le Duan personally took that message to the Central Committee's Ninth Plenum in 1956. But the Central Committee rejected his appeal. To close discussion of any change in party policy Ho Chi Minh told the regroupees in North Vietnam:

To build a good house, we must build a strong foundation. ... The North is the foundation, the root of the struggle for complete national liberation and the reunification of the country. Our policy is to consolidate the North and to keep in mind the South.

Up to now, Diem had not devoted much energy to fight-

Since COSVN's primary responsibility had been to coordinate military activities throughout the country, the Lao Dong party closed this southern office in 1955. Henceforth the two southern regions, Nam Bo in the delta area and Trung Bo in the south-central portion of the country (running roughly from Quang Tri to Da Lat), maintained independent party committees, each reporting directly to the Central Committee in Hanoi.

As Le Duan directed all of these changes from the safety of the U Minh Forest, he could not have been pleased with the developments inside South Vietnam. Diem had succeeded against all odds in consolidating his regime. As the July 1956 deadline for elections approached and passed, North Vietnamese Prime Minister Pham Van Dong sent off a series of letters to Diem demanding consultations for planning elections. Securely ensconced in office, Diem was not answering his mail. The scenarios outlined so confidently by the Lao Dong party in 1954 were but castles in the sand.

Le Duan (far left) and Le Duc Tho (far right) preside over a clandestine meeting of COSVN's Executive Committee held in the Mekong Delta during the French-Indochina War. (Despite the strong resemblance, the man in the center is not Ho Chi Minh. Ho never traveled to the South.)

ing the Communists. A strongly worded Communist policy prohibiting violence on the part of party members, even in self-defense, was an invitation to him. It left the anti-government resistance easy prey for Diem as he moved to counter the last, and most dangerous, threat to his regime. As late as 1956 U.S. officials estimated that from 60 to 90 percent of all South Vietnamese villages not controlled by the religious sects were dominated by Communists. With the elections deadline past, Diem moved with fury to regain control of the countryside. In August 1956 he proclaimed Ordinance Number 47, which made any activity on behalf of any organization designated as "Communist" punishable by death. In order to carry out the ordinance,

Diem organized a broad "Communist Denunciation" campaign, probably one of the two gravest errors of his administration.

Under the campaign every person in South Vietnam was rated by local government officials according to his or her standing as a security risk. The standard was participation in the Vietminh resistance. The category was much too broad, since many of the former Vietminh were not actually Communists or sympathetic to their cause. To make matters worse, Diem also rated individuals according to their family connections with former Vietminh, leaving even apolitical peasants living in fear for their lives.

The Communists suffered severe losses from this campaign. According to a Communist document later captured by American forces, "hundreds of thousands of cadres and people were arrested or massacred." In An Xuyen Province one five-week campaign netted nearly 50,000 "Communists" and their sympathizers. In Tay Ninh Province, long a Communist stronghold, 90 percent of the party cells were destroyed. As the captured document recounted:

Many voices among the masses appealed to the Party to establish a program of armed resistance. In several areas the Party members on their own initiative had organized armed struggle against the enemy. But the leadership of the Nam Bo Regional Committee at that time still hesitated for many reasons but the principal reason was the fear of violating the Party line.

It was Le Duan's objective as head of the Nam Bo committee to change that party line. In December 1956, as he again prepared to make the long and secret trip to Hanoi in the hope of effecting a policy change, Le Duan set down his thoughts in a pamphlet, *The Path of the Revolution in the South*. On the surface Le Duan's tract was a ringing affirmation of existing party policy. "All current international conflicts," he wrote, "can be resolved by peaceful negotiations; the revolutionary movement in various countries can develop peacefully." It went on to point out that the revolutionary forces in South Vietnam were, in any case, too weak to conduct armed struggle. What was needed, he concluded, was "a period of intense political activity in order to rebuild the revolutionary movement in the South." Implicit in this proposal, however, was the possibility of using this revitalized movement to build an armed force.

Le Duan traveled to Hanoi in early 1957 to address the Central Committee. The Central Committee, following the lead of an earlier secret Political Bureau meeting, endorsed the policy outlined in *The Path*, since it involved no substantial change from previous party statements regarding military action. The party, however, did allow for an important change. Certain agents of the party were now permitted to "punish enemies and exterminate traitors." This was the signal for a campaign of violence, one that was carried out subtly, with all possible secrecy. Rank and file party members were kept ignorant of the campaign, lest they be led to believe that a policy of general violence had been declared.

The time could not have been riper for the Communists to step up their activities. Not only had the arbitrary and reckless execution of the "denunciation" campaign stirred wide resentment among the rural population but Diem had compounded the error with his second grave mistake, his very restrictive land-reform program, which, in effect, returned to landlords land distributed to the peasants by the Vietminh. The combination of the Diem government's severe political repression and increasing peasant misery made it easy for the Communists to recruit followers and organize them. The Southern party, while disappointed that the Central Committee still refused to endorse a program of armed struggle, now had on the Political Bureau as a new member and acting first party secretary one of their own, Le Duan.

Comrade party secretary

Le Duan must have received the good news upon his arrival in Hanoi. Truong Chinh had been forced to resign his long-time position as first party secretary in the wake of the disastrous land-reform program carried out in his name in the North. Ho Chi Minh assumed Chinh's former title but asked Le Duan to assume most of the responsibilities. Le Duan was joined on the Political Bureau by Pham Hung, his long-time colleague in Nam Bo.

The ascendancy of these two men was undoubtedly the work of Ho Chi Minh. Ho's participation in intraparty debates was seldom clear. Most observers believe that he remained in the background, letting his "experts" argue policy alternatives. Ho established the goals of the party; the Political Bureau determined the best means to carry them out. Thus his influence was subtle, but in promoting Le Duan and Pham Hung he must have known that he was shifting the center of gravity within the ruling body southward. Le Duan and Pham Hung joined Pham Van Dong and General Nguyen Chi Thanh, both southern natives, and Le Duc Tho, their former COSVN colleague, to give those with a "southern orientation" at least five of the eleven slots in the Political Bureau. Ho was probably signaling a willingness to adopt a new policy toward the South, giving Southerners the decisive voice in the newly constituted Lao Dong Political Bureau. A major shift in Communist tactics, implied by the acceptance of Le Duan's *The Path of the Revolution*, now seemed imminent.

While this inner-party shuffle was under way, in the fall of 1957, Ho Chi Minh chose Le Duan to accompany him to Moscow to celebrate the fortieth anniversary of the Bolshevik revolution and attend the Conference of Communist and Workers' Parties of Socialist Countries. The Vietnamese Lao Dong party had already displayed its displeasure with the direction in which new Soviet leader Nikita Khrushchev was taking the world Communist movement.

In 1956 Khrushchev had opened the era of "peaceful coexistence" with a speech announcing that "peaceful competition" was the "only way open to us." Within days Ho Chi Minh had made public his dissent:

In countries where the machinery of state, the armed forces, and the police of the bourgeois class are still strong, the proletarian class still has to prepare for armed struggle. . . . While recognizing the possibility of reunifying Vietnam by peaceful means, we should always remember that our people's principal enemies are . . . preparing for war.

Traveling to Moscow one and a half years later, Ho sought to gain a codicil to Khrushchev's pronouncements that would exempt Vietnam from the burden of "peaceful coexistence." He found satisfaction in the final communiqué of the Conference of Communist and Workers' Parties. While generally applauding Khrushchev's new line, the assembled delegates allowed that

in conditions in which the exploiting classes resort to violence against the people, it is necessary to bear in mind another possibility—nonpeaceful transition to socialism. Leninism teaches and history confirms that the ruling classes never relinquish power voluntarily.

Returning to Hanoi while Ho remained in Moscow, Le Duan was able to report that the conference had "created favorable conditions for the revolutionary movement in South Vietnam." Scarcely had Le Duan returned from Moscow, however, than the party sent him on another mission in early 1958. His orders were to return to the South and compile a firsthand report on the situation there in order to make a detailed report to the Political Bureau.

It was a time, one Vietcong defector later reported, "when if you did not have a gun you could not keep your head on your shoulders." Southern party leaders knew that Le Duan would have to convey this message to the Political Bureau if the party in the South were to survive. The leaders told Le Duan that "the demand for armed activity by Party members increases daily." Certain individuals, "mostly draft-age youths," the party reported, dug up weapons from hidden arms caches in order "to kill the officials who were making trouble for them." Worse yet, other Communists were deserting the party in disgust, believing that the party would not protect them. Le Duan returned to Hanoi and briefed the Political Bureau. The Lao Dong leaders appeared to have become convinced. They hastily assembled the Fifteenth Plenum of the party Central Committee to meet in January 1959.

No documents have ever surfaced from that fifteenth plenum. No public statements or broadcasts revealed its decisions. But the meeting has taken on a mythical importance in the history of Vietnamese communism. An official Lao Dong history of the party, published eleven years

Land Reform

In the years following the Geneva accords, land reform in the North, not unification with the South, was the main preoccupation of North Vietnam's leaders. The Communists waited until 1956 to implement their long-term program to collectivize all farmland. The Lao Dong party labeled all landlords enemies of the state, including even those who had fought with the Vietminh against the French. Terror followed as the Communists attempted to destroy the landlord class. Early estimates of 50,000 executions proved to be highly exaggerated; more careful studies later revealed that over 1,500 landowners lost their lives in the campaign.

An accused landlord bows his head in penitence during a village meeting.

later, explained why. At that meeting the Central Committee ordered the Southern branch of the party to use "all appropriate means" to bring about the downfall of the "American-Diem" regime:

The direction and task of the South Vietnamese revolution could not diverge from the general revolutionary law of using revolutionary violence to oppose counter-revolutionary violence, rising up to seek power for the people. It was time to resort to armed struggle, combined with political struggle to push the movement forward.

So important was this decision that the Central Committee called for a full party congress, the Third Party Congress, to be held in September 1960. In theory the party congress was the highest policymaking organ of the Lao Dong. In practice, however, it merely rubber-stamped the decisions of the Central Committee. Its purpose was to dramatize the importance of the policy approved by the Fifteenth Plenum and to give the party's new direction the widest possible publicity.

The green light

The decision to authorize an armed struggle against the Diem regime reflected a definite strategic outlook on the part of the Lao Dong leaders. They expected the Southern insurgency to be self-supporting, capable of winning the war with only minimal assistance in men and materiel from the North.

Events, however, were to prove otherwise and required the Political Bureau to reconsider its strategic thinking through three distinct phases. The period of a relatively self-supporting Southern insurgency lasted only until 1964. In that year the Communists determined that while the Southerners had made great progress, the war would be won only if regular North Vietnamese troops provided an extra push to topple the Saigon government. The Southerners, themselves, however, were expected to carry the major burden in the war.

These hopes were dashed by the outcome of the ambitious offensives of 1967-1968 and particularly by the Tet offensive of 1968. The Political Bureau became convinced that their Southern comrades were in fact unable to win the war in the face of concerted American involvement. They thus initiated a third phase, beginning in late 1968 and continuing until the final battle of 1975. The Lao Dong party had come to realize that victory and reunification of the country could be accomplished only by a large-scale invasion of the South by North Vietnam's own troops.

In 1959, however, the Southerners were anxious to translate the Political Bureau and Central Committee decisions into action. In March and April 1959 provincial

In 1959, tribal minorities in Quang Ngai Province join the first Communist-inspired uprising against the Saigon regime.

armed units were formed in the coastal provinces of Quang Ngai and Ninh Thuan, the first assemblage of such forces since the signing of the Geneva accords. Party activists organized an uprising of tribal minorities in western Quang Ngai Province in August. In September Vietcong units ambushed two companies of the 23d ARVN Infantry Division. This was the first offensive action directed against Diem's army. But the Communists saved the fiercest blows for Tet, the 1960 new year. They overran the headquarters of the 23d ARVN Regiment in Tran Sup, Tay Ninh Province, capturing an arsenal of needed weapons. And in the delta provinces of Kien Hoa and Long An they engaged in a period of coordinated uprisings in which armed bands killed or expelled from their villages government officials. In Long An only three government officials had been assassinated in all of 1959, but in one week in January 1960 twenty-six local officials were killed. Many more targeted for assassination fled. An exhaustive study of Long An conducted by an American scholar concluded: "Thus the Party actually *became* the government in considerable areas as early as 1960, gradually expanding and consolidating its grip in the following years."

When the Third Party Congress convened in 1960 it not unexpectedly approved the political report by Le Duan that announced the policy change in the South. But it did so in a manner that must have given the Southerners some pause. It announced the "two strategic tasks for the Vietnamese Revolution at that stage":

First, to carry out the socialist revolution in the North.

Secondly, to liberate the South from the rule of the American imperialists and their henchmen, achieve national reunification and complete independence and freedom throughout the country.

The official report of the congress argued that "these two strategic tasks are closely related to each other and impel each other forward." Yet, it did not leave the matter at that. The party explicitly stated that "to carry out the socialist revolution in the North is *the most decisive task.*" It was clear that the opposition to armed struggle in the South that had dominated the Political Bureau until at least 1959 remained, and it would continue to influence Communist policy. So the Lao Dong party entered the Vietnam War divided over the means to achieve its goals.

The Southern-firsters and Northern-firsters

The two strategic goals defined by the Third Party Congress were not new. They had formed the agenda for the Lao Dong party ever since the signing of the Geneva ac-

Hanoi's Leaders

While Ho Chi Minh, Vo Nguyen Giap, and Le Duan became known to most Americans during the Vietnam War, the Lao Dong party's other leaders remained faceless and often nameless. Yet the men shown here at various stages in their careers all played a vocal and critical role in determining Hanoi's policy toward the South during the 1960s. The Political Bureau's eleventh member, Hoang Van Hoan, was purged in 1976, and photographs of him are no longer available in Hanoi.

Pham Van Dong, prime minister and former foreign minister, was a Southerner by birth but spent most of his revolutionary career by Ho's side in the North. A leading advocate of negotiations, his was an important swing vote in the Political Bureau's factional in-fighting between Northern-firsters and Southern-firsters.

Truong Chinh, a native of the North, was the Northern-firsters' leading spokesman. As the party's leading ideologue, he was especially popular among Lao Dong members. He advocated placing greater emphasis on economic development of the North and an orthodox approach to guerrilla war in the South.

Nguyen Chi Thanh, a native Southerner, ranked second to Giap in the military hierarchy. Long considered a protégé of Truong Chinh, he broke with his mentor in advocating forceful military action in the South, including the commitment of Northern troops. His death in 1967, perhaps during a U.S. B-52 attack, helped tip the balance of power in the Political Bureau back toward the Northerners.

cords. No leading party member ever dissented from them. It was this unanimity toward ends if not means that provided the party leadership with the unity to wage a fifteen-year struggle despite many internal differences. It also explained the absence of any changes in the party's ruling elite except those occasioned by death.

Neither would any party member have admitted publicly that there was any contradiction or tension between the two goals. According to dialectical logic they were mutually reinforcing. Advancing the socialist revolution in the North would provide a strong rear base for liberating the South; the liberation of the South would make the completion of the socialist revolution that much easier. But beyond the abstractions of dialectical logic, in the realm of practical politics, each Political Bureau member realized that the party would have to decide which task received the highest priority.

So long as the party believed that peaceful unification of the country was possible, the tension was minimal. Acting on their own, the Southerners engaged in a political struggle for reunification, while the meager resources of the North were devoted to consolidating Communist rule and extending socialism. But when Diem secured his own rule in the South and refused to hold the 1956 elections, the conflict between the party's two goals became palpable.

Still, for more than two years the party refused to change its policy in the South; it insisted that its members there engage only in political agitation. Thus it was clear that the dominant sentiment in the Political Bureau was to give greater priority to the North. A faction of "Northern-firsters" presented convincing arguments for this emphasis.

The leading members of this faction were Vo Nguyen Giap and Truong Chinh, two powerful voices in the Political Bureau. Both were natives of the North, and pure regionalism might have led them to their policy. Cultural and attitudinal differences between Northern Vietnamese and Southerners were as old as Vietnam itself. Even the nationalist impulse of the Vietminh could not fully overcome them. During the French-Indochina War, Northerners made up the vast majority of Vietminh soldiers; most of the fighting and all of the decisive victories took place in the North. After the war, Northerners like Giap and Truong Chinh may have felt that the few resources and the energy of the Lao Dong party should be devoted to rewarding the people of the North and improving their lives rather than to aiding the Southerners.

But beyond personal predilections, both men spoke for powerful constituencies within the party and the DRV. Truong Chinh's area of expertise was agricultural reform

Pham Hung, a native Southerner and long-time associate of Le Duan, was a consistent supporter of the "Southern-first" position in the Political Bureau. He replaced General Thanh as the head of COSVN in 1967.

Le Duc Tho, although born near Hanoi, became a close associate of Le Duan in the South during the French-Indochina War. Responsible for the training of lower-level party officials, he ensured that war weariness did not affect morale in the North. Considered a moderate by U.S. leaders, he was, in reality, an intransigent supporter of the Southern cause within the Political Bureau.

Nguyen Duy Trinh, a native Northerner who succeeded Pham Van Dong as foreign minister, joined Ho and Dong in a middle faction that tipped the balance between Northern-firsters and Southern-firsters. He was apparently a forceful advocate of negotiations within the party's inner circle.

Le Thanh Nghi, an expert in economic planning, like Hoang Van Hoan (not pictured here), an expert in foreign affairs, probably owed his position on the Political Bureau to his technical skills rather than political prominence. Neither he nor Hoan was considered to have played a significant role in intraparty debates.

Economic development was the highest priority of the DRV during the 1950s. Above. Ho Chi Minh poses with peasants battling a drought affecting agriculture. Below. *In Bac Ninh Province, Ho inspects the plans for a hydraulics network.*

and economic development. In the wake of the disastrous land-reform movement of 1956 he could see that the nation's economy simply was in no position to support an armed struggle in the South. Similarly, Giap was just initiating a program of modernization for the armed forces, which were ill prepared to engage in any Southern adventures. In addition, Giap and the military feared the American reaction to any stepped-up military activity in the South. Should the United States choose to carry the war to the North—either on the ground or in the air—or to permit Diem to use his own troops in similar fashion, the People's Army of Vietnam (PAVN) would be in no position to defend the country.

Historians today are inclined to think that Giap and Chinh were joined by Ho Chi Minh and Pham Van Dong in the Northern-first camp. The one area of party activity in which Ho appears to have played a leading role was in the party's relations with other Communist states. Khrushchev's policy of "peaceful coexistence," already rejected by the Chinese, seemed to veto any armed struggle in the South. Ho would have to secure his relations with the Soviet Union or else find himself unpleasantly committed to the Chinese camp in the nascent Sino–Soviet dispute. Dong was Ho's most intimate comrade. He may have joined Ho out of pure loyalty. In addition, as an architect of the Geneva accords, Dong had already come under strong attack by the Southerners. He may have stuck to the "peaceful unification" line in the hope that his policies would eventually be vindicated.

The elevation of Le Duan and Pham Hung to the Political Bureau in 1957 radically altered the balance of power. Their promotions probably signaled a willingness of Ho, and therefore Pham Van Dong, to change directions, but not immediately. Throughout 1957 and 1958 the Northerners maintained their ascendancy. But events in the South finally compelled the party to make a change. The second-highest party member captured in the South prior to 1968 later recalled:

By 1959 the situation in the South had crossed to a stage which the communists considered to be the darkest in their whole lives; almost all their apparatus had been smashed, the population no longer dared to provide support, families no longer dared to communicate with their relatives in the movement.

Sometime in late 1958 the Political Bureau authorized the turn to armed struggle. In agreeing to the call to initiate armed struggle in the South, the Northerners insisted that the highest priority remain on socialist development in the North.

Truong Chinh explained this decision to the Vietnamese people in April 1961. Writing in *Hoc Tap*, the leading journal of the Lao Dong party, he reminded his readers that the resolutions of the Third Party Congress required that the struggle in the South be carried out "by the southern people themselves." And he added that the Southerners "must not rely on Northern forces." If the Communist party of Vietnam had spoken in the idiom of Lyndon Johnson's west Texas rather than in the jargon of Marxism-Leninism, it might well have said, "We ain't gonna send no northern boys to fight a southern war."

The party had put the Southern insurgents on notice that at best they could expect only minimal aid from the North. The decisions of the Lao Dong party were not, however, empty statements of purpose. Although the party had not committed the DRV government to the struggle in the South, it had, in fact, placed many of the party's own resources at the disposal of the insurgents. Most of these assets were intangible: advice, expertise, and experience in

Ho Chi Minh leads Generals Vo Nguyen Giap (center), Nguyen Chi Thanh (behind Giap's shoulder), and Van Tien Dung (far right) on an inspection of a PAVN unit training in Nam Dinh Province in 1955.

conducting guerrilla warfare. But others were very concrete indeed.

Under the party's direction

The Third Party Congress established the formal structures under which the revolution in the South would be carried out. It urged people in South Vietnam to "establish the worker–farmer–soldier coalition, and it set up a large and united anti-U.S.–Diem National Front." Three months later, on December 20, 1960, the Southern insurgents announced the establishment of the National Liberation Front (NLF).

The concept of a united front had been a standard tool of Communists since Lenin's time. It was not in this in-

stance designed to camouflage the Communists' role in the insurgency. If it were, why would the party have so prominently advertised its call for the creation of the front? The NLF admitted the primacy of the party, as Liberation Radio broadcast to the world in May 1961:

In order to meet the exigencies of the revolution and to meet the new situation which the revolution faces, all of us . . . must strictly execute the basic and immediate mission determined by the party.

Rather, the front was designed to reach beyond the Communists to all of those South Vietnamese in sympathy with the goal of overthrowing the Diem regime. Many of those individuals had no desire to join the Communist party. Nor would the party, which considered itself a

The People's Intelligence

All too often during the Vietnam War, American officials just had to shake their heads in bewilderment. An operation had been planned to attack an enemy force encamped in an isolated village, but when American and ARVN troops arrived the Communists were gone, vacating the village only minutes before the government forces arrived. At the same time, far from the village, South Vietnamese officials plan a happier event. Government representatives will enter a "pacified" village to announce that a new school will be constructed for the benefit of village children. The night before the announcement is made, enemy troops enter the village, assassinate the chief, and destroy a government-sponsored agricultural project. The announcement of the new school is canceled.

In both cases the GVN had been stymied by the extensive and sophisticated intelligence apparatus created in South Vietnam by the Communists with substantial assistance from the DRV's Central Research Agency (CRA). The CRA swung into action in 1954 when thousands of former Vietminh and their sympathizers were asked to concentrate their political agitation in the capital city of Saigon. The Vietminh had attracted the support of a substantial part of South Vietnam's educated middle class, who naturally gravitated to white-collar, managerial employment. In the newly created Republic of Vietnam this almost invariably meant positions in government agencies or in businesses with substantial contact with the government. Thus, at its very birth, South Vietnam's foundation was laid with a "fifth column" whose true loyalty lay with the Lao Dong party.

This fifth column was strengthened by the ineptitude of the Diem government. For every former Vietminh agent who entered into the service of the GVN as a Communist agent, there were others who honestly wanted to give Diem's nationalist government the benefit of the doubt. Pentagon analysts later concluded that these people "resented and feared the communists in the Viet Minh" and "might have been willing to serve the GVN faithfully had it not hounded them out of society." Truong Nhu Tang, a future high official in the NLF, numbered among these former Vietminh sympathizers. He later argued, "Had Ngo Dinh Diem proved a man of breadth and vision, the core of people who filled the NLF and its sister organizations would have rallied to him." Whatever the cause of their sympathy for the Communists, the CIA concluded that by the late 1960s more than 30,000 enemy agents "had infiltrated the GVN's administrative, armed forces, police, and intelligence organizations."

Placement of enemy agents in sensitive positions was, however, only a small part of the Communists' intelligence network. In what the insurgents termed a "People's War," it was natural that the CRA would establish a "People's Intelligence" placed under the immediate supervision of COSVN's intelligence division. COSVN intelligence was divided into three sections: Internal Reconnaissance, External Reconnaissance, and Protection. The first functioned as a secret police within Communist-controlled areas. The last was responsible for protecting high-ranking cadres and securing military and political headquarters. The main burden of supplying information about the enemy fell to the External Reconnaissance section.

The foundation of this effort was the Communists' "People's Intelligence System" in which every person in South Vietnam had the potential of providing the party with valuable information. According to one South Vietnamese study, "The Communists were especially interested in those people whose relatives worked for the GVN." Using the promises communicated through propaganda or the threat of blackmail, the Communists developed a network of informants who were "numerous and ubiquitous."

The Communists were aided by the widespread Vietnamese attitude called *attentisme*, what Americans might call fence-sitting. The main concern of many Vietnamese was to ensure that they were on the winning side in the civil war. During the ebb and flow of battle, the most prudent course seemed to be to provide service to both sides. This could most efficiently be accomplished by living normal day-to-day lives as loyal citizens of the GVN while supplying the enemy with often innocuous bits of information when asked.

The Communists likened this espionage network to an audience watching an actor (the GVN) on stage. Those in the audience (average Vietnamese peasants) are able to view every action of the actor but, being shrouded in darkness themselves, are invisible to those on stage. The South Vietnamese study cited numerous examples:

- A roadside bicycle mechanic provided reports on the volume and direction of military traffic.
- A farmer tilling his land near an airfield counted how many and what types of aircraft took off and landed.
- A peasant woman, working outside her hut, warned, by prearranged signal, of the approach of enemy troops, their size, and composition.

Compounded thousands of times these small pieces of data could net volumes of important information. Noting any unusual departures from normal American or ARVN patterns, COSVN could often predict impending operations. Even minor bits of information, such as the news that the family and relatives of an ARVN officer had left a village "for a few days," might pinpoint the exact location of a government offensive.

It is possible that the work and contribution of the "People's Intelligence" to the Communist effort have been greatly overestimated. The CRA, like any intelligence agency, has revealed few of its triumphs or methods. And yet, even from its failures, Americans have been able to piece together the existence of a patient, resourceful, and extensive spying apparatus. Lacking almost entirely the sophisticated technological gadgetry that characterized much of the American intelligence effort, the Communists were able to mold the people of Vietnam into their most effective weapon.

union only of the most progressive voices in the country, the vanguard of the revolution in Lenin's terms, have accepted those individuals as members. The tactic of the front provided such persons an opportunity to join the anti-Diem movement, while allowing the Communists to control it. As the Third Party Congress put it:

This Front must comprise all the patriotic classes and social strata, the Vietnamese and the ethnic minority peoples, the patriotic parties and religious sects as well as everybody who opposes the US-Diem.

Members of the front were well aware of the role of the Communists in their movement. As Truong Nhu Tang, a non-Communist and former NLF minister of justice, and the highest-ranking member of the front to defect to the West, later recalled upon reading the "Manifesto and Program" of the NLF:

As I read, I had the distinct sense that these historical documents could not have been the work of just the [NLF] leadership group. They had too much depth, they showed too expert a grasp of politics, psychology, and language. I suspected I was seeing in them the delicate fingerprints of Ho Chi Minh. There seemed nothing strange about this. Ho's experience with revolutionary struggle was not something alien to arouse suspicion and anxiety. It was part and parcel of our own background.

Along with the open call for the creation of the NLF, the party also issued some secret orders. It reorganized the party in the South, combining the Nam Bo and Trung Bo regions again into COSVN: the Committee for South Vietnam. COSVN served as a central committee for the Southern branch of the party and reported directly to the party leadership in Hanoi. Nguyen Van Cuc, a civilian and former party secretary of the Saigon-Cholon area, was appointed the first head of COSVN. He later adopted the alias Nguyen Van Linh. His deputy, who served as head of both COSVN's and the NLF's Military Affairs Committee, was Lieutenant General Tran Van Tra. A native Southerner, Tra was a member of the Lao Dong Central Committee. Major General Tran Do, also a Southerner, served as chief political officer in the insurgency. The army, whose first units were formed in early 1959, was christened the People's Liberation Armed Forces (PLAF) but became commonly known by the name given to them by Diem—Vietcong, or Vietnamese Communists.

The Lao Dong also called upon the Southerners to form a new and "separate" Communist party, and on January 1, 1962, the People's Revolutionary Party (PRP) came into being. But it was mostly a disguise. A PRP document captured shortly after its formation declared that the party's creation "is only a matter of strategy . . . to deceive the enemy. . . . Our party is nothing but the Lao Dong Party of Vietnam."

The separate PRP did serve an important function. According to one U.S. Defense Department analysis, the "membership requirements of the PRP are considerably less stringent than in the Lao Dong Party." The Communists, concerned about the quality of their new recruits, usually feared a dilution of commitment if unworthy candidates were admitted to membership. Yet the accelerating pace of the revolution in the South required additional party members to supervise and control the burgeoning movement. Establishing a new and separate party solved the dilemma since recruits to the PRP would not automatically become members of the Lao Dong; this permitted the Northern branch to preserve its higher standards. As another instrument of control, COSVN, the Lao Dong's Southern command center, also served as the PRP's Central Committee.

The party in the North adapted itself to the new policy in South Vietnam. The Reunification Committee established in 1957 to oversee the affairs of the former Vietminh cadres who had regrouped in the North, now began to coordinate the roles that the party assigned to the regroupees in the new armed struggle.

Of equal importance was the creation, in 1963, of the Committee for the Supervision of the South, whose task was to offer overall guidance to the party in the South and to coordinate activities with the PRP. The committee was led by Le Duc Tho and included General Nguyen Van Vinh, one of Giap's deputy chiefs of staff, and Pham Hung, all committed Southern-firsters.

Finally, the Central Military Party Committee, a body that exercised party control over the Ministry of Defense, was assigned to oversee general military affairs in the South. This committee helped the Lao Dong Central Committee develop the objectives for military activities that would then be sent to COSVN. South Vietnam's Central Office was generally given a free hand in developing the tactics by which the party's directives and objectives would be carried out.

Many outside the Communist system find it difficult to comprehend that these party structures did not constitute a system by which Northerners dictated to Southerners. On the contrary, Southerners were well represented on all of these panels; in fact, they dominated them. To the continuing chagrin of the Northern-firsters, the Southerners were in control of their own destiny. What these party organizations did ensure was that the revolution in the South would continue to be controlled by Communists whatever their geographic location.

While most of the assistance that the Lao Dong gave to the Southerners came directly from the party, as opposed to the government, some state agencies did become more deeply involved in the struggle in the South, most notably the DRV's Central Research Agency (CRA). This North Vietnamese equivalent of the American CIA had, since its inception in 1954, devoted most of its attention to intelligence operations in the South. After 1959 it aided COSVN in establishing its own intelligence organization and exercised control over those efforts.

The full extent of Communist intelligence activities are little known (see sidebar, pg. 26). However, it is clear that the establishment of the apparatus was among COSVN's first priorities as the insurgency heated up in the South. The U.S. State Department was surely correct in concluding as early as 1961 that the "intelligence operation in support of the Viet Cong is one of the most extensive of its kind in the world."

While the Third Party Congress had promised the Southerners only minimal material aid, at best, the North Vietnamese government did begin to send to South Vietnam small quantities of critical supplies beginning in 1959. Although the amounts increased yearly, they represented only a very modest contribution to the Southern battlefield through 1963. The overwhelming majority of weapons used by the Vietcong came from caches hidden in 1954 or later, almost exclusively from those captured during military operations. The U.S. Embassy in Saigon estimated that as late as 1963, 92 percent of all Vietcong weapons were secured within South Vietnam. During one eighteen-month period between 1962 and 1964, only 179 of the 15,100 enemy weapons captured were manufactured in Communist countries. The amount of ammunition captured during those eighteen months was barely sufficient to permit one 450-man battalion to fire for more than a half-hour. The Southerners were expected to remain self-sufficient, and the records compiled by the United States government seem to indicate that in large measure they succeeded.

"Northern days, Southern nights"

The Political Bureau did, however, make one critical material contribution to the Southerners' cause, without which it is unlikely that the insurgency could ever have prospered. In deciding to permit armed struggle against the Diem regime, the Lao Dong party committed the redeployment of the former Vietminh regroupees to the Southern battlefield.

By 1959 some 90,000 regroupees had spent half a decade living in the DRV. According to a study of regroupees who were later captured by or who defected to South Vietnamese and American forces, "they did not seem to be displeased with the Communist political system that was being consolidated in the DRV. ... The attitudes of the great majority [including defectors] ... ranged from neutrality to a strong pro-Northern commitment."

The North Vietnamese government had done all it could to foster this loyalty. One regroupee recalled the reception he received when he first arrived in the North:

The Northerners really welcomed us with joy. They had organized a welcoming crowd to take care of us as soon as we dis-

Lugging grenades, PLAF guerrillas fortify their trench positions in central South Vietnam.

embarked. There were flags, crowds, cheers. ... They surrounded us and led each of us to their homes.

The regroupees' gravest problem was loneliness. They received little news of their families in the South, thanks to Diem's postal embargo of North Vietnam. One Southerner, serving in an army unit made up entirely of regroupees, recalled:

In the daytime we worked in the North and we did not have any time to think about our families in the South. But at night when we lay down, we could not help thinking how our families were getting along. We used to tell each other, "Ngay Bac, Bem Nam. Northern days, Southern nights."

After the 1956 election deadline passed, the DRV began to demobilize regroupees no longer fit for military service. Those remaining in the People's Army (PAVN) formed five new divisions composed entirely of Southerners: the 305th, 324th, 325th, 330th, and 338th. Those weeded out of the armed forces were either employed on state farms or learned technical skills that might prove useful to the South.

During the next few years the regroupees became increasingly agitated about the situation in the South. Exposed to the DRV's vilification campaign against Diem and reports of the GVN's repressive measures against families of former Vietminh supporters, many clamored to return South in order to liberate their homeland. By the time that the Lao Dong party decided to initiate the armed struggle in the South, it had succeeded in instilling a hatred of the "American–Diem" regime in the hearts of most regroupees. The party now began to select regroupees most capable of leading the struggle in the South and to prepare them for infiltration.

Regroupees chosen for reinfiltration—both PAVN troops and civilians—were placed in special training programs lasting from several weeks to almost a year. The most important training bases were at Xuan Mai (near Hanoi), Son Tay, and Thanh Hoa. As much as two-thirds of the training was devoted to political work, but specialized military and technical skills were also taught: guerrilla warfare, armor and ordnance, antiaircraft defense, communications, medical training, and transport expertise.

Hanoi's objective in sending down these well-trained and indoctrinated regroupees was to bolster and solidify party control over the insurgency. But they were also selected for their knowledge of the local dialects, customs, and terrain. Yet, all of this planning would prove useless unless the party could find a reliable and secure means of infiltrating these regroupees into the South.

"The Old Man's Trail"

In the first Indochina war the Vietminh maintained communications between North and South through a primitive system of pathways and trails along the Laotian-Vietnam-

A PLAF soldier prepares his mortar for use in the early 1960s. During those years, mortars provided the only form of artillery support for insurgent units.

ese border where French troops seldom patrolled. In the years following the Geneva agreements, jungle growth reclaimed much of the trail. In late 1958, when the Political Bureau adopted the policy that would eventually be approved by the Fifteenth Plenum of the Central Committee in January 1959, it assigned the task of reopening this road to a team of Southerners led by one elderly man. According to legend, this man had extensive knowledge of the old system of paths and, traveling in reverse direction from south to north, selected the most practicable route. In tribute to his efforts, many Communists called the route "The Old Man's Trail," but to the world it became known as the Ho Chi Minh Trail.

Having surveyed the trail, the Lao Dong party now moved to secure the area. The eastern portion of the Laotian panhandle had been a Communist stronghold ever since the French-Indochina War, especially the area around the village of Tchepone, and had been heavily organized by the Vietminh and their Laotian allies, the Pathet Lao. In late 1958 and 1959 the Royal Laotian government in Vientiane began to adopt a more overtly pro-Western orientation and sought to gain control of the area. Hanoi responded by deploying the 335th PAVN Regiment, one made up almost entirely of Laotian regroupees, into

Watching Hanoi

by Douglas Pike

Most of what American officials knew—and didn't know—about the Democratic Republic of Vietnam, both during the war and afterward, came from the work of a small group of specialists who informally became known as "Hanoi watchers." I numbered among these watchers and, in retrospect, would have to characterize our efforts as modest, parochial, and less than adequate. Certainly Hanoi watching never compared with China watching in Hong Kong, in the same and earlier periods, or Kremlinology out of Washington and elsewhere since the 1930s.

Systematic Hanoi watching began in Saigon about 1960, chiefly as a sideline avocation by a few American foreign service and intelligence service officers curious about enemy organization and military structure, political mobilization techniques, and communicational devices. After 1965, with full U.S. intervention in the war, Hanoi watching became institutionalized. Yet, despite the fact that some 465,000 Americans were on duty in Vietnam by 1968, Hanoi watchers never numbered more than a dozen, centered in the U.S. Embassy's Political Section. Among the agencies participating were the State Department's Information Service, the CIA, the Defense Intelligence Agency, and later the Joint U.S. Public Affairs Office.

These intelligence analysts maintained close working relations with the South Vietnamese through various liaison arrangements, most notably the Combined Documents Exploitation Center. CDEC collected literally tons of captured documents and turned their use into something of a cottage industry; the cream of these is now in the National Archives in Washington on some twenty-two miles of 35MM microfilm.

The purpose of all this activity was to divine the strategy of North Vietnam and the Lao Dong party, track Hanoi's relations with its allies, and anticipate its moves at the Paris conference table. Chiefly this effort was the domain of U.S. government intelligence organs and foreign policymakers, displaying lively if shallow interest in the subject. To a lesser extent Hanoi watching was conducted by think tank researchers, often under government contract, and by a few journalists and writers.

The basic task was twofold: collection of information and its analysis. Information came from what were termed "open sources" readily available to the public, such as Hanoi radio broadcasts, newspapers and periodicals, Vietcong propaganda leaflets, and scholarly journal articles. Open sources were augmented by classified material: reports from CIA agents and other covert sources, captured documents and POW interrogation reports, electronic intercepts of Hanoi's coded messages, satellite photos, and rumors and reports picked up by the U.S. diplomatic community.

Hanoi watchers encountered manifold difficulties in their job, but the most important, despite the twenty-two miles of microfilm, was inadequate information. Clearly this represented a major paradox. While far more information was available about the enemy than in previous wars, less could be done with it. The simple fact was that most of the data collected was mere "information pollution" gleaned from incomplete and often unreliable sources.

As in gold mining, the problem was how to recognize and separate the ore from the dross. A classic example of the problem is found in our postmortem of the 1968 Tet offensive. We assembled all of the relevant raw field reports, a stack of paper some three feet high, about 3,500 pages. With the benefit of hindsight it was easy to divide this material into two piles, one predicting an offensive, the other indicating not. It was an uneven pile—15 percent to 85 percent—with the predictive data buried and scattered. Still, 15 percent of it clearly indicated an imminent offensive.

The failure of Hanoi watching was most visible where it counted most—at the top. Intelligence analysts never received much reliable data about the politics of the Hanoi Politburo or doctrinal disputation among PAVN generals. Even accurate biographical data were in short supply. For instance, throughout the war a running argument raged over whether the important leader in the NLF known as *Tran Nam Trung* was an individual or a post held by a succession of individuals. Only after the war, when Tran Nam Trung appeared on the victory parade platform in Saigon, was the argument settled.

Information from "direct sources," defectors from or planted agents in the enemy camp, was also considered dubious. The U.S./GVN succeeded in placing penetration agents in COSVN, but Hanoi watchers did not trust their reports, fearing they were double agents. We never got a truly high-level defector from the enemy side (nor, for that matter, was there ever an important Vietnamese or American defector), a strange occurrence in what was largely a political war. The highest-level defector from the GVN side was a district chief, about to be arrested for corruption. There was not one COSVN level defector, that is Central Committee equivalent in the Leninist organizational structure. The only known American defector of record was Robert Garwood, a Marine Corps enlisted man who turned after he was captured.

Part of the Hanoi watchers' problem was the result of Hanoi's ability to hide both its capability and intentions. Enemy planning was highly compartmentalized

and tightly held. For example, the enemy planned a "Third Wave" to be the culmination and coup de grace of the 1968 Tet offensive. Because the winter-spring campaign did not develop properly in its earlier stages, the finale never came about. Maybe it was to have been Khe Sanh, possibly Hue. So closely held was this secret, however, that to this day we do not know what was to have been the Third Wave. In planning an attack, whether drills in the jungle or sand-table simulations, commanders would rehearse assaults on a dozen different targets, only one of which was the true one, made known only at the last moment.

Another major difficulty was engendered by the sheer complexity of the subject—the decision-making process in Hanoi and its use of a strange new strategy that mixed war and politics. The Vietnam War itself was vastly more complicated compared to other wars. This inevitably led to conflicting perceptions among Hanoi watchers, some of which persist to this day. Was Ho Chi Minh a nationalist first and a Comintern agent second, or vice versa? What was the exact relationship between Hanoi and the Vietcong in the South? Was the long-used distinction among Communist leaders between pro-Soviet and pro-Chinese factions of any significance? These were not matters of factual truth but of perception, differences that may never be resolved.

Perhaps the most serious difficulty Hanoi watchers faced was their lack of status within the American government. High officials in Saigon and Washington regarded their task as an arcane undertaking of dubious value and few took it or its output seriously. Contributing to this low status was a scandalous failure by the U.S. academic community to make any significant contribution to the understanding of events in North Vietnam. While academics vigorously debated the

merits of the war, most of them from the negative side, few did any research on relevant matters, such as the sociopolitical culture of North Vietnam or the all-important operational code of the Politburo in policymaking. Thus Hanoi watchers were deprived of what should have been a major source of aid and guidance, American academia's contribution.

The entire intelligence effort during the Vietnam War was in marked contrast to American efforts in earlier wars. In World War II a vast apparatus attempted to watch Germany and Japan, including even a team of astrologers in London who daily cast Hitler's horoscope simply because he, Hitler, took the stars seriously. Nothing was produced during the Vietnam War remotely equal to Ruth Benedict's *The Chrysanthemum and the Sword*, a brilliant study of the Japanese psyche compiled from a distance.

The saddest epitaph that can be applied to Hanoi watching is that American officials were well aware of its shortcomings but just didn't think that it mattered. Hanoi's capabilities and intentions were simply irrelevant, they thought, when compared to the power and might that America could apply to the war. We suffered from what Aldous Huxley rightly called "vincible ignorance." Americans, both military and civilian, were poorly informed about the enemy, realized that they were poorly informed, but did not think that it would make any difference.

Douglas Pike is a former Foreign Service officer who spent fifteen years in Vietnam as a Hanoi watcher. He is currently Director of the Indochina Studies Program at the University of California/Berkeley.

the area. In 1961, in one of the rare measures in which the Communist leadership committed the resources of the DRV, regular ethnic Vietnamese PAVN forces began to augment the ranks of Communist Laotians. U.S. intelligence estimated that the DRV committed twelve PAVN battalions, totaling 6,000 men, along with another 3,000 North Vietnamese serving in Pathet Lao units, to the offensive. With Soviet planes ferrying North Vietnamese troops to the battlefield, the Royal Laotian government was unable to challenge the Communist control of the panhandle. Faced with a mounting international crisis, the United States government made arrangements for a political settlement at the Geneva Conference of 1962. Under the agreement of July 23, 1962, all foreign troops were to vacate the area.

The American government for the most part lived up to the agreement, withdrawing its uniformed personnel from Laos (although a covert force remained there permanently). The DRV, however, ignored the agreement and instead consolidated its hold on the Laotian panhandle and the Ho Chi Minh Trail.

Primary responsibility for maintaining the trail was assigned to the PAVN 559th Transportation Group, a military unit that would eventually grow to 50,000 strong. Two unique types of units served under the command of the 559th Group: *Binh Tram* units and commo-liaison stations.

A *Binh Tram*, roughly the equivalent of a regimental logistical headquarters, was responsible for securing a particular portion of the trail. While infantry units provided military security, engineer, transportation, and signal elements fulfilled the logistic functions. Whereas the *Binh Tram* were largely responsible for maintenance, commo-liaison stations were concerned with the movement of personnel. They provided food and housing, medical care, and guides to the next station. A station's area of responsibility stretched from halfway between two consecutive stations, thus no member of the commo-liaison team would have knowledge of more than one station.

The way stations were manned by units of fifteen to twenty soldiers and consisted of a medical facility, mess hall, and bivouac site. They were situated one day's march from each other. The DRV established countless commo-liaison stations and spaced them about various branches of the trail so that infiltrators did not pass through each one. Rather, the 559th Transportation Group command assigned each team of infiltrators their own route down the trail, depending on volume of traffic and likely enemy activities.

In the early 1960s the Ho Chi Minh Trail, little more than a network of carefully camouflaged footpaths, was used almost exclusively by infiltrators. As for supplies and materiel, most were brought to South Vietnam by seagoing vessels under the command of the 759th Transportation Group.

Virtually all of the personnel making the long and ar-

duous trip down the trail prior to 1964 were former Vietminh regroupees. Embarking from training camp in regular NVA uniforms, the teams were transported by truck to the Mu Gia or Ne Pa Pass on the North Vietnam-Laotian border. There their uniforms and all means of identity were taken from them, and they were issued the black pajamas typical of Vietnamese peasants. Walking time to the northernmost provinces of South Vietnam required six weeks; the march to the Mekong Delta lasted more than three months. The work of the 559th Transportation Group ended when the regroupees arrived at the South Vietnam border. At that point the PLAF unit to which the regroupees were designated assumed responsibility for the final leg of their journey.

The augmentation of Southern forces by the regroupees began slowly. In 1959 and 1960 a combined total of 3,800 infiltrators made the trip down the trail. That two-year total was equaled by the 1961 figure of 3,700. The number of infiltrators rose to 5,800 in 1962 and dropped to 4,000 in 1963. Sometime in 1964, American analysts believe, the Lao Dong party exhausted the supply of regroupees still fit for military service in the South.

Once in the South, the regroupees played a vital role in the development of PLAF forces. They were not intended to be mere cannon fodder and suffered much lower casualty rates than other VC combat personnel. Rather, they became the "steel frame" of the Communist organization, forming the majority of the insurgents' officer corps and NCOs.

The well-trained and highly motivated regroupees assimilated themselves easily into the NLF and did much to strengthen the political foundation of the insurgent forces. Competent leaders and good soldiers, they subscribed to the Communist goal of leading by example. One captured Southern guerrilla remarked, "In comparison with the fighters and cadres in South Vietnam, the regroupees were militarily and politically better, and also they were the ones who trained the local fighters and cadres."

Some friction did develop between the regroupees and the newer Southern recruits. One PLAF defector complained that the regroupees "behaved loftily" and were favored in promotions and living conditions. But a Rand Corporation study of the Vietcong concluded that whatever antagonisms existed, they "did not appear to have been serious enough to reduce the effectiveness of Front operations."

Insurgent efforts in the early 1960s were, if anything, effective. NLF membership doubled in 1961 and again in 1962. The front regained virtual control of the countryside from the Diem regime. The seeming security and consolidation of Diem's rule in the late 1950s had been illusory. No organized opposition to his government had existed in

Communist troops descend a precarious stairway along the Ho Chi Minh Trail.

those years, and he was able to place loyal officials in villages throughout the country, creating the appearance of "pacification." But this seeming security collapsed in the face of coordinated PLAF activity. Communist concentration on "the assassination of tyrants" was viewed all too often by the local population as just that, elimination of government officials who tyrannized their lives.

If anything, success came to the Vietcong too easily. The Southern-dominated Political Bureau could not help being pleased by the rapid strides made in the South and argued for even greater efforts. But uneasiness still reigned in the minds of many in the Lao Dong hierarchy. In line with the resolutions of the Third Party Congress, they insisted that nothing be done that might spread the war beyond the borders of South Vietnam. An invasion of the North by Diem's South Vietnamese troops, or worse, in conjunction with American troops, would endanger their program of socialist development, if not the regime itself. Moreover, Ho Chi Minh had reason for caution. Ultimately, he realized, North Vietnam had to maintain the support of both the Soviet Union and China. With the dispute between the two Communist superpowers now open and bitter, that had become an increasingly difficult task.

Between Moscow and Peking

Ho's dilemma was simple. Moscow had the wealth and materiel to supply the DRV with its foreign assistance needs but was, at best, lukewarm in its support of the insurgency in South Vietnam. China gave strong vocal support for the liberation of the South and much, often unwanted, advice on how to pursue that goal. But China, engaged in its own process of socialist development, was short on the wherewithal to back up its sidelines cheerleading.

Spurred on by the 1957 resolution of the Conference of Communist and Workers' Parties, on January 6, 1961, just one month after Radio Hanoi announced the formation of the NLF, Nikita Khrushchev did place his stamp of approval on "wars of national liberation." The Soviets, however, privately pressed their comrades in Hanoi to propose a negotiated settlement to their dispute with Diem, or worse, give up hope of reunification. Soviet aid to Hanoi remained meager so that when the DRV announced its first five-year plan of economic development in 1961, Ho was forced to go hat in hand to Moscow to secure the necessary assistance.

Ho's problem was that the Political Bureau had issued a series of bellicose statements in the late 1950s in support of Mao's brand of communism and in contradiction to Khrushchev's policy of "peaceful coexistence." Radio Hanoi broadcast that the DRV would "always stand ready by the side of the CPR [Chinese People's Republic] in its struggle to recover Quemoy and Matsu, and to liberate Taiwan." One British analyst suggested that Ho gave Moscow private assurances that such support to the Chinese was only "empty words" and that North Vietnamese "actions proved that she had not been taken in by Maoist innovations."

However Ho privately handled the two Communist superpowers, he seems to have succeeded. Beginning in 1960 Soviet aid to the DRV, theretofore only about half of what China contributed, began to rise steadily. By 1964 the Soviet Union had supplanted China as the major source of Hanoi's foreign assistance.

It is difficult to know with any certainty how much of that aid was military hardware and how much pure economic assistance. One independent study conducted for the U.S. Army concluded that Soviet aid during the early 1960s "consisted primarily of equipment for factories, oil and oil products, fishing trawlers, lorries, spare parts for machinery, tractors, automobiles, medical equipment and food." The report added that Chinese aid was largely "machinery, road and rail construction materials, and foodstuffs."

However little the amount, foreign military assistance did permit the DRV to begin an ambitious program of military modernization. The origins of the modernization program lay in a debate between "professionals" and "politicians" in the army. After the Geneva agreements, factions within PAVN began to press for greater freedom for the army from party control, to convert the "People's" army into a professional army. While strongly reiterating the principle of party control of the military, the Lao Dong leadership gradually assented to substantial parts of the professionals' reform program. General Giap, a strong advocate of party control, seems to have led the way in steering the middle course.

Much of the modernization program was ideological. Those less fit for military duty, even if politically reliable, were retired from PAVN. Although political indoctrination remained an important part of basic training, the training program increasingly fell under the control of the professionals.

PAVN equipment also underwent major improvements. Here again, Soviet aid, and to a lesser extent Chinese aid, proved crucial. From 1954 to 1962 the number of PAVN infantry divisions increased from six to fourteen. U.S. intelligence concluded that the Soviets and Chinese supplied PAVN with most of its small arms, artillery, tanks, and trucks. In 1960 Giap outlined the purposes of the reform program:

To safeguard the cause of consolidating and building up the North in its progressive advance to socialism, to defend the sovereignty, the territory and the security of the Democratic Republic of Vietnam ... and to be prepared to smash the aggressive plots of imperialism, especially the U.S. imperialists and their lackeys.

At the top of the list came the goal of socialist development. As in most Communist countries, the army was designed to act as an important motor of social change. Training in the army was a crucial element in the political indoctrination of the young, while the army's heavy equipment would prove useful in large-scale public works projects. The assistance PAVN could give to the program of socialist development was probably the crucial reason why the Lao Dong party assented to its modernization.

The goal of national defense, however, cannot be ignored. Party policy still held that the war in the South was to be fought by Southerners, but Giap was also concerned that revolutionary success in the South might spawn an attack on the North. Even against South Vietnamese forces, North Vietnam would have to be well defended. To Giap's chagrin the danger seemed to grow as the insurgency in the South began its third year. In 1962, after a year of intensive study and consideration of policy alternatives, the administration of U.S. President John Kennedy decided to increase substantially America's commitment to South Vietnam and the Diem regime. The inauguration of what the North Vietnamese called "Special War" in South Vietnam sparked another round of debate between the Southern-firsters and the Northern-firsters in the Lao Dong party.

The debate continues

The debate between the two factions had in reality never ended. True, the Third Party Congress had issued the call for an armed insurrection to complement the ongoing political struggle against the Diem regime. The Political Bureau, however, had made no decision on whether the political or military dimension of the revolution was to be emphasized. Naturally the Northern-firsters sought to limit the escalation by emphasizing politics. Le Duan and his allies thought that a solution could come only on the battlefield.

Fundamental to this problem was the task of identifying the enemy in the South and by extension clarifying the goals of the revolution. The crucial question was: Is the revolution in the South an antifeudal or an anti-imperialist movement? Around such arcane subjects of Communist scholasticism depended critical policy decisions.

If, as Le Duan argued, the struggle was first and foremost antifeudal, then it was aimed against South Vietnam's landlord class as well as the Diem regime. The goal of the revolution would be a socialist regime in South Vietnam. Le Duan warned that "some comrades . . . have been deceived by the landlords" and argued that the party should depend on the laboring classes for support.

Truong Chinh, on the other hand, stressed the importance of "getting as many landlords as possible into the Front." He believed that the revolution in the South was anti-imperialist. This meant that all South Vietnamese who, regardless of class, sought to rid the country of the "American-Diem" regime, should be brought into alliance

with the party. The result of such a movement, at least as a first step, would be a democratic South Vietnam in which the Communists would only participate in the government. A truly socialist or Communist-run South Vietnam would come at a later stage of the revolution.

The difference had important strategic implications. Le Duan's program would require the destruction of all anti-Communist elements in the South. General Thanh, probably Le Duan's most militant ally in the Political Bureau, argued that the only way to "solve the contradiction" between Communists and non-Communists was to use "revolutionary violence."

General Giap responded for the Northern-firsters. In 1961 he published the magnum opus of his career, *People's War, People's Army.* Ostensibly a review of the successful strategy he adopted against the French, his book represented in reality a ringing denunciation of the aggressive strategy advocated by Le Duan and General Thanh. He reminded his younger colleagues that "the shifting from political struggle to armed struggle was a very great change that required a long period of preparation." He argued that the liberation armed forces should "primarily be used in propaganda activities." Building a "political base" was far more important than "pushing ahead too rapidly with offensive battles." The Southerners in COSVN allied themselves with Le Duan and his more aggressive strategy. A Communist document captured by ARVN in 1963 attacked "some people" who

wish to restrict the uprising, . . . only construct bases and large forces in a number of mountain areas while the compatriots in the rural delta areas only push the political struggle.

The COSVN leadership called for "inflicting losses on the enemy and isolating him and creating the conditions for the advancement of the armed uprising." The differences between Northern-firsters and Southern-firsters became more acute in 1962 when the United States upgraded its military assistance program in Saigon from an "advisory group" (MAAG) to an "assistance command" (MACV) and introduced 10,000 additional advisers into the country. To the Northern-firsters this was a clear signal for caution and evidence that the struggle in the South was primarily anti-imperialist, i.e., to rid the country of Americans.

"Victory is in our hands"

In February 1963 Minh Tranh, a historian long identified with the Northern faction, published a lengthy article in which he argued that "the South Vietnam revolution must go along a long, arduous, and complicated path and cannot expect an easy and rapid victory." He warned that the U.S. possessed the "most ferocious force" and was "far more cruel and dangerous" than any other imperialist power. Minh Tranh argued that the NLF "must be further developed, and more of the intermediate strata must be

drawn into the revolution," a political process for which "a long period is necessary." And to rub salt into Le Duan's wounds, he concluded:

A revolution develops according to objective laws which exist independent of man's wish. The revolutionary should not rely on his subjective wish but should rely on objective reality.

He added, "Only when sentiment is raised to the level of reason will the revolution be truly stable."

No second-string party cadre answered Minh Tranh. General Thanh himself took pen in hand to respond. "The U.S. imperialists are not invincible," he began. More daringly, he argued that liberation of the South need not await the socialist construction of the North:

The building of the North itself cannot in any way replace the settlement of inner contradictions in the South Vietnam society. . . . If one fears the United States and does not believe in successfully opposing it, and calls on the South Vietnamese people to wait and to "coexist peacefully" with the U.S. Diemists, one will be committing an irreparable mistake.

Finally, against the Northern pessimists, Thanh declared, "Victory is already in our hands."

To American "Hanoi watchers" monitoring the high-level debate, it might have appeared that the Northerners had won. Shortly after publishing that article, Thanh resigned his commission as a four-star general and assumed a low-visibility position in the Ministry of Agriculture. But appearances were deceiving. Although it could not be known at the time, Minh Tranh would never publish another article in North Vietnam. And General Thanh had not been demoted. Rather, he was in hiding, preparing for the most important assignment of his career. Le Duan, too, was lost in preparation. A hastily assembled Central Committee plenum was scheduled for December 1963, the ninth plenum since the Third Party Congress.* Le Duan as first secretary of the party would deliver one of his most important speeches. The subject matter was, as usual, arcane—modern revisionism in the world Communist movement. But every delegate knew that much more was at stake. Just one month earlier the first Communist goal in South Vietnam had been reached. The hated regime of Ngo Dinh Diem was overthrown.

* Central Committee plenums are numbered consecutively, beginning anew with each party congress. Thus the Fifteenth Plenum of January 1959 was the fifteenth such meeting following the Second Party Congress. The Ninth Plenum of December 1963 was the committee's ninth meeting since the Third Party Congress.

The first armed unit in the Saigon area readies for action in 1961. The unit reflects the diversity of such early guerrilla units, including a political cadre (in white jacket), a regroupee from the North (top row, center), and PLAF regional forces (wearing soft hats). The helmets worn by the men in the front row were captured from ARVN troops.

A Race Against Time

The year 1963 was a lucky one for the Communists. The Communists, however, never liked to depend upon luck for their success. For all their belief in historical inevitability, the Communists strove for absolute control over events and 1963 befuddled them. True, the year began predictably enough. In January, PLAF forces gained their most decisive victory to date at Ap Bac in the Mekong Delta. By destroying a vastly superior ARVN force supported by helicopters, the insurgents showed that they could, indeed, defeat South Vietnam even in the face of an increased American presence in South Vietnam.

Otherwise, as the months passed, the NLF watched nervously from the sidelines as some of the most decisive events in the war paraded by them. Beginning in May and continuing throughout the summer, Buddhist protests brought the Diem government to a virtual standstill. Following its policy of not joining movements it could not control, the NLF watched. Then the dispute

between Moscow and Peking flared into verbal fireworks, and the Lao Dong party could only plaintively call for unity. Finally, on November 1 the Communists watched again, in amazement, as the regime of Ngo Dinh Diem was overthrown—not by a general uprising of the people, as the Communists had predicted, but by a well-coordinated coup carried out by Diem's "chief executioners," the generals of ARVN.

As welcome as the coup was to the Communists, its immediate aftermath might have given the Lao Dong leadership some pause. The generals, whose army, the Communists charged, had tyrannized the people of South Vietnam, were being hailed as heroes. And more amazingly, the man whom the insurgents considered the chief puppeteer, the American ambassador in Saigon, Henry Cabot Lodge, was cheered wildly when he appeared in public.

The Northern-first faction in the Political Bureau pointed to this response as evidence of the weakness of the Southerners' strategy. By devoting too much attention to military struggle and placing too little emphasis on political organization, the NLF had failed to galvanize anti-Diem sentiment into a "broad, united front" capable of bringing the Communists into the government. The Southern-firsters, however, could point to Vietcong military victories, which had destroyed Diem's strategic hamlet program and paralyzed the government outside of the major cities. The Southerners wanted to step up the military pressure, but because the supply of regroupees had been almost exhausted, this could be accomplished only by committing regular PAVN forces. With one eye looking askance at the Southern organization and the other warily watching U.S. reactions, the Northerners argued for a less risky political struggle. With the debate in the Political Bureau reaching a high pitch, the Lao Dong Central Committee convened for its Ninth Plenum in December 1963.

The modern revisionists

Now officially bearing the title of party first secretary, Le Duan addressed the Central Committee with the Political Bureau's political report. Ostensibly, the first secretary's talk was a denunciation of the "modern revisionists" of the Soviet Union. Modern revisionism was the Chinese term for the policy advanced by Khrushchev under the banner of "peaceful coexistence." This policy stated that since general war in a nuclear world was unthinkable, communism would have to advance through peaceful competition. Through economic development, the Communist countries could surpass the standard of living of Western nations and thereby attract the peoples of the world to its

cause. Le Duan now joined the Chinese in accusing the Soviets of betraying the revolutionary spirit of Marx and Lenin.

The real target of Le Duan's polemic, however, was the modern revisionists within his own Lao Dong party. The policies advocated by the members of the Northern-first faction of the party were in remarkable harmony with those of Khrushchev. They had argued that political struggle rather than military efforts should be emphasized in the South, and they had made the economic construction of the DRV the number-one priority of the party.

Le Duan attacked them on all fronts. He maintained that the imperialists "want war and not peace. ... We carry out the offensive to prevent the imperialists from creating war, thereby insuring peace." More important, Le Duan rejected the priorities established by the Third Party Congress in 1960. He charged that "he who speaks of compromising with imperialism to build economy and regards this as the number one requirement, willingly or unwillingly only hinders the progress of revolution."

By suggesting that those accused might be "willingly" hindering the revolution, the party first secretary was charging them with the most serious of Communist sins: counterrevolutionary attitudes. It was a hint that a purge in the party might be near.

The import of what Le Duan was saying could not have been lost on informed party members. The spokesman for the party's Political Bureau was relegating the Northern-firsters to the Soviet camp while casting the fate of the party with the Chinese Communists.

The Ninth Plenum of the Central Committee did not act merely as a rubber stamp for the first secretary's report. Le Duan later revealed that the meeting lasted "over ten days" to discuss his report "thoroughly and carefully," language that suggests sharp debate in the Lao Dong hierarchy. But the Political Bureau maintained its unity. For Truong Chinh it must have been particularly painful, even galling. He was widely known as the most "Maoist" of the Vietnamese Communists, but Le Duan had placed him in the Soviet camp. In the end, however, it was Truong Chinh who, in the name of party unity, strode to the platform to ask the Central Committee to approve Le Duan's report.

This much was all duly reported in Hanoi's papers. But another part of Le Duan's report was considered much too sensitive for such publicity. It was revealed only when a copy of a letter from Le Duan to COSVN was captured by American forces in 1966. In his letter Le Duan did offer one concession to the Northerners. The Communists must "restrict the war within the limits of the South," Le Duan told COSVN leaders, and added, the "principle of protracted war had been heavily stressed" at the Ninth Plenum.

But then came the new policy, the reason why he had so vituperatively attacked the Chinh-Giap faction. The Central Committee established a new principle of "racing against time in order to achieve the ultimate victory in a

relatively short period of time." He added that primary emphasis lay in "building up the party's military arm in the South." For this, it was "time for the North to increase aid to the South; the North must bring into play its role as the revolutionary base for the whole nation."

Giap's worst fears of 1959 had come true. His own army was being committed to the struggle in the South, to "achieve the ultimate victory in a relatively short period of time." Le Duan had few words of comfort for those who feared that this would spark a forceful reaction from the U.S. He dismissed the possibility as "remote . . . because the U.S. cannot evaluate all the disastrous consequences she might bear if she wages the war on a larger scale." He merely urged that the party "positively prepare" for any eventuality. Two years later Pham Van Dong revealed to a Western journalist that the Political Bureau "had been surprised" by the American commitment of ground combat troops and implied, according to the journalist, that the party had "miscalculated the reactions of the U.S. government."

Le Duan's presentation to the Central Committee was one of the most remarkable speeches given by a Lao

Ambush complete. PLAF guerrillas steal away with valuable weapons after ambushing a small South Vietnamese unit in the Mekong Delta in the early 1960s.

Dong leader during the course of the war. Seldom were differences of opinion within the ruling body so transparently presented to the North Vietnamese public, and even more rarely did one member so stingingly attack his colleagues and their followers. The reasons for this departure from the usual practice of compromise and mollification of the minority were the momentous decisions announced by Le Duan. The Political Bureau was, in effect, destroying the tenuous compromise made at the Fifteenth Plenum in January 1959 and endorsed at the Third Party Congress. The revolution in South Vietnam had, in effect, replaced socialist construction of the North as the number-one priority of the Lao Dong party.

More important, Le Duan and his followers erased the thin line separating Lao Dong party support of the revolution in the South from active involvement of the entire government and society of the DRV. The Political Bureau had decided that North Vietnam could no longer sustain a pol-

41

icy of "guns and butter" and had opted for guns. Henceforth, every family in the North would be dramatically affected by the war in the South. The people would be asked to sacrifice future economic development in the struggle to reunite their country. They would be asked to sacrifice their sons to the war effort in the South. And although Le Duan had brushed aside the possibility, everyone knew that they risked seeing their own country engulfed in the destruction of war.

The Ninth Plenum had scarcely ended when its decisions took on a concrete reality. Across the border from China came a stream of military assistance, mostly in the form of small arms. Within months a Chinese-manufactured version of the Russian AK47 assault rifle had become the standard infantry weapon, not only for PAVN troops but for PLAF main force units as well. Meanwhile, in a move that only Ho Chi Minh could have arranged, a high-level delegation from the Lao Dong headed by Le Duan left for Moscow. The resulting communiqué was, as expected, cool, but the two Communist parties vowed to maintain "correct relations." For its part, the Vietnamese removed any possibility of an anti-Soviet purge in their own ranks by promising "to struggle for the sake of unity" even with revisionists. In order to maintain some influence in Hanoi, the Soviet Union continued its assistance to North Vietnam without interruption.

The Communist high command

In the meantime, General Giap and his General Staff were busy at work. Ironically, most of PAVN's leaders, including Giap, had vigorously opposed the decision to commit regular North Vietnamese troops to the war in the South. Now it was their responsibility to develop plans for executing the party's resolutions.

Exactly one year after the meeting of the Ninth Plenum, in December 1964, the first organized PAVN unit, the 95th Regiment of the 325th PAVN Division, entered GVN territory. From this point on, PAVN would play an increasingly important, ultimately decisive, role in the South.

The DRV Ministry of National Defense coordinated the planning for this deployment. The ministry was led by the Military High Command, headed by General Giap, minister of national defense, and consisted of the General Staff and three directorates. The General Staff directed operations, collected intelligence, developed plans, and oversaw personnel. The General Logistics Directorate assumed responsibility for logistical support, including medical services. The General Training Directorate carried out both individual and unit training, while the Political

Highlanders carry provisions to Communist troops in western Thua Thien Province, South Vietnam. The commitment of PAVN troops in 1964 greatly increased the Communists' need for food.

Directorate was the official party organ within the military, responsible for maintaining ideological reliability in the armed forces and overseeing most nonmilitary activities, including party meetings, study sessions, and entertainment. It also supervised the system of political commissars.

The Lao Dong's Central Military Party Committee linked the High Command to the party's Central Committee and Political Bureau. This party organ, wholly outside the governmental structure, enabled the Lao Dong party leadership to maintain strict control over the Ministry of Defense. In reality, it became an interlocking directorate, since the highest-ranking military men served alongside civilians on the committee. It was this system that placed Giap in the uncomfortable role of executing, as minister of defense, plans he had opposed as chairman of the Central Military Party Committee and member of both the Central Committee and Political Bureau.

The DRV High Command and the Lao Dong's Central Reunification Committee shared responsibility for COSVN activities. Until 1965 it was assumed in Saigon that COSVN directed all insurgent activities in South Vietnam. However, the two northern provinces of South Vietnam, Quang Tri and Thua Thien, which included Hue, had until 1954 been a part of Vietminh Region IV, which stretched across the DMZ. This rump region, known as Tri-Thien-Hue (TTH), may always have acted under the direct control of the High Command. In June 1966, as part of a larger reorganization of Communist geography, this command arrangement became clear. In addition, Region V (Trung Bo) was divided into two commands, the Western Highlands Front Command (or B-3 Front) and the reduced Region V, consisting of the remaining coastal provinces. The B-3 Front was autonomous only in military matters. It remained a part of Region V's party structure. The three new divisions were counterparts to and not subordinates of COSVN, although they maintained liaison with the Central Office (see chart and map, right).

At the strategic level, party influence dominated. When a Southern command required additional troops or supplies from the North, it petitioned the Central Reunification Committee, which took up the request with the Central Military Party Committee and, if necessary, with the Central Committee or Political Bureau. The results of those party deliberations were then passed on to the DRV's High Command, which coordinated their execution with the Southern command.

The provision of PAVN troops to the South began with conscription. In accordance with the 1959 draft law, all males between the ages of sixteen and forty-five were subject to a two-year term in the military. In 1964 this term was increased to three years, and in April 1965 service was extended "indefinitely." Those not exempted or deferred (the DRV, like the U.S., granted student deferments) awaited induction to begin their basic training.

Basic training

To prepare new recruits for combat in the South, the PAVN High Command modified its basic training program. It was modeled on the Chinese army's training method, which stressed the central role of political training to motivate soldiers and to avoid reliance on sophisticated weaponry and foreign aid. Chief of Staff General Van Tien Dung explained, "Military cadres must at the same time be political cadres, and . . . armed forces must at the same time be political forces."

The emphasis on political indoctrination began with basic training. Beginning with a five o'clock reveille, recruits underwent seven hours of intensive training six days a week. Four days were devoted to military training, the other two to political indoctrination. On Sundays recruits were given leave to visit their families.

After basic training, the recruits were asked if they wanted to volunteer to fight in the South. In the early years of the war, the system of volunteers seemed to work well enough. Many chose to do so on their own. Recalcitrants were coaxed into doing so largely through peer pressure. PAVN had little need to rely on threats or brandishments. If nothing else, many recruits believed that service in the South would benefit their later careers.

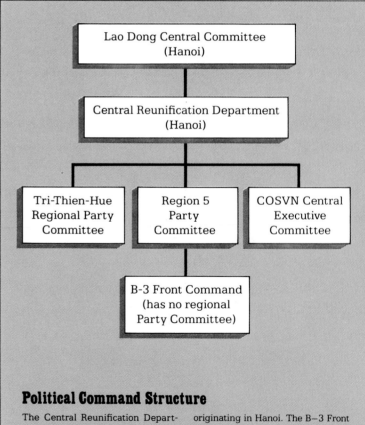

Political Command Structure

The Central Reunification Department of the Lao Dong's Central Committee supervised all party activities in South Vietnam. The regional party committees of Tri-Thien—Hue, Military Region (MR) 5, and COSVN implemented orders originating in Hanoi. The B-3 Front was only a military command and not a political entity. It therefore had no regional party committee and fell under the political jurisdiction of MR 5.

But, even among the true volunteers, few were enthusiastic about their assignment. One North Vietnamese later captured in the South estimated that "only 20 percent were enthusiastic about going South" and that he "was very worried about our trip South." Yet he volunteered because "I felt that it was my duty." This POW said that as many as 10 percent of the soldiers "boldly returned their personal effects and weapons and asked to go home." Most of these men, however, were persuaded to go by indoctrination and education. The only punishment for their earlier recalcitrance was to be criticized before their squad and platoon. Reindoctrination was not, as some might imagine, a program of terror and coercion. One recruit who experienced it explained to his American captors:

The cadre mobilized my spirit and told me that I could not stay behind because all my comrades were going. He said I was strong and healthy, so I should go South. My comrades were all very sad at first but the cadres mobilized their spirits and then they began to feel all right about it.

Later in the war, as manpower needs increased, the volunteer system was continued, but most soldiers who went South were simply chosen and informed while en route where they were going.

Once selected, soldiers designated for service in the South assembled at special military and political training centers. By the mid–1960s PAVN had established at least twenty-six training camps. The six–month specialized training course was organized around the monsoon cycle. Instruction ran from June to December so that the recruits were ready for the infiltration trek during the dry season.

PAVN military training was surprisingly conventional. Instruction centered around the use of rifles, mortars, and assault techniques. Notably absent was substantial training for jungle survival and combat. The course did stress physical endurance and march discipline in preparation for the walk south. The conditioning included marching with sixty–five–pound packs, simulating the thirty–mile–a–day hike over rugged terrain.

Political indoctrination, in contrast, was intense. One POW reported:

The soldier's supreme duty is to fight on the side of the Revolution. . . . The Revolution is going on in the South. North Vietnamese fighters must go there to fight on the people's side to free them from the yoke of American imperialism.

The recruits were given an optimistic view of the battlefield situation in the South. The men heard that the PLAF suffered few losses and controlled two–thirds of the country. While instructors conceded that American forces were well armed, they reported that GIs lacked motivational

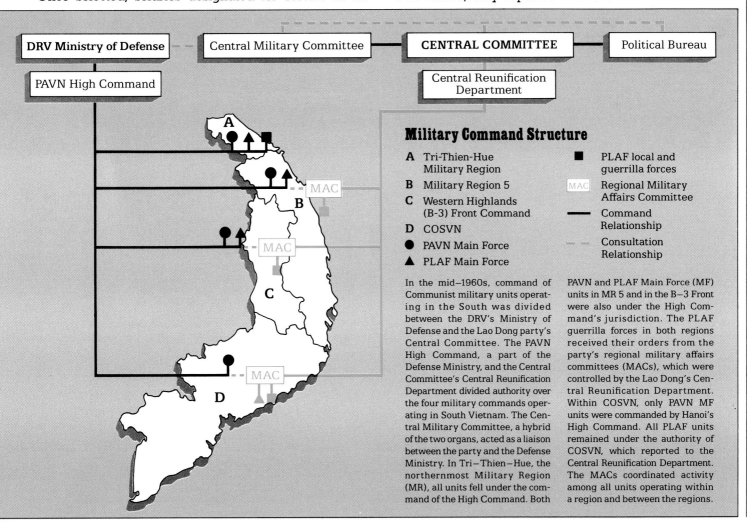

Military Command Structure

A Tri-Thien-Hue Military Region
B Military Region 5
C Western Highlands (B-3) Front Command
D COSVN
● PAVN Main Force
▲ PLAF Main Force

■ PLAF local and guerrilla forces
MAC Regional Military Affairs Committee
── Command Relationship
-- - Consultation Relationship

In the mid–1960s, command of Communist military units operating in the South was divided between the DRV's Ministry of Defense and the Lao Dong party's Central Committee. The PAVN High Command, a part of the Defense Ministry, and the Central Committee's Central Reunification Department divided authority over the four military commands operating in South Vietnam. The Central Military Committee, a hybrid of the two organs, acted as a liaison between the party and the Defense Ministry. In Tri–Thien–Hue, the northernmost Military Region (MR), all units fell under the command of the High Command. Both PAVN and PLAF Main Force (MF) units in MR 5 and in the B–3 Front were also under the High Command's jurisdiction. The PLAF guerrilla forces in both regions received their orders from the party's regional military affairs committees (MACs), which were controlled by the Lao Dong's Central Reunification Department. Within COSVN, only PAVN MF units were commanded by Hanoi's High Command. All PLAF units remained under the authority of COSVN, which reported to the Central Reunification Department. The MACs coordinated activity among all units operating within a region and between the regions.

DRV Ministry of Defense — Central Military Committee — CENTRAL COMMITTEE — Political Bureau

PAVN High Command

Central Reunification Department

zeal. ARVN was dismissed as a force with low morale and an aversion to combat.

Shortly before a soldier headed south, his food ration was quadrupled. One NCO reported that he could eat anything he wanted, including beef, pork, fish, cake, fruit, sweets, sugar, and milk. A PAVN trooper received two green uniforms, a pair of black pajamas, two pairs of underwear, a sheet of nylon, a cotton tent, a cord to transform the tent into a hammock, a pair of rubber sandals, a canteen, some medical supplies, and a seven days' ration of dried food. He carried his own personal weapon, either an AK47 or a semiautomatic carbine. Heavier weapons, including mortars and Chinese recoilless rifles, were infiltrated separately into the South.

Into the South

Now ready for infiltration, the soldiers began the easy part of their journey, traveling by train, truck, or boat to the Laotian border. From there they began a march of varying length down the Ho Chi Minh Trail, destined for a PAVN base area along the Laotian–South Vietnamese border. From there, troops could easily infiltrate into the South. PAVN maintained four major base areas, each serving as a conduit into different military regions in the Southern battlefield. Those heading for TTH Military Region either infiltrated directly across the DMZ or grouped in Base Area 604 (the numerical designations are American) along Route 9 or Base Area 611 adjacent to the A Shau Valley. Reaching the latter two defiles required twenty days. Men destined for Region V headed to Base Area 614, also near the A Shau, while those en route to the B-3 Front infiltrated from Base Area 609, a fifty-day trip from Vinh, including the march down the Ho Chi Minh Trail.

Until 1965, Transportation Group 559's commo–liaison chain extended only to Base Area 609. In that year PAVN began an extension of the Ho Chi Minh Trail, known as the Sihanouk Trail because it connected to a network of paths in Cambodia. The trail opened in May 1966, permitting Hanoi to resupply and reinforce COSVN in the Nam Bo region.

The Ho Chi Minh Trail, which prior to 1965 had been used almost exclusively to infiltrate personnel into South Vietnam, also became the main conduit for transporting supplies to the South. As a consequence, Transportation Group 559 began to improve the trail network. It constructed over 200 miles of two–lane dirt roads capable of accommodating truck traffic. By early 1968, 10,000 trucks could move down the trail at one time. The improvement of the trail, however, made the network a more conspicuous target of American bombing.

The North Vietnamese took several steps to limit the impact of bombing. Perhaps most important, infiltrating PAVN soldiers were restricted to the old pathways, while the improved roads were reserved for materiel. Since the trucks were the main target of U.S. bombers, infiltrating soldiers were thus largely immune from air attack. Captured PAVN soldiers reported that as many as 20 percent of all infiltrators did not complete the journey down the trail, but the vast majority of casualties resulted from disease, primarily malaria, and injuries sustained while marching over the rugged terrain. These POWs estimated that only 2 percent of the infiltrators were wounded or killed by U.S. bombing.

The volume of traffic moving down the trail increased yearly from its modest beginnings in 1964. In that year, 12,000 PAVN regulars reached South Vietnam. The following year the number doubled and may have tripled. Estimates for 1966 range from 58,000 to 90,000, and infiltration continued at the same pace through the first six months of 1967. The total number of PAVN troops reaching the South between 1964 and mid–1967 was about 150,000. Due to losses suffered in battle, however, no more than 50,000 PAVN soldiers were actually serving in the South at any one time, a modest number compared to the nearly 500,000–man American force fighting in Vietnam by mid–1967.

These numbers swelled, however, when the Communists began to reinforce their fighting strength in preparation for the great offensives of 1967 and 1968. In the second half of 1967 another 60,000 Northern troops reached Southern borders. And in 1968 more than 200,000 PAVN soldiers infiltrated, a figure equal to the total of the previous four years.

The PAVN "grunt"

PAVN soldiers somehow gained a reputation as fanatical, almost superhuman, fighters. In fact, they experienced war much as all soldiers do. In particular, they experienced a disillusionment that in many ways mirrored that of their American counterparts. Above all, PAVN soldiers were afraid, and with good reason. Of the 200,000 who infiltrated before 1968, few expected to avoid death or capture. Said one recruit after his capture, "I went to the South to liberate the Southerners and had no hope of returning." Nor did desertion offer any hope: "Had a man from my unit defected he would have been captured by the guerrillas; had he gotten lost he would have been captured by the ARVN."

PAVN soldiers also suffered from living conditions immeasurably poorer than those of the Americans. The diary entry for January 1966 of one Mai Van Hung reads:

How unbearable life is! Worse still there exists no stream in which to bathe except a mudhole large enough for a water buffalo to wallow in. How dreary is the life of a member of the Liberation Army! There is nothing for the Lunar New Year Celebration! I feel sad beyond words.

Like many American soldiers, PAVN troops were

shocked by the discrepancy between the propaganda they
heard in basic training and the
reception they received in the
South. One PAVN grunt re-
ported:

The cadre said that when we
reached the South we would be
welcomed by the people. But when
we did reach the South we didn't
see anybody coming out to welcome us. I thought the North had
sent us to liberate the South, and yet
people in the South expelled us
from their houses.

To their amazement, PAVN
soldiers, like the Americans,

*PLAF training mirrored the dual military-political in-
doctrination of PAVN. Above, guerrillas receive
bayonet training. Below, Political studies.*

they were told that they were
fighting to oust the American in-
vader. Reported one soldier, "I
saw that all who get killed and
wounded in this war are Vietnamese. When I thought about
that I felt we should not drag on
this war."

These problems were exacerbated as the vision of a quick
victory, as widespread in 1965
among PAVN troops as among
Americans, began to recede. In
1967 a survey of POWs revealed
that only 20 percent foresaw a
victory for the NLF, another 20
percent believed that the GVN

were isolated from the local population in the interest of
security and to prevent incidents with the villagers, particularly women. This annoyed the soldier who was told that
two-thirds of the South had been liberated: "We spent all
our time completely cut off from the people."

The PAVN grunts were also shocked to find that they
spent much of their time fighting fellow Vietnamese, when

would triumph, but 60 percent were uncertain. In the end,
PAVN soldiers were confronted with the same question
that gnawed at many Americans. "In what way does this
war benefit us?" Mai Van Hung plaintively asked in his
diary.

But despite all of these setbacks, deprivations, and dis-
illusionments, PAVN did not collapse from low morale. On

47

the contrary, its fighting effectiveness remained high. What made the morale of a PAVN unit something more than the morale of its individual soldiers, indeed, what made PAVN more than the sum of its parts, was a network of support that began at the top and reached down to the lowest grunt—a system that formed the soul of PAVN, a program developed and administered by the Lao Dong party.

Party and army

At the top of this system stood the PAVN High Command's Political Directorate, whose head was the chief political officer in the armed forces. Operating under his guidance were political officers, often called political commissars, assigned to each unit down to company level. The system of political officers paralleled that of the military officer corps, with the commissar holding the same rank as that of the unit commander.

Political officers had to belong to the "hard core" of the Lao Dong party with a class background of poor farmer, landless farmer, or laborer. American students of the DRV have largely focused on the potential for friction between political and military officers in the exercise of unit command, especially over military matters. And indeed, this was a source of continual concern at PAVN's highest echelons. The formal relationship between the two officers changed over time, reflecting the general tactical direction taken by the PAVN High Command. When military activity was emphasized, military commanders held the upper hand. When political struggle dominated, more power accrued to the political commissar. In all instances, each officer held the right to appeal decisions of his counterparts to higher authority.

However intriguing this dual command structure might be to westerners, it was not the most important function of the political commissar. Rather, in his day-to-day work he had to act as a combination chaplain, psychologist, older brother, confidant, and entertainer. PAVN soldiers, like Americans, spent much of their time battling boredom. The commissar organized study groups, cultural events, and entertainment programs and was available for private discussions to boost the morale of individual soldiers. In short, he was the representative of the party within the army and was expected to be an exemplary revolutionary fighter.

The most important responsibility of the political officer was to conduct the weekly criticism/self-criticism sessions. These sessions were conducted at every level of PAVN, from platoon to division. But the cornerstone of this system lay even deeper in the PAVN hierarchy—in the army's basic unit, the three-man cell.

The three-man cell was one of the Chinese Communist practices adopted by PAVN to control its troops and, above all, to maintain their spirit. Soldiers were organized into three-man units before they traveled south. One trooper, usually a recently promoted NCO or a two- to three-year veteran, assumed leadership. During battle, a soldier was expected to stay close to his cell mates. One POW relates, "If a cell member split from his cell during combat, our actions would become uncoordinated and our casualties would be higher."

The cell was one tool used to prevent desertion, but POWs pointed out that it was insufficient. "If a man wanted to desert he could easily do so . . . during rest-period after lunch or at night when he was alone. The three-man cell system does not require that cell members should always be close to each other, . . . only in battle."

Cell members typically formed strong personal bonds, as described to an American interrogator:

Whenever we were together, we spoke about our daily work, our family, our health, our joys and worries, so that we knew one another better. We also practiced self-criticism, so that we would be guided in our thinking.

The practice of self-criticism was the cement that glued together the three-man cell and with it the entire army. One American who studied the practice concluded:

Probably this form of psychological control—which is distantly related to, but entirely different from, indoctrination—is one of the principal bonds by which the PAVN army . . . is held together.

Criticism/self-criticism sessions provided an emotional catharsis for the PAVN grunts. They were encouraged to relate all matters that troubled them, even to criticize their superiors. The individual soldiers had ambivalent feelings about the sessions. It was fine to be praised and a form of relief to be able to talk about matters that caused trouble. But to become the object of criticism was something that every soldier feared. In the process of being criticized he could become completely isolated from his peers.

The sessions were probing. Superficial explanations of misbehavior did not suffice. For example, confessing concern about family in the North was not an acceptable explanation for perceived cowardice. Accusers continued to press until the soldier admitted his cowardice, his fear of the enemy and of death. Such practices were probably effective in changing behavior—a form of depth psychology—but must have been searing experiences for North Vietnamese twenty-year-olds no more willing to search their souls than a twenty-year-old anywhere.

The effectiveness of criticism/self-criticism cannot be underestimated. Many transgressions that in other armies might be punished by death—desertion, refusal to fight, disobedience—were punished in PAVN solely by public criticism.

Despite the effectiveness of the Communist control system, some PAVN soldiers did rally to the GVN. A study of over 200 deserters ascertained that not one had done so because of ideological disaffection or attraction to the South Vietnamese government's cause. Most rallied to the

Vietcong Snapshots

These snapshots, confiscated from a captured Vietcong, depict the life of a guerrilla at war and peace. *Above*, guerrillas complete a successful sapper attack by looting a South Vietnamese compound (left) and then nurse their wounded (right). Meanwhile, parents of PLAF soldiers receive accolades at a special Lao Dong rally. *Below*, the recruit poses with his family before reporting for duty.

GVN side because of hardships experienced in the South. Ironically, several ralliers indicated that their decision to defect was an outgrowth of self-criticism sessions. Forced to acknowledge their own fear of war, they opted out in the only way they knew—by surrendering.

In general, however, the process of self-criticism served PAVN well. For an army committed to fighting as long as necessary until victory was attained, for soldiers whose duty tour was "for the duration," a method of continual revitalization and renewal was essential. It was this process more than any other factor that made ordinary peasants into the tenacious fighting force that PAVN became. Combining the Confucian value of self-improvement with the Communist vision of the ideal revolutionary, the Lao Dong party was able to fashion this personal sense of struggle into a military strategy.

The ice tong of struggle

Unlike their counterparts in the United States, Giap and his senior aides in the Defense Ministry did not have to worry about the development of a strategy. Such decisions were reserved for the Political Bureau, and the Lao Dong leadership was well versed and experienced in the doctrine and strategy of revolutionary warfare. In Giap's own *People's War, People's Army* and Truong Chinh's *The Resistance Will Win*, the Political Bureau had, quite literally, written the books on the subject.

At the base of Communist strategy was the concept of *dau tranh*, usually translated as struggle or struggle movement. The Vietnamese term, however, fuses the internal and external substance of the word. *Dau tranh* was not only a struggle against something—U.S. imperialism—but also a struggle within oneself to become an ideal revolutionary. In Vietnamese, therefore, it suggests a total commitment to the cause. As one party member put it, "The essence of existence is *dau tranh*."

As a strategy, *dau tranh* takes on two forms: *dau tranh vu trang*, armed struggle, and *dau tranh chinh tri*, political struggle. Whether emanating from the Asian *yin yang* or Marxist dialectics, the two forms of *dau tranh* cannot be separated. Like half of a set of ice tongs, a single form is useless in itself.

Neither *armed struggle* nor *political struggle* has in Vietnamese quite the same meaning as its English equivalent. While *armed struggle* includes warfare, it also encompasses assassination and terror. Similarly, *political struggle* goes beyond the forms of traditional politics to include political coercion, or as Douglas Pike defined it, "politics with guns."

Political struggle assumes three different forms called *van*, or action programs. *Dan van*, action among the people, represented the program adopted in areas under Communist control. Here the insurgents could begin the construction of a socialist society in the South and provide

a safe haven for their troops. The second action program, *binh van*, or action among the military, concentrated on ARVN and attempted to undermine morale and gain converts within the South Vietnamese armed forces and government bureaucracy. As many as 12,000 *binh van* cadres were allocated to the effort during the war. Since the collapse of ARVN was a long-sought goal of the Communists, *binh van* was constantly emphasized in strategic planning.

At the heart of political *dau tranh*, however, lay *dich van*, action among the enemy. Under this banner the insurgents engaged in the full range of psychological warfare that marked their efforts. Ranging from ideological proselytizing in government-controlled villages, to whispering campaigns and rumormongering, to efforts at undermining the South Vietnamese economy, *dich van* sought to rot the government from within. Nor was *dich van* limited to South Vietnam's borders. It encompassed Communist efforts to influence public opinion throughout the world, in the United States, and among America's allies; to gain support in the Third World; and to bolster relations with Communist countries.

Political struggle in the form of the three *van* programs when combined with armed struggle constituted the entire practice of war engaged in by the Vietnamese Communists. As Douglas Pike put it:

Every act, every guerilla ambush or military attack, every propaganda broadcast, each Ho Chi Minh speech, every communist mission abroad, every Party cell in the village to the Politburo in Hanoi—all came within the scope and framework of these two kinds of *dau tranh*.

The climax of Communist strategy lay in the concept of *Khoi Nghia*, or General Uprising. Some observers, including Pike, have suggested that *Khoi Nghia* served only the purpose of a social myth, that is, one that may never come true but whose importance lies in the willingness of people to believe in its truth. Certainly *Khoi Nghia* served that function. In contrast to American strategy, which could never quite explain how the war would end victoriously, the General Uprising provided an awe-inspiring image to both the leaders and their followers of how victory would be obtained. The people, united, would spontaneously arise and cast aside the hated enemy government and army, already in its death throes when caught between the tongs of armed and political *dau tranh*.

But the concept of General Uprising also resolved a very real ideological impasse for the Vietnamese as they adapted Maoist revolutionary theory to Vietnam. In Vietnam as in China, revolution would expand from sparsely settled mountains to highly populated rural areas, finally isolating the major urban areas, where bourgeois and antirevolutionary ideology was strongest. Mao could depend upon the sheer mass of China's rural population to provide the final push to liberate the cities. South Vietnam's 16 million people could not provide the same force as China's half-billion. To resolve this dilemma, the Vietnamese Communists adopted the General Uprising. The final liberation, the liberation of the cities, would come not from an external assault as in China but from an internal explosion, the rising of the people.

No description of Lao Dong military strategy is complete without including the concept of protracted warfare. Drawing from Vietnam's own 2,000 years of history and from the Marxist belief in historical inevitability, the Communists believed firmly that time was on their side. A drawn-out conflict, therefore, could only aid them. Endless war was not a Communist goal but a means to achieve victory. Basic Communist strategy held that the armed forces should always be *capable* of fighting a protracted conflict, and virtually every Lao Dong military plan at least bowed in that direction. The mere threat of protracted conflict strengthened not only military *dau tranh* but also political *dau tranh* and particularly *dich van*, action among the enemy. The enemy could be demoralized as much by the prospect of no end to a war as by the war itself.

The strategy of *dau tranh* and protracted conflict

formed the bible of revolutionary warfare as practiced by the Vietnamese Communists. So sacred was this doctrine, no member of the party ever dared attack it directly. It was, in fact, one of those articles of faith that bound the members of the Political Bureau together through all of the years of factionalism. But, like any sacred text, it was subject to interpretation, or in military terminology, to tactical flexibility. The strategy prescribed that the Communists use a combination of political and military struggle to achieve their goals but did not reveal in what combination. It was the task of the Political Bureau to determine which of the two impulses was to be emphasized, and this responsibility provided the Northern-firsters a continuing opportunity to press their case against the conduct of the war in the South.

At the Ninth Plenum of the Central Committee in December 1963, the Lao Dong party approved the policy advocated by Le Duan and his allies of "racing against time

Members of the NLF organize and entertain residents of a South Vietnamese village during a nocturnal visit in 1965. Such meetings were an essential part of "action among the people."

in order to achieve the ultimate victory in a relatively short period of time." By augmenting PLAF forces with regular PAVN troops, the Southern-firsters believed that they could make the "puppet army [ARVN] disintegrate in a basic and irretrievable manner," as Le Duan later described the goal.

The race against time

The Communist forces came very close to achieving their aim. By the spring of 1965, they had destroyed virtually every ARVN reserve battalion. This meant that beleaguered Saigon units could no longer expect *any* reinforcement when surrounded by enemy forces. All that the Communists need do was to mass superior forces against individual ARVN units and slowly destroy them, what military specialists call "defeat in detail."

The Communist plan was ultimately foiled by the introduction of American ground combat forces. In this desperate situation, U.S. troops served as a replacement for

A B-57 light bomber stands in ruins, testimony to a guerrilla attack on Bien Hoa air base on October 31, 1964, in which five B-57s were destroyed and four Americans were killed.

the ARVN reserve battalions and prevented insurgent forces from defeating ARVN in detail. Le Duan's operating assumption, that the American government would not commit substantial numbers of its own troops to the conflict, had proven to be a grave mistake. Even after the United States had initiated its modulated program of bombing North Vietnam—Operation Flaming Dart and Operation Rolling Thunder—Le Duan's faction had pressed forward believing that the bombing had come too late to alter the situation on the Southern battlefield. But the introduction of combat troops in March, followed by a major build-up in July, had turned the immediate tide of battle.

Within the Political Bureau, however, the second-guessing went beyond blaming the setback on the deployment of American troops. Le Duan had strong words for General Giap, who had taken twelve months after the Ninth Plenum to infiltrate the first PAVN regiment into South Vietnam in December 1964. Le Duan charged that a chance for victory had been lost because of foot-dragging on the part of "some comrades," adding, "efforts were not appropriately made to give strong impetus to the movement so that the war situation could be rapidly changed." But Le Duan's opponents refused to accept the blame, and

they focused attention on the controversial commander of the Southern forces.

Although the Americans did not learn of it until 1966, sometime in 1964 General Nguyen Chi Thanh, having withdrawn from public view the previous year, surreptitiously made his way into South Vietnam to assume the command of COSVN. Replacing Nguyen Van Cuc, a civilian, Thanh's appointment undoubtedly reflected a decision to emphasize military *dau tranh* in the South. In a remarkable parallel to the strategy that General William Westmoreland adopted for American troops the following year, Thanh wanted to draw ARVN forces into the highlands where his now superior forces could destroy them through attrition.

In order to accomplish his goal, Thanh had to militarize the entire movement in the South. Political organization, especially in the heavily populated Mekong Delta and in urban areas, was de-emphasized in favor of the recruitment of military personnel. Military training of these new recruits dominated political indoctrination. Moreover, the regional and local forces—the guerrillas proper—became little more than adjuncts to the main force units. Ill-trained and poorly experienced guerrillas were rushed into main force units to replenish their ranks as casualties mounted under the quickening tempo of the fighting. Thanh had, in effect, mortgaged the future of the revolution in his "race against time."

Thanh's gamble seemed to be paying off until American combat troops arrived in South Vietnam. Not only did ARVN suffer serious setbacks, but the revolutionary movement in the South gained adherents and popularity. An estimate later prepared by MACV and the U.S. Joint Chiefs of Staff concluded that "by the fall of 1964 ... the National Liberation Front enjoyed the active, willing cooperation of more than 50 percent of the population in South Vietnam." Yet, at the end of 1965, victory was rapidly slipping away as the Central Committee assembled for its Twelfth Plenum.

"Victory within a relatively short period of time"

Like many Lao Dong policy discussions, what is known about the debate at the Twelfth Plenum has largely been learned by inference. The following April (1966), the leaders of the Lao Dong addressed the National Assembly, presumably to brief the parliament on the results of the Central Committee meeting. Giap's speech, alone among the leadership, was never printed in Hanoi's newspapers. Giap disappeared from public view until the end of the summer. Thanh later wrote that there had been "some ideological wavering" within the party during that period and charged that some had wanted "to stop when the revolution required that one continue to progress." That spring, General Nguyen Van Vinh secretly traveled to

COSVN headquarters to brief the Southern leaders on the results of the Twelfth Plenum and admitted that a faction in the party was "afraid of the Americans, dared not to fight them. It kept on discussing and arrived at no conclusion."

The nature of the criticism offered by Giap, Truong Chinh, and the Northern-firsters can be inferred from their writings. At the heart of the matter they believed that Thanh's failure was, as one authority on North Vietnam put it, "the result of the faulty strategy he was following."

In Giap's view, the decision to concentrate energies in the highlands had led to an uneven development in the *dau tranh* strategy. Giap's watchwords were "coordinated and independent fighting methods" employed in the "three zones." The three zones were the highlands, where Main Force units would be most effective; the populated coastal regions (the rural zone) in which lower-level guerrilla fighting was most appropriate; and urban areas, which required political proselytizing and organization punctuated with occasional terrorist activities. These tac-

A dead woman, victim of a Vietcong terrorist attack on the U.S. Embassy in Saigon on March 30, 1965, lays amid the burning debris.

Modernizing PAVN

After the Vietnam War, many "armchair generals" believed that a critical weakness in the South Vietnamese army (ARVN) had been the elaborate program carried out by American advisers in the late 1950s to create a conventional fighting force. If this were so, it was also a debility the North Vietnamese army (PAVN) had to overcome as well. The fact was that after the Geneva agreements, both sides held the same goal—to protect themselves from an invasion by the other. Ironically, these very policies to enhance self-defense exacerbated fears of invasion by the other, thus making further modernization seem even more necessary. To add to the irony, both sides, fearing that self-defense required the ability to counter a conventional military attack, organized their new forces in ways that were ultimately inappropriate for the war they would find themselves fighting by the mid-1960s.

After 1954, the DRV leadership recognized the need to convert its essentially guerrilla force into a modern, professional army to defend and consolidate the newly created socialist state. The military leadership ordered the formation of new divisions, integrated the "regroupees" into the regular army, and weeded out those unfit for service. It also established separate commands for national defense and internal security.

PAVN's "peace-time modernization program" went into high gear in 1957 when the military command realized that modernization required the creation of regularized ranks and an officer corps. In April 1958 the DRV enacted the "Law Es-tablishing a System of Service of Officers." The statute replaced the Vietminh-era scheme of assigning a "functional commander," like a regimental or company commander, who bore the responsibilities but not the status of an officer, with a formalized hierarchy of ranks, promotions, and pay scales, along with representative epaulets and insignias. The leadership established officer training schools that emphasized modern combined-armed tactics in place of "revolutionary" guerrilla techniques. The military command also developed specialized branches and programs to train technicians manning these new units.

After approving these initial moves toward professionalization, the Lao Dong party became wary that a "purely bourgeois, militarist" viewpoint might dominate in the "people's army" and instituted a series of political reeducation programs for PAVN personnel. The party intended to raise the "socialist consciousness" of the men and eliminate any nationalist or liberal ideas that might have lingered from the National Front ideology of the war with the French. The training included courses in Marxist dialectics, the principles of collective leadership, and the role of an officer in a socialist army in guiding and educating his troops.

While both party and army leaders agreed that modernizing PAVN was a priority, the development of a regular armed force created tension between the political and military authorities, fueling arguments about how to proceed. Basically, party officials feared that too great an emphasis on "professionalism" and technology would detract from the political work required to maintain a revolutionary people's army. Because of the preeminence of the party in a socialist society, Lao Dong leaders considered the party's control of the military essential. As generals Vo Nguyen Giap and Nguyen Chi Thanh noted in 1958: "We must not neglect building the army politically and ideologically because of regularization and modernization; on the contrary, we must unceasingly strengthen the political consciousness of the army ... [so that] the army will serve its revolutionary mission."

The debate between the party "politicians" and the military experts gave rise to another controversy summed up as "men versus weapons." The proponents of the "soldier-as-politician" viewpoint touted the supremacy of men over technology, stressing that the ideological commitment and motivational zeal of the "armed masses" could supplant the role played by modern weapons and techniques. The "professionalists," on the other hand, believed that technological factors were of equal importance to human elements. They felt that if an army was to be successful in modern times, it must keep up with scientific advances. No one, however, challenged the importance of the party's role in the military. Lieutenant General Hoang Van Thai wrote an article that appeared in the December 1960 edition of *Hoc Tap* and honored the "decisive role of man" in the army but also emphasized the need to modernize and master skills, because "either we will progress to acquire new technique, or we will be exterminated."

Although North Vietnam continued to upgrade its forces with more advanced Soviet- and Chinese-supplied weapons and training techniques, the debate subsided by 1960 with a decision to adopt an official doctrine of "men over weapons." Party theory was not the only factor in reaching this conclusion. The simple fact was that the North had limited material resources, which made the adoption of a "human factors," revolutionary approach, the only real option for the DRV.

Even though the decision was a defeat for the most extreme program of the military professionals, the clear trend in PAVN throughout the early 1960s proceeded toward greater modernization and professionalization. By the end of 1963, however, as the prospect of introducing regular PAVN units into the intensifying conflict in the South grew imminent, the leadership began to scrutinize even more closely what it had created. Meanwhile in the South, the conventionally trained ARVN was finding itself increasingly ill prepared to wage its war against the guerrilla insurgents. The irony of the parallel modernization programs on both sides of the DMZ was played out in early 1965, as regiments of the 325th PAVN Division filtered into South Vietnam to meet the regular forces of ARVN in the irregular, guerrilla warfare of the central highlands.

tics were to be employed in their respective zones "independently," that is, by conducting each type according to the abilities of the forces and actual situation in each area. At certain crucial points all three fighting methods in all three zones would be coordinated into a general offensive.

This was Giap's method of conducting revolutionary warfare and he found Thanh's performance wholly inadequate. Communist activities in the lowlands were so sporadic that General Westmoreland later wrote that in 1965 "Viet Cong operations in the Delta remained at a low level of intensity and thus offered a lesser immediate threat." Equally important, urban organizations remained undeveloped. During the 1965 Communist offensive no major city or provincial capital was captured and held by insurgent forces. Giap was, in effect, accusing Thanh of a most serious Communist sin: inattention to the political dimension of warfare.

With the Le Duan faction still dominating the party's deliberations, the Political Bureau and Central Committee again brushed aside the arguments of the Northern-firsters and approved a continuation of Thanh's tactics. Captured documents revealed that the Central Committee called for "tremendous efforts" to result in a "decisive victory within a relatively short period of time." As Le Duan later explained in his letter to COSVN, "victory on the battlefield is the decisive factor for the solution of the overall war." He called for the further development of revolutionary forces in the South, in "particular the military force."

The struggle of the Northern-firsters

The Twelfth Plenum represented yet another clear defeat for General Giap and Truong Chinh. Still, they did not give up the fight. There was much in the resolutions of the Central Committee that remained open to interpretation and emphasis. The Lao Dong leadership continued to pay lip service to "protracted conflict" and recognized the weakness of the guerrilla movement in the South, calling for its improvement and increased emphasis on political organization. As the number of American troops in South Vietnam continued to rise, reaching the 200,000 mark in early 1966 and passing 400,000 by the end of the year, the Northern-firsters had further ground for questioning tactics that, in their view, played directly into the hands of Americans.

Northern-firsters argued that guerrilla tactics were more appropriate than main force tactics since they risked less exposure to American firepower. Naturally then, political *dau tranh* should be emphasized over military *dau tranh*. In these circumstances the Southerners could revert to the principle of "self-reliance" and cease calling for PAVN reinforcements.

Northern-firsters also looked starkly at American strength. America could never be defeated in a conventional sense because of its insurmountable advantages in technology and manpower. It could only be worn down in a war of wills. Ultimately, peace talks would have to negotiate the U.S. out of the war, following a period of "fighting while talking." The current policy to reject all negotiations was thus in error.

At the root of the entire debate lay the goal of the war. The Southern-firsters still hoped for a quick victory, arguing that the "race against time" could produce a "decisive victory within a relatively short period." The Northern-firsters called for a return to protracted conflict of at least two stages: first, wearing down the Americans and forcing their withdrawal, and only then, confronting ARVN and the Saigon government directly.

There was much logic on the side of the Northern-firsters, but Le Duan and Thanh were equally certain of victory. Le Duan, displaying his obeisance to the concept of protracted war, pointed out that the struggle in the South was already more than a decade old and that calling for protracted war "does not mean the war ... is only at its beginning." As for Thanh, he refused to consider any alternative to his offensive strategy: "If we want to take the defensive position, we should withdraw to India," he wrote.

By the end of 1966, however, Thanh's tactics began receiving criticism from a new source. The general's own subordinates in COSVN argued that he had misused Southern guerrilla forces and complained that "leadership over the guerrilla war" had increasingly fallen to military commanders, often from PAVN. The old-line Southern cadres were pushed to the side.

With the debate over the conduct of the war swirling from one end of Vietnam to the other, the Central Committee convened for its Thirteenth Plenum in December 1966. On the basis of its resolutions it appears that, in fact, two plenums were held, one in December and the other in January.

During the December meeting, the Lao Dong leadership reaffirmed the basic tactical emphasis adopted twelve months earlier despite the lack of success on the battlefield and the barrage of criticism both north and south of the DMZ. While this seemed to confirm the continued dominance of Le Duan's faction within the leadership, it made one major change in strategy that showed the first fissures in the Southern-first alliance. Acting against the long-held opinion of Thanh and Le Duan, the Central Committee resolved that "in view of the character of the war, diplomatic struggle has an important, positive, active role." For the first time, the Central Committee showed a willingness to open negotiations with the United States and assigned the Political Bureau the task of determining when and under what conditions those talks could begin.

Until the Thirteenth Plenum the position of the Lao Dong on negotiations had been simple: the party would only accept a U.S. surrender. The "Four Point" plan presented by Pham Van Dong in April 1965 had required the U.S. to "withdraw from South Vietnam all U.S. troops, military personnel and weapons . . . and cancel its 'military alliance' with South Vietnam." It also demanded that the U.S. halt its bombing of the DRV by ending all "acts of war against North Vietnam." For the next year and a half the DRV refused to budge from this formula. Pham Van Dong and Foreign Minister Nguyen Duy Trinh, both members of the Political Bureau, were known advocates of opening negotiations, but the dominance of Le Duan's faction within the ruling body seemed to preclude any strategy that would detract from the pursuit of a quick victory.

At the December meeting a subtle realignment of factions must have taken place. For the first time since 1957, Pham Van Dong and Trinh allied themselves with the Northern-firsters. It is possible that Ho Chi Minh joined them as well. The results of that realignment became apparent within one month. On January 28, 1967, Foreign Minister Trinh announced that if the United States wanted negotiations "it must first halt unconditionally the bombing raids and all other acts of war against the DRV." After that, he added, "There could be talks between the DRV and the United States." Nowhere did he mention the withdrawal of American forces from South Vietnam as a precondition. It represented the first victory of the Northern-first faction in the Political Bureau since 1959. The Northern-firsters had long argued that the war in the South should not endanger the socialist construction of the North. Nearly two years of sustained American bombing north of the DMZ had not succeeded in paralyzing the Communist war effort, but it had made impossible progress in economic development. In January 1967 the Political Bureau decided to take steps to return to the spirit of the resolution of the Third Party Congress. The North was to be spared as much as possible from the destruction of the war of liberation in the South.

The Southern-firsters' last stand

The results of the first session of the Thirteenth Plenum suggested the creation of the third faction within the Political Bureau, a middle group including Ho, Pham Van Dong, and Trinh. On the question of negotiations they were willing to side with the Northern-firsters. But on the conduct of the war, they continued to stand beside Le Duan and their commander in the field, General Thanh. The significance of this new faction could not have been lost on the Southern-firsters. It could well swing to the side of Giap and Truong Chinh on other questions as well. It was probably, then, with some sense of desperation that Thanh and Le Duan considered their options for 1967.

Most observers speculate that it was Le Duan who presented to the second session of the Thirteenth Plenum the blockbuster resolution in January 1967. Having not yet succeeded in winning a "decisive victory within a relatively short period of time," Le Duan now asked the party to in-

struct the Southern command to win "a decisive victory . . . in the *shortest time possible.*"

In approving this resolution, the Central Committee, as usual, left it to the Political Bureau and its Military Affairs Committee to develop the military and political plan for carrying out the decree.

It is clear that a strenuous debate took place within the party leadership over how to define a "decisive victory" and how to do so in the "shortest time possible." It is likely that General Thanh, presenting the military plans for the Southern-firsters, called for a fairly conventional "general offensive." Many observers believe that he and Le Duan wanted to attempt one all-out effort to win the war on the battlefield. They hoped to destroy ARVN and thus cause the collapse of the Saigon government.

No copy of the original plan proposed by Thanh and Le Duan has ever been revealed, but something like it must have been presented to the party leadership, for during the first four months of 1967 the Northern-firsters responded with a series of articles with a single theme: the importance of guerrilla warfare. Giap, himself, took a positive tone in a speech presented to leading North Vietnamese military commanders. "It is obvious," he told them, "that developing guerrilla war to an increasingly high level is one of the main duties . . . in bringing the resistance to final victory." Another article published under the pseudonym Cuu Long took a more critical stance. Cuu Long charged that the Southern leadership "has not yet kept up with the developing war's requirements [the entrance of the Americans] and with the immense potential of the masses [developing guerrillas]." He castigated Thanh for a "bureaucratic, superficial, and lazy" approach to his duties and blamed it on a "rightist, negative" attitude that "feared difficulties and hardships."

In July the Southern-firsters were dealt a severe blow. The DRV announced that General Nguyen Chi Thanh had died of a heart attack in a Hanoi hospital. One of the two most vigorous proponents of the Southerners' cause, and their leading military spokesman, was silenced just as the party was making one of its most momentous decisions. Political Bureau member Pham Hung received the appointment to replace Thanh, and he arrived at COSVN in the early autumn of 1967. While Pham Hung was a long-time associate of Le Duan, the selection of a civilian to replace Thanh may have signified a decision on the part of the Political Bureau to reemphasize political *dau tranh* in the continuing struggle.

During this factional fighting the Military Affairs Committee continued to formulate its plans to carry out the resolutions of the Thirteenth Plenum. On the basis of those resolutions, Le Duan and Thanh's plan for a general mili-

A PAVN soldier pays the price for North Vietnamese intervention during the American operation Masher/White Wing in February 1966 in Binh Dinh Province.

tary offensive was approved, and the High Command immediately began the task of providing the necessary troops for the Southern battlefield. But it appears that the Southerners' original plan was substantially modified. In addition to the general offensive, the party drew up and approved plans for an all-out effort by the guerrillas in rural areas, an effort that was intended to culminate in a final general uprising and victory. The author of such a plan could be none other than General Vo Nguyen Giap.

Why did Giap, who for nearly a decade had urged restraint and caution on the Southern battlefield, suddenly execute an abrupt about-face, not only approving the general offensive but adding to it the more ambitious program of a general uprising?

In the first place, the PAVN commander was faced with a fait accompli. The party had approved the general offensive, and it had become his duty as minister of defense to execute the policy whether he approved of it or not. What he succeeded in doing, however, was to integrate the conventional military offensive into his own theory of revolutionary war. The plan he developed would have three distinct phases. In phase one, independent fighting methods would be employed in all three zones. Huge conventional battles would be initiated in the highlands, guerrilla activities in the lowlands would increase dramatically, and urban organization would be heavily emphasized. In phase two, all three methods would be further intensified, this time in a coordinated effort to hand ARVN a crushing defeat and instigate mass uprisings throughout the country. Phase three would be the crowning blow, a decisive and coordinated strike employing Main Force, guerrilla, and political activities at a major target, possibly Saigon, to overthrow the South Vietnamese government.

The plan had much to recommend itself to Giap. While PAVN forces would be extensively employed, especially in phase one, the main burden would fall on the Southerners themselves. They would have to recruit, train, and deploy the guerrilla forces and coordinate the final uprising. The NLF, not PAVN, would have to bear the major burden.

If the offensive achieved maximum success, it would bring a great victory to the Communists and there would be enough glory for all to share. If it failed, however, the Southerners would suffer the most and the weakness of their organization would become obvious to all in the Political Bureau. It would be the Southern-firsters' last chance.

Giap's plan appealed to the other factions within the Political Bureau as well. For the Southern-firsters it represented a chance to end the war quickly, their major goal since 1964. On a tactical level, destruction of ARVN forces remained the highest priority, and to accomplish this the

PLAF was being augmented with a massive infusion of regular PAVN troops, just as the Southerners had requested. For the newly formed "negotiations faction" within the Political Bureau—Pham Van Dong, Ho Chi Minh, and Nguyen Duy Trinh—Giap's plan also offered great promise. While they had already altered the DRV's negotiation strategy, limiting the preconditions for talks to an end to the American bombing of the North, they still believed that successful talks required a major show of force on the battlefield. General Vinh told the leaders of COSVN, "As long as [the Americans] still believe that if they introduce more troops they can win, they will pursue the war. As soon as they see that no matter how many troops they introduce they are still defeated, then their aggressive will will be crushed." Giap's offensive might well bring the Americans to that point.

To this the Northern-firsters, including Truong Chinh, could nod in agreement. If the offensive resulted in the opening of negotiations and the cessation of the bombing of the DRV, one of their principal goals would be reached. The war would again be confined to the Southern battlefield and the North spared the destructiveness of the air attacks. In addition, the Northern-firsters readily approved of Giap's reemphasis on guerrilla warfare and political *dau tranh*, and the plan to confront the American forces in phase one.

Giap's three-phase offensive became best known for its second phase: the Tet offensive of 1968. But it is as a total plan that one must assess its goals. It is precisely because Giap offered something to every faction in the Political Bureau that this task becomes difficult. COSVN informed its Southern cadres that the decisive victory Giap's plan promised would result in the liberation of the South. But only to them and the Southern-firsters in the North did the winter-spring campaign take on the semblance of a "go for broke" effort. The other factions in the Political Bureau were willing to settle for a much less ambitious "decisive victory." For them the victory would not mean the end of the war in the South but the inauguration of a new phase in the struggle, one that would bring the Communists closer to ultimate victory.

The winter-spring offensive

Giap launched phase one of his offensive in October 1967, directly assaulting American fighting positions along South Vietnam's borders. Relying heavily on Main Force units, PAVN attacked at Con Thien, Loc Ninh, and Dak To to test American reactions. As expected, MACV rushed its

Antiaircraft guns in North Vietnam's panhandle protect trucks headed for the Southern front in the mid-1960s.

troops to the battle sites to reinforce U.S. positions and to engage Giap's troops in General Westmoreland's long-sought set-piece battles. The cost of the intelligence gained by Giap, however, was high. Over 5,000 PAVN troops were killed in the battle of Dak To alone. Guerrilla activities also intensified during the three months of phase one as attacks on South Vietnamese officials and civilians both increased by more than 60 percent over previous months.

The result of the independent phase of the offensive was inconclusive; the loss of some of his best PAVN forces must have been painful to Giap. Overall, however, the situation must have looked promising to him as he maneuvered to initiate phase two, scheduled to begin in January 1968. Surrounding the U.S. Marine base at Khe Sanh, the general could be confident that the Americans would respond by reinforcing the border regions. PLAF Main Force and guerrilla units moved into position to attack American military installations and take on ARVN in head-to-head combat. In the cities, urban guerrillas and propaganda experts, whose ranks had been greatly increased by a massive recruitment drive characterized mostly by impressment, waited anxiously for the beginning of the lunar new year, Tet 1968. They hoped to celebrate it with a "decisive victory," only days away.

In Hanoi, in the Political Bureau and Foreign Ministry, there was also a burst of activity. On December 30, 1967, just as phase one of the offensive was ending, Foreign Minister Nguyen Duy Trinh reiterated North Vietnam's bargaining position but with a slight alteration crafted to catch the ears of those versed in diplomatic nuance. Instead of stating that negotiations *could* begin once the United States stopped the bombing of the North, he now promised that such talks *will* take place once the airplanes were grounded. Trinh and Pham Van Dong realized that the American response would come only after the Communists punctuated their newest "peace feeler" with their most ambitious offensive in the South. If the prongs of military and political *dau tranh* worked in coordination, negotiations could begin. And for the Northern-firsters, that would mean a respite from the bombing and an opportunity to begin again on their first priority—the reconstruction of the North. After three years of bombardment and destruction under the most extensive and intensive strategic bombing program in history, that would be victory enough.

PLAF main force soldiers race into battle hauling a 12.7MM machine gun behind them at the outbreak of the Tet offensive in February 1968.

Ho Chi Minh Trail

Just as the U.S. military build-up in South Vietnam during the 1960s symbolized the expansion of America's involvement in the Vietnam War, so too did the development of the Ho Chi Minh Trail represent the escalating and ultimately decisive role the North played in the conflict. The maze of rudimentary paths and trails that snaked through the sparsely populated forests and hills along the Laotian border served through 1964 as the main infiltration route for increasing numbers of Communist troops, mostly regroupees returning South. Starting in the mid-1960s, substantial amounts of supplies began filtering down an expanded and improved trail, in addition to ever-increasing numbers of regular PAVN soldiers. After 1968, the Ho Chi Minh Trail became the North's main conduit to the Southern battlefield and a true symbol of the "North Vietnamization" of the war. At the same time the trail network came under the increased pressure and harassment of stepped-up U.S. interdiction campaigns.

On the North Vietnam side of the border a convoy of supply trucks winds through the Truong Son Mountains toward Laos in 1959.

After American aircraft began regular attacks against the trail, PAVN engineering squads were kept busy repairing the damage caused by U.S. air strikes. Top. A soldier directs truck traffic through a heavily bombed portion of the trail. Above. Members of the 39th Engineering Battalion fill bomb craters in a devastated area. Right. Using hand tools and bulldozers, an engineering unit widens a mountainous section of the Ho Chi Minh Trail.

Scouts perched atop a mountain watch for approaching enemy aircraft to warn infiltrating soldiers of their approach.

A soldier leads a column of elephants transporting weapons to Communist forces in the central highlands.

Left. A truck carrying PAVN regulars crosses a rickety bridge along a coastal route of the trail.

Fortress North Vietnam

December 1, 1966, was one of those rare days during the winter monsoon when the skies over Hanoi shone clear and bright. The respite from several weeks of clouds and steady rain was not welcome, for U.S. bombers, no longer grounded by the monsoon overcast, suddenly swooped down in waves over the outskirts of the city. Twenty U.S. Navy jets damaged the Van Dien truck depot and army barracks just five miles south of the center of Hanoi, while sixty air force F-4C Phantoms hit the Ha Gia oil facility north of the city. For the next two weeks air strikes rocked the Hanoi area. On December 4, American warplanes pounded the railroad switching yard, only four miles from downtown Hanoi. And on December 13 and 14, U.S. bombers again attacked the Van Dien military installations and the Yen Vien railroad yards.

The December air raids against Hanoi marked the beginning of a new, and potentially devastating, phase of the American bombing of North

Above. *Hanoi residents rummage through the smoldering remains of their homes after a U.S. air attack in December 1966.*

Vietnam. Since the start of the U.S. air campaign, code named Rolling Thunder, in March 1965, American bombers had been striking ever closer to North Vietnam's industrial heartland and most populous region. In June 1966, 116 U.S. Navy and Air Force planes had for the first time blasted petroleum storage tanks in the port of Haiphong, a portent of what would soon befall the nearby capital of Hanoi. By year's end, military and industrial facilities in North Vietnam's major cities were becoming targets for U.S. air power. Although President Johnson prohibited American planes from attacking residential sections in central Hanoi and Haiphong, he gradually approved military targets well inside the boundaries of both cities.

North Vietnamese leaders dreaded the prospect of U.S. air attacks on their urban industrial and population centers, but they were well prepared for them. Following the United States's Tonkin Gulf retaliatory air strikes called Operation Pierce Arrow in August 1964, according to North Vietnamese Army Chief of Staff General Van Tien Dung, "Our party soon realized that the United States might carry out the plot to prosecute a war of destruction against the North on a permanent basis." As a precaution, the Political Bureau enacted a sweeping measure to reduce the vulnerability of its urban population to the American bombing. On February 28, 1965, it ordered all persons not directly involved in wartime production or combat to evacuate the country's major cities as a preventive "anti-aircraft measure."

Preparing for the worst

The order initially affected only children and the very old. But inasmuch as 40 percent of the North's population was under the age of fifteen, a substantial number of people were involved. By the end of 1965, for example, as many as 100,000 people had left Hanoi. Nearly 400,000 more followed in 1966. Hanoi's mayor, Tran Duy Hung, recalled, "In 1964 [after Pierce Arrow] we began discussing preparations for air raids on Hanoi. In 1965 we put the plans into practice, and we prepared our minds for the coming fierce battle against the enemy." In January 1966 the Soviet newspaper *Pravda* reported that of Haiphong's 230,000 people, some 50,000 children and a part of the adult population had been evacuated. Other cities, like Nam Dinh, Thanh Hoa, Viet Tri, and Vinh, also began dispersing their inhabitants to the countryside.

After the U.S. bombing of Haiphong in June 1966, the North Vietnamese government expanded its evacuation

Preceding page. *PAVN soldiers ready a Soviet-built SA-2 missile for launch during an air-raid alert in 1972.*

decree in Hanoi to include everyone not "truly indispensable to the life of the capital"—not just the very young or elderly but mothers, artisans, teachers, shopkeepers, and laborers. Other cities followed suit. As an inducement, the authorities issued certificates entitling evacuees to 30 percent fare reductions on trains and 20 percent on buses and boats. The French newspaper *Le Monde* reported in July 1966 that as many as 10,000 people were leaving Hanoi each day by truck, car, bicycle, or on foot.

Daily, throughout North Vietnam's cities, families had to split up. At bus and train stations, and on streets outside their homes, husbands and wives took leave of each other, many facing separation for the first time. Tearful children departed from their parents, as they joined their schoolmates heading for strange locales. Being uprooted was particularly hard on the elderly who were wrenched from the relative comforts of their city homes to face the rigors of life in the countryside.

Those who tried evading evacuation from the cities risked more than the danger of air attacks. Urban authorities took a street-by-street census and marked each person's ration card "essential" or "nonessential." People designated nonessential would no longer receive food rations in the city. In effect, those who did not comply with evacuation faced starvation.

Many government personnel also took flight from the cities. In Hanoi the Political Bureau ordered the entire government administration, except for the office of the president, the governing council, and the heads of ministries, to move to sites at least twenty-four miles outside the city. In late 1966 French journalist Jacques Decornoy wrote that some government officials had retreated from Hanoi to a hamlet on the edge of the city. By the spring of 1967, the general directorate of the North Vietnamese railroad system had been newly located in a one-story residential building outside the capital. Tens of thousands of government officials from provincial and district capitals around the country also shifted their offices to more secure sites away from the cities.

In addition to the government administration, other important urban institutions such as hospitals and schools had to evacuate. Many of North Vietnam's 480 hospitals and health clinics, for instance, abandoned their urban facilities for temporary ones in the countryside. The evacuation of schools coincided with the mass transfer of urban youths to country havens. The North Vietnamese newspaper *Lao Dong* announced that during 1966 approximately 230,000 students from Hanoi were attending schools outside the city. The 710 students of the North's top-ranking high school departed Hanoi for a site in the Tu Liem District, twelve miles beyond the city limits. In 1965 British journalist James Cameron witnessed the dedi-

Thick black smoke rises from Hanoi's petroleum storage tanks struck by U.S. aircraft on June 29, 1966.

cation and closing of Hanoi's Polytechnic University, all in one day. "There took place a strange and fanciful ceremony," he wrote. "There were hours of vigorous oratory and many distinguished guests in the auditorium. And the moment the ceremony was over, the University closed down." When Australian journalist Wilfred Burchett, much favored by the Communists and decidedly sympathetic to them, asked a Polytechnic professor, "Isn't it [the closing] an awful waste?" the professor replied, "We must prepare for the worst."

Breaking down industry

The most difficult problem for North Vietnam's evacuation drive was what to do with its industrial facilities and factories, most of which were concentrated in Hanoi, Haiphong, Nam Dinh, Thanh Hoa, and Viet Tri. In 1965 North Vietnam's economy was still primarily agricultural. According to a U.S. Senate Armed Services Committee report, "The significant industrial facilities could be counted on your fingers." Of the North's 1,000 industrial enterprises, only a few were equipped for the production of heavy goods and the processing of raw materials. These included the Haiphong Cement plant, the Hanoi Machinery factory, the Thainguyen Iron and Steel Combine, the Hanoi Vehicle Repair and Assembly plant, the Hanoi Rubber Products plant, the Haiphong Phosphate Fertilizer plant, and the Viet Tri Chemical plant. The majority of the North's industries manufactured light products such as matches, textiles, sugar, beer, and canned fish and oils. Overall the country's industrial output was small, roughly $1 billion in 1965, and industry employed only 30 percent of the work force.

Even this modest industrial base had been a costly achievement for the Lao Dong party. Starting with the few industries left by the French, the Political Bureau had painstakingly developed the North's industrial capacity throughout the 1950s and early 1960s. Industry's contribution to the gross national product jumped from 31.4 percent in 1957 to 53.7 percent in 1964. Besides its economic importance, industrialization held ideological significance for North Vietnam's Communist leaders. They adhered closely to Lenin's maxim that "the material foundation of Socialism can only be mechanized large industry."

Despite the value of the North's heavy industry, however, the Political Bureau in 1965 reluctantly shelved its long-term goal of a centralized industrial sector. Confronting the U.S. bombing of its precious industrial resources and determined to pursue the war in the South, the Political Bureau decided to dismantle and disperse as many of its industries as possible. Although the Thainguyen pig iron works and the Haiphong Cement plant could not be moved, many other urban industrial operations were transferred from the cities to other locations. The party newspaper, *Nhan Dan*, deemed this "the most

urgent and vital task of the people's air defense." Every kind of factory—shipbuilding, machine parts, truck assembly, canning, fertilizer, paper, and textiles—was broken down into smaller production units and transported from Hanoi, Haiphong, Nam Dinh, Viet Tri, and Thanh Hoa to rural or suburban spots judged safer from the bombing. Most of the 7,000 employees of Hanoi's main textile mill, for example, evacuated in 1965 to villages thirty to sixty miles from the city. Workers also removed sections of Viet Tri's industrial complex, which contained a sugar refinery, a plywood factory, a fruit cannery, and a surgical dress factory. Nam Dinh's rice mill relocated, as did 80 percent of Haiphong's handicraft producers and similar manufacturers from Vinh and Thanh Hoa. In many of North Vietnam's once-bustling factories an eerie silence soon replaced the whir of the assembly line. Only the floor bolts remained where machines and equipment once stood.

By 1967 the drain of people, institutions, and factories imparted something of a ghost-town atmosphere to the North's main urban areas. Hanoi's population plummeted from more than a million to about 500,000, Haiphong's from 250,000 to 150,000. Viet Tri lost half of its 40,000 inhabitants, and Thanh Hoa appeared almost completely deserted. "We consider that our city has ceased to exist," Thanh Hoa's mayor lamented in early 1967. Meanwhile the influx of hundreds of thousands of urban evacuees into suburban and rural communities created enormous logistical problems for local governments. The authorities required local residents to assist newcomers in obtaining shelter. In some cases villagers had to share their own already overcrowded homes with as many evacuees as they could accommodate. Rural farming cooperatives offered them a chance to work the land and to procure food and housing for their families. The government also recruited thousands of evacuees to resettle in the relatively underpopulated and undeveloped highlands. Some ended up in hastily put together relocation camps, short on water, sanitary facilities, and other essential services.

For the most part, evacuees had to fend for themselves. Although food, medicine, and building materials were in short supply, the abundance of manpower was an asset. Officials quickly organized work battalions for the construction of shelters and homes, schools, health and hospital facilities, and buildings capable of housing factory equipment and workshops. North Vietnamese officials claimed that despite the dislocation caused by the evacuation, 4 million students were still attending primary and secondary schools. At a typical evacuation school in Tu Liem outside Hanoi, students attended overcrowded classrooms and spent the rest of their time building and maintaining new facilities or growing food and tending farm animals. While many older students set up hostels and did their own cooking, caring for the younger ones, especially those separated from their parents, was the responsibility of teachers. The government provided some money for room and board and textbooks but not enough to supply even the basic educational needs of students and teachers.

In 1966, at the transplanted facilities of the medical school of the University of Hanoi, Professor Tham Trong Tao, the deputy director of the medical faculty, described the school's swift relocation from Hanoi. "In the course of five weeks," he said, "we built dwellings scattered across the entire region: living rooms, dining rooms, bedrooms and lecture rooms, laboratories and libraries made of bamboo and palm leaves." Like many evacuation officials, Professor Tham gave glowing reports of the esprit de corps and high spirits of his students. Students, however, did not find the realities of their situation so easy to bear. For Vietnamese youths a university education meant status and an escape from manual labor. Many students, therefore, grumbled about their living conditions, physical labor, and primitive equipment. Some bitterly resented the regimentation.

Wherever evacuees settled, the government provided at least one health clinic for each evacuee community. But many displaced urban hospitals were unable to keep to the standards of the medical care they had dispensed from their modern urban facilities. In 1966 Wilfred Burchett paid a visit to one. Outside an ancient Buddhist pagoda, he reported seeing patients from an evacuated Hanoi hospital laid out in camp beds. "A white-gowned nurse," he wrote, "pedaled with her hands an upturned bicycle, wires leading from the ordinary cycle lamp dynamo into a small cabin. Inside the cabin under the feeble light of a six-volt lamp, a surgeon and nurses bent over a patient for a stomach operation." When Burchett commented on the hospital's primitive conditions, a public health official gave him the standard line about being prepared for every contingency: "Our surgeons and medical team must prepare for the worst. They must get used to operating under emergency conditions."

The North Vietnamese displayed remarkable resourcefulness in dispersing their industrial facilities, establishing

Children from Hanoi attend kindergarten at an elementary school evacuated from the city to a nearby rural area. They spend part of each day in the concrete bomb shelter (middle right) practicing air-raid drills.

new sites for them, and then restoring them to operation. Across the countryside industrial workers reinstalled machines, assembly lines, and raw-material processors in old farm buildings, garages, and cabins, as well as in newly built sheds of bamboo and thatch. A March 1966 North Vietnamese magazine article suggested that even caves could be suitable industrial sites. A 1967 article in the North Vietnamese journal *Common Sense Science* instructed workers to select locations near power lines but at least two kilometers from any strategic target.

One branch of the Hanoi Machinery factory was nothing but a cluster of huts surrounded by rice fields. The huts contained Soviet machine tools for making cutting gears and trucks for bearing the finished gears to a sub-assembly workshop where other machine tools were manufactured. Wilfred Burchett described a machine-tool factory in a large cave. "A famous old grotto with a hundred yards or so of rock above it was inhabited by bats and a few statues when I first visited it," he wrote. "Now there was the steady hum of machinery. Galleries which led off in all directions from the mouth of the main grotto had been reinforced, generators installed in some; lathes, borers, grinders, and polishers in others."

North Vietnamese leaders put the best possible face on their large-scale evacuation and the economic decentralization it entailed. They portrayed it not as a retreat from U.S. bombing attacks but as a tactical step to preserve the North's ability to continue serving as a base for Communist forces in the South. "We have a word for that," an official informed Harrison Salisbury in 1967. "It's *sotan.*' It doesn't really mean evacuation. It's more like regrouping in order to fight better and reduce losses and to repair damage which has been suffered in combat. It's not a passive word—it's an active word."

Digging for safety

North Vietnam's leaders recognized that evacuation made their people, essential services, and production facilities less vulnerable but hardly immune to U.S. air power. Accordingly, in 1965 they initiated a nationwide civil defense program. Civil defense officials supervised a huge effort to construct enough bomb shelters to accommodate all of the North's 18 million people. Every day, in cities and villages around the country, people had to devote their scant "leisure" time to digging bomb shelters. Often the scraping and clanging of shovels and pickaxes could be heard into the night. The shelters consisted of a concrete pipe about three feet in diameter that was set five feet into the ground and covered with a lid of concrete or bamboo. It was just large enough to hold a man or woman of average size.

By 1968 these one-person shelters were everywhere, in parks, streets, back yards, and rice fields. The government claimed there were 21 million of them. The country resembled a giant honeycomb. In 1968 a civil defense worker remarked to an American journalist, "Manufacturing [shelter] cylinders is one of our principal industries now." Civil defense officials also constructed larger concrete and steel shelters in basements and sewers. The relatively few factories and workshops remaining in the cities had the most extensive ones. At a Nam Dinh textile mill, for example, workers cut deep shelters into the extrathick cement floors under their milling machinery. Other factories were crisscrossed with long trenches connecting several big shelters. Because of the importance of factory operations, civil defense specialists issued them a torrent of instructions on the latest innovations in shelter design and continually conducted inspections and air-raid rehearsals for the workers.

Out in the villages, according to the North Vietnamese government, peasants dug some 30,000 miles of trenches. Every village hut or building contained a safety bunker. A four-foot-deep trench connected each house, enabling villagers to move about during an attack. Some trenches had roofs of woven bamboo and wickerwork screens. At an evacuated agricultural school in Hoa Binh Province, students moved about through straw-lined tunnel trenches three and a half miles long.

In the very heavily bombed areas along the coast to the DMZ, the North Vietnamese in 1965 introduced the concept of what they called "combat villages." These strongly fortified communities were similar to the "strategic hamlets" initiated by the Diem regime in South Vietnam during the early 1960s. Combat villages possessed many types of defense. Besides the standard one-man and communal shelters, villages near the DMZ believed vulnerable to attack or used as way stations for infiltrating the South had fortifications against commando raids, enemy helicopter landings, and enemy tank attacks. Peasants had to erect supply depots and ammunition depots, gun emplacements, and other strong points and even dug moats and trench barriers.

Wherever they lived, city or country, digging, installing, and maintaining civil defense shelters became a daily ritual for North Vietnamese civilians. The authorities required Haiphong residents to have four shelters each: one at their work place, one along the route they traveled to work, one where they ate, and one where they slept. The government urged people to treat their shelters like a second home, but most needed no prodding. For despite their outward pose of fearlessness and defiance, the North Vietnamese people harbored an intense fear of the destructive power of U.S. air attacks. Not surprisingly, they treated their shelters as home, cleaning them often and stocking them with dried food, first-aid kits, and escape tools.

In cities air-raid sirens and loudspeakers gave people advance warning of approaching U.S. aircraft. If the

Workers manufacture agricultural equipment in a cave turned machine shop in Dong Hoi in 1967.

planes continued on course, the sirens sounded additional warnings indicating that all public areas such as markets, stores, transportation terminals, and theaters should be evacuated. When the planes came within fifteen miles of the city, the signal ordered all people to rush to the nearest shelters. *Nhan Dan* repeatedly reminded urban dwellers to remain in the shelters until the all clear was issued. For those crammed into the small one-person shelters, the minutes, or sometimes hours, until the all clear sounded could be harrowing. Beyond the withering heat and claustrophobia was the constant terror that a close hit by an American bomb could instantly turn their tiny shelters into coffins.

In 1965 the journalist James Cameron experienced an air raid at Haiphong. "At half past ten [in the morning]," he wrote, "the sirens went. Within minutes the big park area in the center of town was immobile and silent except for the whistle of the air raid wardens chivvying the ignorant or the careless into the shelters." According to John Colvin, British consul general in Hanoi from 1966 to 1967, whenever it was even remotely possible that American planes would strike Hanoi or Haiphong, civil defense authorities took no chances. "Even when an attack was manifestly not against the city," he observed, "but against targets in the outskirts or even farther away, the Democratic Republic of Vietnam would insist on declaring an air raid on Hanoi itself. The sirens wailed up to 30 times a day."

The air-raid-alarm setup in rural areas did not work as smoothly. Most people lived in widely dispersed villages, and it was harder to predict exactly where U.S. bombers were heading as they streaked across the countryside. To spot the bombers as early as possible, villages erected watchtowers. Throughout the day, peasants perched atop them scanned the skies for planes. When a plane was sighted, they banged a loud drum or gongs to alert villagers. For farmers in outlying fields, watchmen also raised flags that could be seen from afar. A yellow flag meant pre-alert, a red one imminent attack. At night, bright red-and-yellow lamps replaced the flags. The vigilance of plane spotters was thus crucial to villages. Civil defense officials schooled them thoroughly in the identification of every U.S. attack aircraft from the B-52 to the A-4D to the F-105.

When not hastening to their shelters, North Vietnamese civilians found that U.S. bombing constantly overshadowed their existence in other ways. Since U.S. bombers generally confined their raids to midday hours, in the cities stores and government buildings opened only from six to eight or nine in the morning and from seven to ten at

---

Seeking refuge. Opposite. Peasants dig one-man bomb shelters along a rural road in 1972. Right, top to bottom. An air-raid alert in Haiphong; nurses shuttle babies to a shelter underneath a Hanoi hospital; a young girl takes cover.

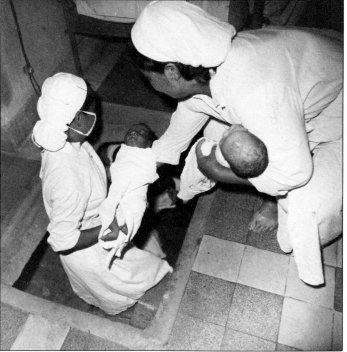

night. This forced people to spend their mornings and evenings in long lines at shops to buy scarce supplies of food and other goods. In Hanoi the only places still in business were government-run department stores, food-rationing centers, and some bicycle-repair and barbershops. During a 1968 trip to North Vietnam, a Philippine journalist, Amando Doronila, described life in Hanoi as "harsh and inflexible. The city rouses at cock's crow. The Vietnamese have learned that it is not safe to go out in the open between 9:00 A.M. and 2:00 P.M. when the skies are brightest."

The bombing threat also significantly disrupted the normal regime of urban workers, especially those employed in industry. The wartime workday lasted from 5:00 or 6:00 A.M., with a midday break from 10:30 to 2:00, until late in the evening. Since so many workers labored long hours with little time to shop or prepare meals, city officials organized collective kitchens where a worker could leave his stew pot in the morning and pick it up fully cooked at night. By the end of 1967, collective kitchens were serving around 90,000 people.

The bombing severely hampered the ability of workers to perform their jobs. Continually interrupted by bomb alerts, electricity cutoffs, and machinery breakdowns, they were hard pressed to keep even skeletal operations going, much less meet demanding production quotas. Official directives about "operating the machines faster when the alert is over to make up for the idle time spent in the shelters" added more pressure. In some factories workers were ordered to stay by their machines during raids to minimize delays. They called themselves "suicide squads."

Many urban workers endured the strain of separation from their evacuated families, a traumatic blow to the traditionally close-knit Vietnamese family. Although it supplied no statistics, in 1968 the government cited a disturbing rise in the number of divorces precipitated by the evacuation. Thousands of husbands and wives whose jobs kept them in the city tried to hold their families together by visiting them on the weekends. The evacuation thus produced a new social phenomenon in North Vietnam: commuter marriages. A printer named Hiep at Hanoi's Tien Bo printing works, for example, had recently been separated from his wife of three months, a graphic artist who had been evacuated with her factory. Hiep had seen her only once in eight weeks, having bicycled eighty kilometers to her evacuation site and back in one day.

Parents worried particularly about the welfare of their children. Because they knew that villages often lacked proper sanitary facilities, parents making the trek from the city to see their children often carried cans of clean water. A physician named Phuong had to send her two boys, eleven and thirteen, to an evacuated school thirty-five kilometers from Hanoi. "Once a month I cycle there and back," she said. "I can do it in a day, but it's hard to come home to an empty flat."

Beyond the city limits, where 80 percent of the North's population inhabited thousands of villages, coping with the bombing proved equally difficult. The evacuation thrust hundreds of thousands of city people into the normally closed, custom-bound world of the village. Peasants did not respond enthusiastically to decrees about accepting evacuees into their homes or about moving out of their houses to provide classrooms until new schools could be built. Nor did they take kindly to the intrusion of "city slickers" who ignored village mores and violated social and religious taboos. Villagers also resented sharing their already meager supplies with outsiders.

Many evacuees, on the other hand, did not easily adapt to village life. They found living conditions there primitive and oppressive. Besides inadequate sanitary, housing, and medical facilities, evacuees encountered diseases like malaria, typhoid, and cholera. Unacquainted with manual labor, they had to perform such backbreaking tasks as farming, dike building, and canal digging. Many unhappy evacuees clamored to return to the cities, but the government enacted travel restrictions to keep them out.

Particularly eager to go home were the evacuees the government had dispatched to resettle the highlands. A government official noted that "the majority of the township people have never gone too far away from home, and most of them have never done any manual work in their lives. ... A number seemed to be worried about the deadly climate." Even urban party cadres balked at assignments to the highlands. Some cadres, an official said, "believed that only idle families or those having difficulties were expected to take part in the campaign. ... There were still others who preferred to stay [in the city] because they were allergic to hardship." Despite official restrictions, in 1966 tens of thousands of highland settlers had either packed up for their city homes or wrangled jobs elsewhere.

Life underground

To the people of North Vietnam's southern panhandle, the adversities and discomforts of their countrymen seemed minor inconveniences. Because it contained key transportation routes, supply depots, and military facilities, the southern panhandle was one of the most frequently bombed areas of the North. The almost continuous bombardment by U.S. aircraft, the U.S. 7th Fleet off the coast, and the long-range artillery of American installations across the DMZ compelled the people to alter their way of life radically. Air attacks occurred as often as every thirty minutes. By 1967, incessant bombing forced most of Vinh's 72,000 people to evacuate. In March 1967 Lee Lockwood of *Life* magazine recorded nineteen separate attacks in and around Thanh Hoa.

This steady bombardment so endangered lives, agriculture, and industry that whole communities took to living and working underground. In Quang Binh, families lived in bunkers set four feet underground, which they entered by crawling through holes on all fours. Every village carved out underground food storage rooms, as well as barns and stables for animals. Thanh Hoa and Vinh Linh built huge labyrinths of underground shops, markets, schoolrooms, hospitals, communal kitchens, and sleeping quarters. One of these vast subterranean refuges at Vinh Linh contained long tunnel entrances that led to a series of large chambers barely lit by gasoline lanterns. Deeper still, through the narrowest of passageways, were meeting rooms and dormitories.

Farmers generally holed up in these bunkers during the day, emerging for several hours at dawn and dusk to cultivate their fields. Meanwhile, industrial workers operated machines in underground workshops. Most resembled that of engineer Vo Thung near Thanh Hoa, which fanned out into several caves. Each one had truck-repair machinery for thirty employees. "The Americans wanted to bomb us back into the Stone Age," remarked Vo Thung. "But I am sure they did not think it would turn out like this."

North Vietnamese officials played down the physical strains on people compelled to live and work underground. They portrayed them as willingly, even cheerfully, adapting to their molelike existence. But life underground proved to be a depressing, unhealthy, and exhausting ordeal. Deprived of sunlight and fresh air, sometimes for weeks at a time, many people developed serious eye and respiratory ailments. Poor sanitation and dank conditions, along with rats, snakes, and an exotic variety of biting insects, bred disease and skin infections. Because smoke would signal their presence, people usually went without hot food. On top of that was the nagging fear of an air strike powerful enough to bury them alive. While going underground may have provided North Vietnamese civilians a haven from the rain of fire above, it tested to the limit their psychological and physical endurance.

Military versus civilian targets

No matter where or how they sought refuge, however, the North Vietnamese could not block out the destruction of the U.S. bombing. For the people of the cities the bleak

After spending the 1967 Tet holiday with relatives in Hanoi, evacuees buy bus tickets to return to the countryside.

During a 1967 air attack U.S. bombs, directed at a nearby railroad overpass, destroyed these residential buildings on Nguyen Thiap Street in downtown Hanoi.

reality of explosions, fires, and casualties was no longer confined to a faraway battlefront in the South. Soon the scars of the bombing were visible throughout all of the North's urban areas. By 1968 air attacks had destroyed Hanoi's railroad yard, most of its major bridges, the main power plant, and dozens of factories and warehouses. In April 1967 Agence France Presse called Haiphong's industrial sector "a wasteland." At Nam Dinh American air attacks left its industrial and transportation facilities in rubble. In 1966 journalist Harrison Salisbury wrote in the *New York Times* that he saw "nothing there but devastation."

Despite U.S. efforts to restrict Rolling Thunder to military targets and personnel, bomb damage to nonmilitary structures and residential sections was considerable. For one thing, many military targets, especially in cities, lay adjacent to civilian communities. For another, the Pentagon overestimated its ability to conduct the pinpoint bombing that it claimed would prevent civilian casualties and destruction. North Vietnam did not release civilian casualty totals, but in 1969 a U.S. intelligence study estimated that Rolling Thunder produced 52,000 civilian deaths. At least several hundred thousand more, North Vietnam claimed, suffered wounds. As late as 1986, there were no authoritative figures on the dead and wounded.

During visits to North Vietnam, American, as well as French, journalists confirmed Hanoi's allegations of civilian casualties and damage. After a bomb strike in Hanoi in August 1967, for instance, the American broadcaster, David Schoenbrun, reported that "an entire row of houses on Hue street, more than half the street long, had been wiped out, plus an area going back some 50 feet deep to the street behind. . . . Two bodies were stretched out on the sidewalk, covered with canvas." In the fall of 1967 an Agence France Presse reporter, B. J. Cabanes, surveyed bomb damage in civilian areas of Haiphong. He found that "whole neighborhoods had been demolished, houses were gutted, trees were slashed, and much of the city was pocked with craters." At Phu Ly and Phat Diem near Hanoi, houses, Catholic churches, schools, and hospitals were badly damaged by bombs.

British philosopher Bertrand Russell's International War Crimes Tribunal denounced Rolling Thunder as "genocidal" and "terror bombing." Some American antiwar leaders, like Dave Dellinger, echoed the charges. Rolling Thunder, however, never approached terror bombing of civilians. Another American journalist, William Baggs of the *Miami News*, wrote from North Vietnam in 1968, "There is not a hint that the American strategy has been to obliterate Hanoi: Surely with the competence of the United States Air Force, all of this city could be reduced to broken bricks and scattered glass on any one afternoon." Felix Greene, a *Look* magazine reporter in North Vietnam in July 1967, asserted that "the numbers of people killed relative to the intensity of the bombing has been

very minor." Even Vietnamese officials privately conceded that the American policy was not to annihilate civilian targets. "I don't think the Americans were trying to bomb our cooperative," Do Tien Hao, manager of the Yen Duyen cooperative confided to *New York Times* correspondent Fox Butterfield in 1969. "The railroad runs just over there," he said. "Some of the pilots got nervous and dropped their bombs on anything they could see."

Rolling Thunder planners were guilty of exaggerating the accuracy of their bombs and pilots and of failing to anticipate civilian losses in lives and property. The frequency and extent of civilian casualties and damage contradicted the much-vaunted precision of American bombers. In 1967 Washington acknowledged that some bomb damage to nonmilitary persons and targets was unavoidable. American officials in Thailand explained that "bombing instructions are not always as precise as they might be. Targets of opportunity are not defined exactly, and pilots, for varying emotional and personal reasons, decide that a bullock or a windmill is a suitable military target."

That American bombs inadvertently fell on them was small consolation to North Vietnamese civilians killed or injured. When a misdirected bomb exploded above the houses on Pho Nguyen Thiep Street in Hanoi on December 13, 1966, killing five and injuring five, the people reacted with bewilderment and frustration. Harrison Salisbury observed, "The bombing would go down in history as one of the senseless accidents of war–death inflicted by a man who did not even know he was causing it." If anything, the randomness of the death and destruction made civilians even more apprehensive. William Baggs reported evidence that "random bombs have fallen, that people have been killed. You are often introduced in sidewalk conversations to the fear among people that they never know where the next stray may strike."

On April 14, 1966, Tran Dang Hoi of Nam Dinh left home with her sisters to buy food for the family observance of their father's death. While she was away, a bomb demolished her house. Amid the debris she found the bodies of her husband, brother, and five-month-old child. "I didn't expect that the death anniversary of my father would also be that of my husband, brother and child," she said bitterly. At least one thing was certain: the Hanoi regime's evacuation and dispersal of its population and its extraordinary civil defense program greatly minimized the number of civilians harmed by Operation Rolling Thunder.

A steel curtain

North Vietnam's evacuation program acknowledged the country's inability to deny the Americans air superiority. Nevertheless, Hanoi sought to make U.S. pilots pay a high price for their forays into its territory. When the United States first unleashed bombers against the North during

Antiaircraft artillery batteries in Hanoi fire at U.S. planes attacking the Bac Giang bridge (left) and the Long Bien bridge (below).

Operation Pierce Arrow in August 1966, North Vietnam's air defense was rudimentary. Its air force consisted of thirty training aircraft, fifty transports, and four light helicopters. The North's entire arsenal of air defense weapons was made up of but 700 conventional antiaircraft guns and twenty outdated early warning radar systems. By the time Rolling Thunder got under way in March 1965, however, Hanoi had deployed thirty MiG-15s and 17s from the People's Republic of China at Phuc Yen airfield near Hanoi. Each of these Soviet-designed subsonic fighters was armed with 23MM and 37MM cannons and capable of carrying rockets.

By mid-June 1965, additional MiG-15s and 17s from the Soviet Union boosted the North's air fleet to seventy fighters. Several months later, Soviet supersonic MiG-21s arrived. To support jet operations, the North Vietnamese expanded their existing airfields: Phuc Yen and Gia Lam near Hanoi, Cat and Kien An near Haiphong, and Dong Hoi along the DMZ. They also began constructing four more tactical jet airfields, such as the one at Kep north of Hanoi.

Between 1964 and 1966 North Vietnam increased its antiaircraft artillery (AAA) threefold to about 7,000, ranging from 12.7MM to 100MM guns. The North's air defense commanders concentrated most of their AAA firepower in the industrial corridors from Haiphong to Hanoi. According to U.S. Air Force General William Momyer, "The AAA defenses within thirty miles of Hanoi and ten miles from Haiphong were comparable to those found in World War II around key industrial areas and in the Korean War around the airfields along the Yalu and near Pong Yang. Many experienced pilots said the Hanoi flak was the worst in the history of aerial warfare, and it may well have been." American pilots certainly thought so. On missions around Hanoi they ran such a menacing gauntlet of AAA that they nicknamed it "Dodge City." Journalist

David Schoenbrun wrote, "Hanoi looks like an armed porcupine, with hundreds, probably thousands, of spiny, steel gun snouts sticking out beyond the tops of trees."

Several thousand Chinese and Soviet advisers trained hundreds of Vietnamese AAA crews. By 1967 these guns were capable of shrouding North Vietnam in a curtain of steel, spewing about 25,000 tons of ammunition each month at American planes. Over the course of the war AAA accounted for 60 percent of U.S. air losses, a total of 750 planes. In 1966 air-war analyst Sam Butz said of the North's AAA performance, "Overall in World War II enemy anti aircraft guns accounted for about half of the U.S.A.F. losses by shooting down one in every 200 flights. German gunners had the most practice and the best score. They knocked down one in 170. This is not as good as the North Vietnamese in 1965, and the German targets were far easier."

North Vietnam's air-warning systems ranged from sophisticated radar to a tool as simple as binoculars. In areas most frequently attacked, AAA units called "Combat Standing Teams" were kept on continuous alert. A French Communist journalist, Marceline Loridan, interviewed members of an AAA crew near the DMZ. "One must really be on top of them to see the guns," she wrote. "Half buried and completely covered with foliage, they look like large bushes." "The best time to get a plane," one AAA gunner told her, "is when it is diving to drop its bombs. When it is coming straight in, one aims at the nose and the belly and wham!"

The most sophisticated weapon trained against American planes was the surface-to-air missile (SAM). In the spring of 1965, U.S. aerial intelligence photographs revealed that the North Vietnamese had obtained and installed Soviet radar-directed SAM-2 missiles. These SAM-2s could strike planes at altitudes of 20,000 to 30,000 feet.

On July 14, 1965, a SAM from a site near Hanoi downed a U.S. Air Force Phantom. By September 1967, North Vietnam had as many as 200 SAM sites operational, at least 60 of them protecting the Haiphong-Hanoi military complex and the lines of communication running south through Thanh Hoa. Its missile supply exceeded 500. Fortunately for American pilots, SAM-2s could sometimes be outmaneuvered if spotted or forced off course by electronic jamming. Another technique was to fly below the SAMs' effective altitude.

In 1965 Soviet technical advisers, along with several hundred East Europeans, began teaching Vietnamese

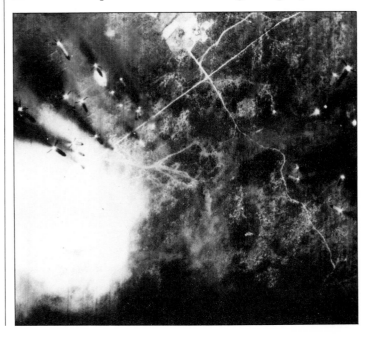

Left. *A U.S. fighter unleashes rockets that destroyed a camouflaged surface-to-air missile (SAM) site near Dong Hoi in November 1966. Opposite. A USAF reconnaissance photo of a SAM station reveals four missiles poised for launching. A semicamouflaged vehicle (right center) contains missile guidance and control equipment.*

missile crews how to set up and operate SAM sites. They found it a daunting task. Vietnamese crews received less training than those of other countries. Many were simply reassigned infantry troops. Some were teen-aged draftees with no prior military experience. One missile trainee told Polish reporter Monica Varnenska, "We had in a very short period of time to become familiar with the specifics of missile firing, to learn how to use this weapon effectively, and, what is most important, to service it." Vietnamese commanders said their "soldiers made up with enthusiasm what they lacked in training."

American intelligence accused the Soviets of coordinating the SAM system against U.S. bombers. Soviet involvement in the SAM system, however, was apparently minimal. While gratefully accepting hardware and advice, the North Vietnamese military brooked little interference by outsiders. Soviet and East European advisers griped about North Vietnamese SAM crews firing missiles "as if they were machine guns." "If they had skilled technicians," said one Russian, "they would get a far higher total of U.S. planes with the SAMs. They really don't know how to use them." North Vietnamese stubbornness on this point infuriated another Communist missile specialist. "We came to them and offered them our expertise," he said. "They refused."

The North Vietnamese rebuffed criticism of their inexperience in handling complicated weapons. "We are fully aware of the value and significance of modern technology," said a government official. "In Hanoi, in Haiphong and elsewhere, the Yankees get a taste of Soviet rockets and Soviet flak." Moreover, the North Vietnamese took pride in the ways they adapted advanced Soviet weaponry to the conditions of their country. A North Vietnamese commander boasted of having "developed a truly Vietnamese technique for employing the missiles. Had we not decided to do so, the Americans could have destroyed them all. The foreign friends who gave us the missiles said they should be positioned in hardened sites. But we thought that the Americans, if they discovered the sites, would concentrate their bombing on them. We would not have one SAM left. We disregarded instructions and handled the missiles on the move."

In addition to making the SAMs mobile, the North Vietnamese employed other tactics to increase the effectiveness of their antiaircraft fire. Sometimes they erected a mock SAM battery alongside a camouflaged AAA battery. When American planes dove to bomb the SAM battery, the AAA guns would then open fire at close range. Commanders also coordinated the placement of SAMs with AAA batteries to achieve maximum air coverage and catch U.S. planes in a vicious crossfire. Nevertheless, North Vietnam's "kill ratios" with SAMs were disappointing to Hanoi. Although SAMs forced U.S. planners to devise expensive electronic countermeasures to throw them off course, and compelled American pilots to alter their tactics and flight patterns, the North Vietnamese launched over 5,500 missiles during Rolling Thunder but brought down only 117 planes.

Battle of the skies

To the hazards already confronting U.S. pilots in the skies over North Vietnam, Hanoi's leaders added another: Russian-made MiG-15s and 16s. Russian instructors trained prospective North Vietnamese pilots at schools in the Soviet Union. Like missile trainees, these pilot candidates had scant technical knowledge, much less flying experience. One pilot, for example, confessed to having never even ridden in a car before his flight course. As a result, he said, he had continuous bouts of motion sickness: "The comrade mechanics had a hard time cleaning the floors of the plane. I then used handkerchiefs and threw them out after each attack. As many handkerchiefs were wasted, I shifted to a new method by using a football inner tube. This could be washed after using."

As one might expect, North Vietnam's novice MiG pilots did not fare well in their initial encounters with highly trained American fliers. During engagements in the summer of 1965, U.S. planes easily shot down five MiGs. Until the end of 1966, MiGs flew only at irregular intervals, as little as one engagement per month. Meanwhile, North Vietnam's MiG force grew from 30 to 115 and included faster MiG-21s armed with heat-seeking missiles. In April 1967, the U.S. decided to bomb the MiG bases. U.S. bombers regularly attacked Kep, forty miles north of Hanoi, and Hoalia, twenty miles west. They hit Kienan five and a half miles southwest of Haiphong, as well as Catbi, two miles southwest. By August American commanders believed they had eliminated the MiG threat. On the seventh Lieutenant General William Momyer of the 7th Air Force stated that "we have driven the MiGs out of the sky for all practical purposes. The MiGs are no longer a threat."

Such confidence was premature. After improving its pilot training, the North's air force suddenly rose up in September 1967 to rechallenge American fighter-bombers. In two months MiG pilots knocked down 6 U.S. planes, while losing only 2 of their own. The number of MiG sorties gradually rose to twenty a month. Although throughout Rolling Thunder the U.S. lost 48 planes to 111 MiGs, in the interlude, November 1, 1967, to November 1, 1968, the North Vietnamese outdueled the Americans, downing 18 U.S. aircraft while losing 17 of their MiGs. The MiG did no more than the SAM to deter American bombers from their missions, but it did disrupt American attack plans and forced the U.S. to raise the number of its fighter escorts.

One of the more unusual features of North Vietnam's air defense was its grassroots arm, a steady hail of small-arms fire directed at low-flying U.S. planes. During Rolling Thunder, the North Vietnamese government armed hundreds of thousands of civilians—farmers, factory workers, and teachers, among others—with rifles, automatic weapons, and machine guns. It encouraged them to shoot at U.S. planes in the hope that a lucky hit might bring one down. Harrison Salisbury reported in the *New York Times* that at a textile mill in Nam Dinh he "saw stacked beside almost every production post a rifle. Some were propped beside open windows. . . . At the sound of the air raid sirens the workers would grab their rifles and take up posts at the windows and on the roof to fire back at the American planes."

Although the Hanoi government bestowed medals on marksmen who supposedly shot down U.S. planes, American records for Rolling Thunder show no U.S. planes downed by small-arms fire. In any case, by arming its

cars, ships and boats, and buildings were wiped out, the Pentagon reported. North Vietnam's Ministry of Heavy Industry said that U.S. bombers had ravaged 390 factories and workshops. As for a dollar figure, in August 1967 Secretary of Defense Robert McNamara estimated that the bomb damage inflicted on the North amounted to $350 million.

A persistent coping

Beyond its physical destruction, the bombing severely impaired the North's economic and social life. In 1967 Admiral Ulysses S. Grant Sharp, commander in chief Pacific, concluded that "as a result of the increased might and ef-

people to fire on U.S. planes, Hanoi reduced their sense of helplessness and enabled them to vent their frustration.

By the time it ended in November 1968, the American Rolling Thunder operation had chalked up some impressive statistics. During three and a half years of bombing, in which an average of 800 tons of bombs, rockets, and missiles rained down each day, Rolling Thunder, according to Pentagon statistics, caused immense damage to North Vietnam's military and economic infrastructure. American planes destroyed or damaged almost every major target, including 25 percent of the North's military barracks, 76 percent of its ammunition depots, 87 percent of its petroleum storage capacity, 18 percent of its supply depots, 78 percent of the country's power plants, 12 percent of its ports, 36 percent of its railroad yards, 23 percent of its airfields, 50 percent of its bridges, and all of its iron and steel plants. Tens of thousands of trucks, railroad

Major N. P. Burkov of the Soviet air force briefs PAVN pilots at a training center in the U.S.S.R. in October 1968.

ficiency of our attacks, the Hanoi regime faces mounting logistic, management and morale problems. Repair, reconstruction and dispersal programs are consuming increasing human and material resources which otherwise would contribute to the Communists' combat capacity in South Vietnam. We believe that about 500,000 men have been diverted to such activities." There is no precise information from North Vietnamese sources to corroborate this American assessment, but it is a credible one.

Despite all the statistical indicators of success, however, Rolling Thunder failed on two important counts. It pressured but did not persuade North Vietnamese leaders to yield politically nor did it prevent them from continuing their military intervention in the South. From the start they had showed themselves firmly resolved to prosecute the war no matter what the consequences. In 1965 Prime Minister Pham Van Dong told journalist James Cameron the bombing "is costing us terribly dear. I am not acting when I say that I am obliged to cry—literally cry—at the suffering and the losses. And they will get worse, make no mistake." But when asked if North Vietnam could "lick the most powerful nation in the world," Pham Van Dong stoutly replied, "The one thing old revolutionaries have to be is optimistic. ... We do mean what we say." Luu Quy Ky of the Cultural Relations Ministry said, "Hanoi can be razed to the ground, but everything is prepared even for this eventuality."

By dispersing its industries the North preserved enough of its economy to keep the country going. A 1980 Pentagon study concluded, "The U.S. bombers destroyed the main centralized industries, but there were scores of smaller plants turning out war and consumer goods in each province. In effect a sizable proportion of the DRV's smaller war-essential manufacturing capacity was beyond the effective reach of any but the most indiscriminate and inefficient air attacks."

In reaction to the destruction of their electrical plants, for example, the North's factories switched to manual tools and labor. The 2,000 small diesel generators distributed in 1967 were more than sufficient for dispersed workshops. As for the North's manpower shortage, more than a million women took the places of their husbands and sons serving in the military. By 1967, women formed 70 percent of the agricultural work force, 50 percent of light industrial labor, 60 percent of government employees, 30 percent of heavy industrial workers, and 45 percent of doctors and pharmacists.

What Pentagon planners did not realize until later was the extent to which the North's advance planning and the sheer endurance of its people could foil devastating bomber raids. Foreseeing the eventual destruction of their fuel storage centers, for example, the North Vietnamese secreted tanks holding up to 3,300 gallons of petroleum near all major transportation routes. Trucks and trains rolled at night to avoid daylight bombing, and the transportation repair effort was enormous—and constant. Over a million people labored round-the-clock to repair the damage inflicted each day on North Vietnam's transportation system. Their motto: "The enemy destroys, we repair. The enemy destroys, we repair again." The state required farmers and other workers to devote several days each month to transportation repair and to supply gravel and other road-paving materials. Along every major highway lay piles of stone and sand and stacks of wood for filling and patching bomb craters. No sooner had the smoke from bombs cleared than beaverlike road crews would set to work repairing the damage.

North Vietnamese engineers devised some ingenious methods to keep open the thousands of bridges linking the country's railroad and highway network. If a bridge was partially damaged, they propped up the remaining structure. If a bridge was completely toppled, they improvised with temporary spans, the most basic consisting of arm-thick bundles of bamboo stalks that floated on waterlike pontoons. Steel-wire-bound wooden boards were laid across the bamboo. Repair crews also lashed together flat-bottomed boats about three feet wide and sixteen feet long, then constructed roadways of bamboo poles or boards across the top of them. To shield these bridges from attack when not in use, one end was cut loose during the day and the bridge was pulled along the shore and camouflaged. Where river conditions permitted, engineers discovered that they could build a "sunken span" just beneath the surface of the water. Trucks could still cross it, but water concealed it from reconnaissance planes and bombers.

Sometimes the sole recourse to ensure the flow of traffic was simply the physical exertion of the people. On roadways and paths, caravans of peasants bore loaded baskets on the ends of long flexible poles extended across their shoulders. Some rode bicycles that could carry more than 100 pounds in two baskets attached to either side of a wooden platform over the front wheel. Others pushed bicycles equipped to handle over 600 pounds each. Whether

riding or walking, these human "pack trains" endured a grueling experience. In addition to pushing cruelly heavy loads along dirt roads and paths caked with mud and rutted with potholes, they labored through suffocating humidity, insect-infested jungles, and continual pressure to reach their destination with speed.

CINCPAC's Admiral Sharp had once defined Rolling Thunder as a way of pressing North Vietnamese leaders until they cried "uncle." But one crucial element that Pentagon analysts could not tally in their bombing statistics was the stamina of the Vietnamese people. The privations of war were nothing new to them—they had just endured seven years of struggle against the French. After all, said a Hanoi official, "we fought the French and the Japanese. Now we are fighting the Americans. Most of our population have, in the course of their life, experienced nothing but war, so in one sense it seems normal to them."

The North Vietnamese even saw their poverty as a source of strength. "We are poor and the Americans are rich," Vu Trong Kinh of the State Cultural Commission declared. "But we have very little left to lose, and they have everything to lose." A Foreign Ministry official in Hanoi put it this way, "We are like a little animal pitted against a dinosaur. We will survive, but the dinosaur will not."

American policymakers ultimately recognized that such defiant declarations were more than bravado. In 1967 Secretary of Defense Robert McNamara informed the Senate Armed Services Committee that "morale in North Vietnam appears to be holding up fairly well despite the heavy burdens upon them ... it is unlikely that we can break the morale or weaken it so as to change the course of political action in that country by alternative air campaigns open to us." In 1971, attempting to explain the inability of Rolling Thunder to break North Vietnam's resolve, former Secretary of State Dean Rusk concluded, "I personally ... underestimated the persistence and tenacity of the North Vietnamese."

Hanoi-Moscow-Peking

While the preparation, flexibility, and perseverance of the North Vietnamese enabled them to outlast Rolling Thunder, without huge and steady doses of Chinese and Soviet aid they could not have sustained the acceleration of their involvement in South Vietnam. Throughout the 1950s and early 1960s, North Vietnam's relations with China were es-

At Hanoi in 1968 a convoy of trucks, the last carrying petroleum, crosses the Red River on a pontoon bridge made of bamboo poles lashed to wooden boats.

Mission from Moscow

Opening a new era of increased Russian assistance to the DRV, Soviet Council of Ministers' Chairman N. S. (Aleksei) Kosygin led a delegation to Hanoi in February 1965. During his visit, Kosygin announced that the Soviet Union would provide North Vietnam with huge amounts of economic and military aid, including sophisticated weaponry. The Kosygin mission heralded the Soviet Union's eventual replacement of China as the DRV's principal ally.

Pham Van Dong (left) accompanies Kosygin (right) and members of his entourage on a visit to the Yen Cho farm cooperative.

Above. *The motorcade of the Soviet delegation headed by Aleksei Kosygin is welcomed by large crowds in Hanoi.*

At a conference in Hanoi, Lao Dong party leaders (right side of table, from right to left) Truong Chinh, Le Duan, Ho Chi Minh, Pham Van Dong, an unidentified aide, and Vo Nguyen Giap discuss their aid requests with the Soviet delegation.

pecially cordial, while Hanoi's attitude toward Moscow during that period was cool, if not frigid, because of its aversion to Premier Khrushchev's doctrines.

Late in 1964, however, as it geared North Vietnam for U.S. bombs and the escalation of its military involvement in the South, Hanoi approached the Soviet Union in search of substantial amounts of economic and military aid. Both Premier Pham Van Dong and Party First Secretary Le Duan led foreign-aid delegations to Moscow. The Political Bureau explained its new attitude toward the Soviet Union by pointing out to the Lao Dong party rank and file that it was Khrushchev, now removed from power, who was responsible for "revisionism," not the Soviet party as a whole.

The new Soviet Premier Leonid Brezhnev and Prime Minister Aleksei Kosygin were receptive to North Vietnam's courtship. New trade agreements between the Soviet Union and North Vietnam were signed in January 1965, and a far bigger military aid breakthrough for Hanoi came in February 1965 during a visit by Aleksei Kosygin to Hanoi. In a farewell speech, Kosygin revealed the Soviet Union's open-ended commitment "to strengthen the defense potential of the DRV and to hold frequent exchanges of views."

Following a series of talks in April and September, Soviet ships bearing more than $300 million of military and economic aid began steaming into Haiphong Harbor. In addition to MiGs, SAM missiles, and other air defense equipment, Soviet military assistance included rocket launchers, tanks, coastal artillery, gunboats, 14,000 trucks, and small arms and ammunition. Economic aid included machine tools, electric generators, petroleum, and mining equipment, as well as rice and bicycles. The Soviets also dispatched several hundred economic and industrial advisers to North Vietnam and invited over 1,000 Vietnamese students to study at Russian technical schools.

Several strategic considerations underlay the Soviet policy switch. Brezhnev and Kosygin were unwilling to write off Southeast Asia to China's sphere of power. They treated aid to Hanoi as a counter to Chinese charges that Moscow was "soft" on wars of national liberation and to restore Russian prestige among Third World countries. In backing North Vietnam, the Soviets could reassert their leadership of the international Communist movement.

Peking reacted quickly to what it called Moscow's "intrusion" in Southeast Asia. In July 1965, China signed the first of several new assistance pacts with Hanoi, a $200 million deal covering "national defense and economic supplies." Chinese military aid included rifles and automatic weapons, pistols, grenades, and such heavier weapons as 37mm and 57mm artillery, mortars, and recoilless rifles. Economic assistance consisted of more than a million tons of rice, railroad cars, blankets and uniforms, powdered milk, and even such things as Thermos bottles. In addition, Peking sent 40,000 workers to help North Viet-

nam repair the vital rail links along the Chinese border.

In this concrete way, North Vietnam was the beneficiary of the growing rift between the U.S.S.R. and China: between 1965 and 1970 it received nearly $3 billion of Soviet economic and military assistance. Chinese aid topped $1 billion. The Russians and Chinese also tried to outdo each other with promises of combat support if necessary, though those were never tested.

Instead of welcoming the Soviet-Chinese rivalry for its favor, North Vietnam strove, in its limited way, to bring the two Communist powers together. More than any other Communist leader Ho Chi Minh consistently called for unity among socialist countries. In part his motive was ideological. He believed that only a unified Communist front could successfully challenge the "economic and military imperialism of the West." There were selfish reasons, too. He felt that unqualified support by all Communist countries would minimize North Vietnam's reliance on a single source of aid and maximize its flexibility to conduct the war as Hanoi saw fit.

Despite Ho Chi Minh's personal and diplomatic maneuvers to close the Sino-Soviet breach, however, North Vietnam found itself caught precariously between its two feuding benefactors. In 1965 Soviet-Chinese bickering threatened to interrupt the flow of aid to the North. The Chinese not only refused to grant Russian requests for cargo-plane landing rights but began delaying the supply trains that carried nearly 70 percent of the military aid from the Soviet border to the North Vietnamese frontier. On April 22, 1966, Soviet Defense Minister Rodion Malinovsky asserted that "assistance for the people of Vietnam would be more efficient would the Chinese not hinder these efforts." The Chinese response was blunt: "Malinovsky is a liar." Later the Soviets accused the Chinese of pirating equipment from Soviet military shipments bound for the North. Moscow radio also accused the Chinese of "stealing jet fighter planes" and of "raiding Soviet missiles."

In 1967 North Vietnamese leaders reached an understanding with China to facilitate the unimpaired passage of Soviet-aid trains. As insurance, Vietnamese soldiers began meeting Soviet trains at the Russian border and escorting them across China to the North. Still, there were occasional aid blockages. The Soviets, fed up with Chinese intransigence, started expanding Haiphong's port facilities to reduce their reliance on trans-Chinese land routes.

Other Soviet-Chinese matters bedeviled North Vietnam. In 1965 and 1966 the Soviet Union pressured Hanoi to negotiate with the United States. Although the Soviets eventually eased its pressure for peace talks, North Vietnamese leaders remained anxiously concerned that Russians might someday cut a deal with the U.S. toward a diplomatic settlement. China was an even greater cause for concern. Not content to allow North Vietnam to steer a

Chinese workers shout pro-Vietnam, anti-U.S. slogans at a Peking rally in 1965. The posters of Ho Chi Minh and Mao Tse-tung indicate Hanoi's continuing close ties with Peking.

neutral path in the Sino-Soviet dispute, China insisted that Hanoi take its side. Peking also badgered North Vietnam to pursue a protracted war strategy that would bog the U.S. down in Southeast Asia yet avoid drawing China into an escalating conflict. In a 1965 essay, "Long Live the People's War," Chinese leader Lin Piao proclaimed that Mao's doctrine of people's revolutionary war, not big-unit, semiconventional tactics, would bring victory to Communists in every country. He further contended, with Hanoi in mind, that only by relying on its own resources, not outside aid, could a nation like North Vietnam defeat U.S. "imperialism."

China's intentions were obvious both to Hanoi and the Soviet Union. By advising Hanoi to fight a low-level, self-supported people's war, China hoped to check the Soviets' use of aid to penetrate Indochina. Aggravated by Chinese "interference," Hanoi reaffirmed its independence of judgment and action. In 1966 First Party Secretary Le Duan put China's protracted war strategy in a Vietnamese perspective. "We cannot adopt the revolutionary struggle of other countries and practice it in our own country," he wrote. "Those who do not understand the people and history of Vietnam cannot understand the strategy and tactics needed in the Vietnamese revolution."

By 1968 doctrinal disagreements and diplomatic strains had brought Hanoi and Peking near estrangement. The Chinese alienated Hanoi by criticizing the large-scale 1968 Tet offensive and by lashing out at North Vietnam for entering talks with the United States that spring. Still, North Vietnam's leaders managed to continue getting what they wanted most: reassurances from Moscow and Peking of additional support for 1969 and 1970. So long as its pipelines from these essential aid sources remained intact, Hanoi retained a strategic initiative.

Yet some trends disturbed the North Vietnamese. Chinese aid between 1968 and 1970 showed a marked decline from $200 million to $150 million. In turn, Soviet aid in 1970 now comprised more than two-thirds of North Vietnam's outside assistance, unsettling evidence of increasing North Vietnamese dependence on a single ally. Then, in 1971, hints of a rapprochement between the United States and China reached Hanoi. This cast the future of North Vietnam's deft middle road policy between Moscow and Peking into shadowy doubt.

Mobilizing the Home Front

In 1965, a decade after his Vietminh front had vanquished the French, ending their occupation of the country, Ho Chi Minh found himself once more summoning his people to war. This time, he told them, the "colonialists" were the Americans in South Vietnam and the "sacred" cause to drive them out and reunify the country. Above all, the struggle required the absolute commitment and participation of every person. "Everybody is against the enemy," his mobilization order proclaimed, "each citizen is a soldier, each village, street, plant is a fortress, each party branch a command post on the national salvation anti-American battle front. Build up the rear zone into a self-exerting spiritual source, a source of material for the front line."

Lao Dong leaders recognized that accomplishing their objectives in South Vietnam demanded not only the complete mobilization of North Vietnam's people and resources but the utmost effort, devotion, and talent of its party

cadres. As early as April 1964 the party urged its cadres to commit themselves totally to the "liberation of our South Vietnamese compatriots." In the beginning of 1965 the party gave Lao Dong cadres their home-front mission: "Stimulate and lead production and fighting; understand party politics and help party bases and branches both correctly interpret and implement these policies; pay attention to and improve the material and intellectual life of the masses; and mobilize and educate the masses."

From the Political Bureau and the Lao Dong Central Committee down to the village, the party's presence and authority were pervasive. Party officials at every level of government, for example, transmitted and executed policies and directives emanating from the party Central Committee in Hanoi. Although it sometimes overlapped in function with the government bureaucracy, the party existed as a separate and distinct decision-making body. Each district, the basic administrative unit of North Vietnam, was headed by a party committee composed of a chairman, a secretary, a few assistant secretaries, and a standing committee. This committee was responsible for interpreting and executing party policies as they applied to its district. Below the party committee, each district had party units ranging from three-cadre cells to village and cooperative subcommittees. Other party members oversaw administrative organs handling finances, law enforcement, and taxes. In addition, party officials galvanized and controlled the general population through numerous trade, political, educational, and cultural associations. Since all North Vietnamese had to belong to at least one of these groups, no person or facet of society escaped party oversight and direction.

The evacuation and dispersal resulting from the bombing, however, did force the party to alter somewhat its rigid structure. After much debate, the party Central Committee in 1965 decided to decentralize the government and, in effect, party operations. The Central Committee gave both local officials and party organs more authority to deal with the myriad local problems of the evacuation and mobilization programs. This form of administrative and economic self-sufficiency, the party felt, would allow the central government and party leadership to focus more on the larger issues of the war while encouraging more interaction and efficiency among local officials.

This decision also had a strategic purpose. In case U.S. or South Vietnamese forces ever launched an invasion of the North, each self-sufficient region would be better able to defend and sustain itself. A State Planning Commission official asserted, "We must apply the principle of becoming self supporting on a national and regional basis. Each zone should become . . . economically autonomous, ready to combat the enemy's attacks, whenever they come, however they come, and from wherever they come."

Instead of the usual detailed directives on how each province and district should run its affairs, central party planners now issued only general policy guidelines, allowing local officials to interpret and execute them. By the end of 1967 provincial and district officials and cadres were enjoying more latitude and responsibility than ever before. In the Hanoi area, for example, the district committee handled a wide number of duties that formerly belonged to the central government: agricultural production, communications and transportation, village trading cooperatives, education, and commerce. While it was relinquishing direct management over certain local economic and social activities, however, the central government and party leadership maintained several indirect controls over what took place in the countryside. Province leaders, for instance, were selected and trained by the party and tended to adhere closely to the central party line. Since the party held a monopoly on the means of production, as well as access to technology and development funds, local administrators inevitably had to conform to broad party guidelines. The party also made sure that provincial and other upper-echelon cadres conducted frequent checkups of local operations. To encourage leaders to keep abreast of what occurred in their districts, the party revived an old motto: "To be like the people, with the people, and among the people."

In order to cope with wartime mobilization, Lao Dong leaders reluctantly increased party membership from 800,000 in 1965 to over 1 million in 1968. In North Vietnam the Lao Dong party was not a mass organization but an elite of men and women chosen according to stiff standards of loyalty, personal commitment, indoctrination, and ability. In June 1966, the party Central Committee initiated an accelerated training program for more persons of leadership potential with scientific, technical, and economic backgrounds. Those admitted to the party received certain privileges of special status—free housing, medical care, and hospital treatment. They also got larger food rations and admittance to state stores for imported goods. When they retired, all party members could count on a pension and a state-financed burial.

Because military mobilization had cut deeply into the availability of qualified men, party leaders turned to young people and women. People under twenty-five made excellent party recruits, in the words of *Nhan Dan*, because they were "enthusiastic about the revolution, have good health, are cultured and usually absorb new things easily." By 1972 some party cells reported that 70 percent of their members were under thirty, including sig-

---

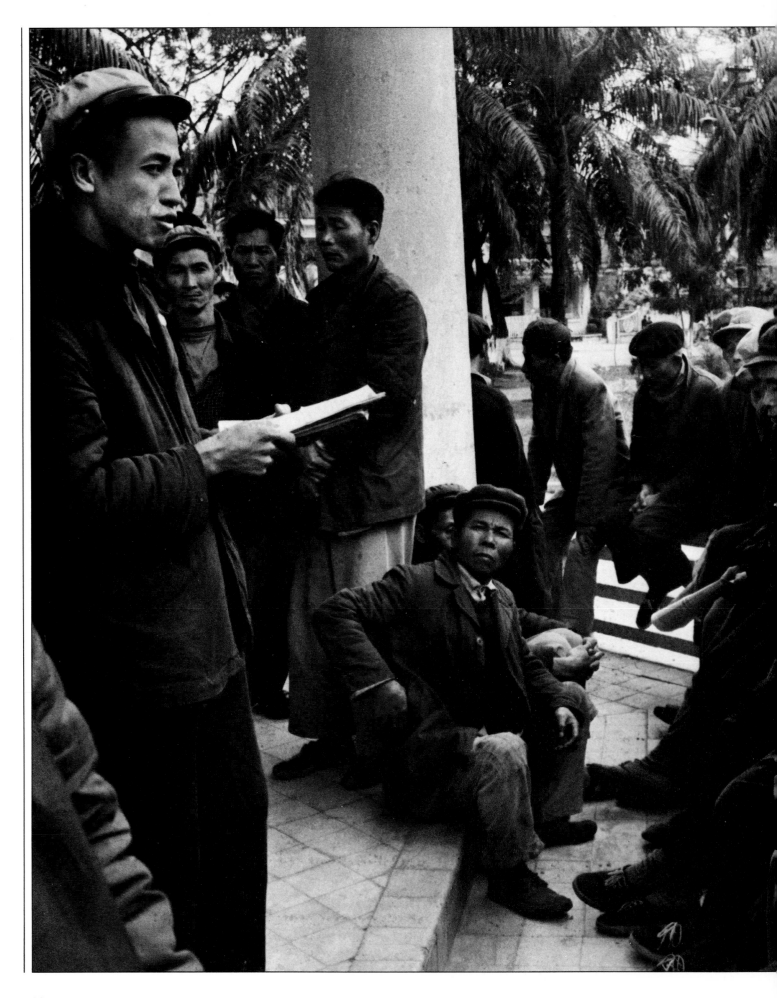

nificantly large numbers of women. Mobilization had already intensified the country's reliance on women. In the spring of 1965 the party had given every woman "three responsibilities: to replace the men who were called from the fields and factories for combat duties; to take charge of their families; to join militia units to take part in combat when necessary." By 1967, 70 percent of farm workers were women. The number of women in nonfarm jobs was up as well, from 348,000 in 1965 to 1,290,000.

Many men in the party reacted coolly to the influx of women members. According to *Nhan Dan*, some made known to party leaders that "if female cadres are promoted we will leave," or "if you bring her into the deputy slot then be prepared to replace me," or "we men took the wrong road in coming into these branches." In 1967 *Nhan Dan* criticized men who still believed a woman's place was in the home. It spoke of party members who disparaged women and considered it "the duty of their wives to serve them."

The party sent workers out among the masses with an exhortation from Ho Chi Minh. "Let us not be seduced by wealth," he bade them. "Let us not be discouraged by poverty. Let us suffer hardship now in order to enjoy happiness in the future." Many party officials, however, failed to live up to expectations. The projects and new responsibilities imposed on them by the bombing, for example, caught many of them unprepared. A *Nhan Dan* report revealed that "some cadres who previously did political work now manage a work camp of several thousand people, but they do not know how to direct or lead in their new jobs." "Waste is rampant," asserted one party provincial committee chairman. The dispersal of industries, he continued, had exposed many "weaknesses and obstacles" among cadres.

Some became overly bureaucratic and arrogant. Others, according to a report by Le Duc Tho in 1966, "degenerated into bureaucratic, dictatorial, and arbitrary elements concerned only with their private and individual interest." Even though in 1967 Ho Chi Minh warned that "we fear no enemy except bad and corrupt cadres," some continued using their positions to enrich themselves and their families through bribery, theft of state property, and embezzlement of government funds. In September 1968, for example, Radio Hanoi deplored "rowdies who have colluded with a small number of aberrants in state organs and enterprises to steal raw materials and goods." Party officials in charge of agricultural cooperatives falsely reported grain production, then sold what they had skimmed for a profit. Others took bribes in exchange for favors such as higher ration allotments and work points. A Miss Ty, the assistant director of the Phu Do cooperative

At the port of Haiphong in 1967, a stevedore foreman, who doubles as a party cadre, leads fellow dockworkers in a self-criticism session.

Vietnam's Veterans

In sharp contrast with the chill that greeted many American soldiers returning from the war in South Vietnam, the North Vietnamese warmly embraced their veterans as national heroes. Medals, honors, and titles were conferred upon dead soldiers and special memorials and cemeteries dedicated to their memory. Junior high school students deemed it an honor to visit the families of killed or wounded soldiers, often helping out with the household chores. To "remind the people of their gratitude to those who have sacrificed themselves in the interest of the nation," in 1969 the government declared July 27 Wounded Soldiers and Dead Heroes Day.

The North Vietnamese people accorded military veterans more than pomp and circumstance. Gratitude for their sacrifices translated into policies and programs designed to aid veterans in their return to civilian life. Wounded soldiers received free medical care, and amputees got allowances for artificial limbs. Government agencies and enterprises reserved 5 percent of their jobs for disabled veterans, who were hired without the usual period of apprenticeship or probation. The government also encouraged local training and employment of veterans in areas "compatible with their health, capabilities, and cultural level." Wounded veterans were particularly recruited for training as teachers, cadres, and skilled workers. Veterans also benefited from supplementary education and training programs. Vocational and professional schools reserved places for disabled soldiers. In addition, veterans benefits included extra rationed goods, transportation discounts, and free postage.

During the war, the government addressed the needs of the families of military personnel as well. When a soldier left for the South, his wife or mother got his salary for the first few months. The state provided funeral expenses and insurance compensation for those killed in action. Families of deceased soldiers were entitled to food, allowances, medical care, and assistance in the repair and construction of homes. Children of veterans enjoyed preferential treatment, such as special tutoring, in the schools. Sons of veterans entering the armed forces could choose their branch of service, including the option of avoiding the South.

The government's concern for the plight of veterans was more than humanitarian. Aid to veterans helped prevent

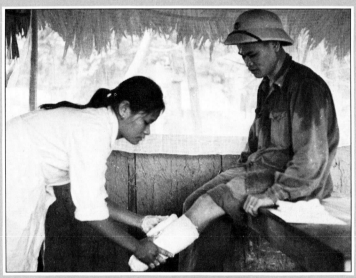

A PAVN soldier, one of North Vietnam's several thousand amputee war veterans, is fitted for an artificial leg in 1975.

the growth of a discontented political bloc that could challenge the government's authority and war policies. North Vietnam did in fact experience some veterans problems. While the government officially recognized the returnees as "men of high quality, political consciousness, and a sense of organization and discipline," and thus "a great source of labor," many disabled veterans (no statistics are available) remained unemployed and dependent on government subsidies. They were, said one newspaper, "like fish out of water." The hundreds of thousands of veterans and family members eligible for assistance nearly overwhelmed the local authorities responsible for their care.

There were frequent complaints in the press of inefficiency in the distribution of soldiers' benefits. In Dong Ma, for example, support funds to the families of dead soldiers fell short by as much as 15 percent in 1969.

Like their American counterparts, North Vietnamese veterans sometimes found readjusting to the home front difficult. Press accounts criticized some combat veterans for "unsoldierly behavior," such as wearing nonregulation clothing, like oversized sunglasses, walking arm-in-arm in the streets, rowdy behavior in buses and train stations, and playing radios at full blast and food fighting in public. One policeman recounted an incident in which he tried to stop a soldier who ran his bicycle through a red light. Instead of stopping, the culprit sped off shouting, "I've just come from the front and I don't know a red light from a green one."

In February 1974, fifteen vets were jailed in Hanoi for fighting and other public disturbances, and some less-than-honorably discharged veterans were caught with stolen submachine guns that were used "purely for dishonest acts." Three months later, a company-sized group of crippled veterans, unhappy with unemployment, lack of food, and inadequate accommodations, staged an armed uprising in Thanh Hoa, seizing the provincial administrative office. It took an entire regiment to put down the protest.

For many North Vietnamese veterans the final victory over South Vietnam in April 1975 did not fulfill their dreams of peace and of returning home to their families. Military occupation kept tens of thousands of them below the seventeenth parallel for years after Saigon surrendered. For some North Vietnamese troops the fighting never really ended. In 1985, while American veterans were putting the war behind them through memorials and national reconciliation, North Vietnamese veterans of twenty years of warfare in South Vietnam were still slogging through jungles and rice fields, at war with nationalist guerrillas in Cambodia.

near Hanoi, got caught for embezzlement and grain theft.

Village officials often justified their actions by arguing that party work overtaxed themselves and their families. One said, "The state trade agencies do not provide enough consumer goods for the people and the party members . . . so the problem of corruption and petty bribery and misuse of public property cannot be avoided."

Villagers, who were at least as much burdened by the war, were not sympathetic to such excuses. One popular ditty about shady cadres went like this: "Alas, my uncle, let us work as two, so the co-op director can buy radios and bicycles. Alas, my uncle, let's work as four, so the cadres can have their houses full of extra rice. Alas, my uncle, let's work as five, so the cadres can lie down in bed and enjoy the eating."

What most alarmed party leaders were signs of disenchantment with the war among party workers. In 1966 Le Duc Tho referred to "doves and peaceniks" in party ranks. "A small number of cadres have developed erroneous thoughts," he wrote. "They entertain subjectivism and pacifism, slacken their vigilance and fail to get ideologically ready for combat." Party leaders also bemoaned ideological quarrels among members over whether to follow a pro-Soviet or pro-Chinese line. They chastened them for "failure to associate themselves with reality, to take pains to go deeply into the reality of our country."

Periodically party "minipurges" followed public airings of cadre misdeeds, mismanagement, and slackening in revolutionary fervor. In 1967, for instance, the party instituted an open criticism and self-criticism campaign after which 200 to 300 members were ejected from the party. Similar "purification" drives took place in 1969 and 1970. Those deemed unfit were luckier than their counterparts in some other Communist countries. Instead of facing harsh penalties, they usually just lost their party membership and were demoted to lesser positions.

Hanoi watchers like British historian P.J. Honey and some experts in the U.S. State Department and the CIA sometimes interpreted party troubles in North Vietnam as symptoms of a political breakdown. They read too much, however, into Hanoi's sometimes hysterical-sounding reactions to party malefactors and malcontents. Although corruption, factionalism, and apathy did beset the Lao Dong, this never much impeded the party's home-front mobilization. Rather than openly acknowledging the shortcomings of their own directives and programs, Lao Dong leaders often tended to use party officials as whipping boys, thereby deflecting public dissatisfaction away from their policies onto those responsible for carrying them out.

A rifle in one hand, a plow in the other

While promoting economic and political decentralization, Hanoi's mobilization produced an extraordinary militarization of North Vietnamese society. Between 1965 and 1975

the North's military forces rose from 250,000 to 650,000, giving it the fourth largest standing army in the world. In 1965, as the war in the South intensified, the North Vietnamese government indefinitely extended the tours of conscripts already in service. While in the United States President Lyndon Johnson rejected military requests to activate the U.S. reserves, in Hanoi the government called up reservists as early as 1966.

All North Vietnamese males when they turned eighteen had to register for the draft. Unless deferred because of physical problems or occupational specialties, students were eligible for service within a year and a half after graduating. In 1967 the government raised the upper draft age from twenty-five to forty-five. As the size of the draft pool declined in the late 1960s, boys as young as fifteen were inducted. By the 1970s, lowered draft standards permitted the military to take 120,000 of the 190,000 males who came of draft age each year.

The draft in North Vietnam was nearly universal. Still, family considerations sometimes overrode obligations to the state. Some government officials and party members, for instance, managed to keep their children or relatives out of the military. One tactic was to get a son accepted into a foreign study program in the Soviet Union, China, or Eastern Europe. Another was to fit him into a draft-exempt government job. The party press widely ridiculed such evasions, but that did not stop them.

Although far fewer in number than in the United States, North Vietnam also had its share of draft dodgers. Some youths feared going south, whence they knew so many soldiers did not return. In urban areas draft-age males changed residences frequently to avoid their conscription notice. In villages peasants frequently shipped off their sons to friends or relatives in another district. At one village in Hai Duong Province in 1970, thirty-seven young men called up for service fled to other villages. Parents and friends lied to security agents about their whereabouts. When arrested, draft dodgers could be sentenced to three- to six-months' imprisonment, and on release they would be inducted.

Believing revolutionary ardor necessary to good soldiering, the North Vietnamese preferred recruitment to conscription. In 1965 the government promised a variety of benefits to attract new recruits. Joining the army, for example, entitled an enlistee to admission into the Labor Youth Group, which in turn brought several privileges and perquisites. Said a captured North Vietnamese soldier in 1967, "If you and I both sat for an exam and we both came out with the same mark, I, a Labor Youth member, would pass. You, not being a member, would not." More important, Labor Youth Group membership was a step toward acceptance in the Lao Dong party, an especially attractive prospect for peasant youths.

Appeals to the patriotism of parents were another aspect of the recruitment program. The government honored mothers and fathers of volunteers as "revolutionary heroes" and awarded them medals and tributes. In 1967, Ha Tay Province party officials presented "War of Resistance medals" to nearly 300 parents whose sons "enlisted in the army to fight the United States and save the nation." Newspapers published stories about parental sacrifice and patriotic devotion. In 1971 *Tien Phong* recounted the example of a woman named Duy, who had volunteered her four oldest sons to fight. When one of her sons was killed in combat, her youngest son, Kinh, asked to take his place in battle. "Some people," *Tien Phong* stated, "told her that she [Duy] had already contributed enough. But with gratitude to the revolution, how could enough be given in return! For national salvation, to guard her home, she would not protect her son or spare her wealth." In another instance a mother intervened in support of her only son, who pleaded with the army to accept him. He wrote to the recruiters seventeen times, the last time in his own blood, but to no avail. Finally, his mother took her son to party headquarters and insisted, "You must allow my child to go and kill the aggressors in order to avenge his father who was murdered by the French." Her son got his wish.

Recruiters attempted to dissuade wives from discouraging their husbands from military service. The government made much of a case in Nam Ha Province, where a young wife named Hai was hailed for deciding, after only one month of marriage, to encourage her husband, Sau, to join the military. "Both fighting the enemy and maintaining production," she reportedly told him, "are necessary. Presently the district is recruiting youths into the army. I will stay home and substitute for you in farming." After Sau was killed in battle, Hai persuaded the army to let her go to the front to avenge him. "I have selected the combat road," she was quoted as saying, "because it demands sacrifice but glorifies the fatherland."

The North's recruitment effort also tried to instill in youths dreams of glory, action, and victory. Newspapers regularly published accounts of battlefield heroes and triumphs. In 1970, for instance, *Quan Doi Nhan Dan* (People's Army) lauded the feats of Nguyen Chon, "a superior party member, a sharp cadre, and an unmatched hero. He is one of the most beautiful flowers among the ranking heroes and soldiers fighting on the great front line." Others published letters purportedly from troops at the front that spoke glowingly of valiant deeds, esprit de corps, and rousing victories. One letter said, "The red flame of victory is running high. . . . Here in the South one big victory follows another, and I'll keep attacking as long as there are enemy posts and towns." Another spoke almost joyously of "climbing heights through clouds to the battlefield" and of singing martial tunes. What did not get into print were uncensored letters like this one found near Kontum by American troops in 1969. "I am crying while writing this letter to you," wrote the soldier to his parents.

"Our surrounding areas are mountains and we can not find anything to eat. Consider me dead."

Party appeals to nationalism and duty induced many North Vietnamese youths to join the military. In 1970 *Quan Doi Nhan Dan* mentioned a fresh recruit who so yearned "to triumph over the American bandits" that he daily "practiced volleyball, weight-lifting, high-jumping, and running" in order to pass his physical. A history student, Tran Kim Dinh, quit his studies at a school in Quang Binh Province in 1971 to head for the front "with the spirit of my forefathers and with a great pride in the Vietnamese land and people." The motivation of some enlistees was similar to that of their young American counterparts: peer pressure and breaking away from family. A volunteer named Vinh explained, "I wanted to keep up with my contemporaries. Many soldiers are under social pressure from their friends to volunteer."

The North Vietnamese military advised instructors "to be gentle with new recruits. Most of them are used to family and village life. Army life is new and boring to them unless there are enough activities. Therefore they are easily homesick." To ease the transition from civilian to military life, the military set up morale-building programs. Instructors regaled their youthful recruits with stories of combat and heroism from the resistance against the French, as well as the fighting in the South. They gathered their troops to hear radio broadcasts that described military victories against the Americans or South Vietnamese. The military also tried to improve living conditions for the troops. "We have failed to overcome the temporary difficulties concerning the life of troops," *Nhan Dan* stated in 1965. "Many army units are trained in the open and outside the barracks. One must provide good tents and planks to serve as wooden beds for the units stationed in the open air."

During the war as many as 200,000 PAVN soldiers remained stationed near towns and villages around the North. They served as reserve troops for the front and performed such logistical and support functions as maintaining supply and communication lines and repairing equipment. The troops also oversaw the preparation of home-front defenses, the training of civil defense and militia forces, and the placement and operation of antiaircraft artillery.

The deployment of regular military forces throughout the countryside had a political purpose, too. Party members hoped that close contact between soldiers and civilians would imbue the people with discipline and with affection for the army. "We must understand," said Lieutenant General Song Hao, head of the party's General Political Directorate, "that . . . the leadership of the Party determines that our army is really a people's army,

A young boy in Hanoi plays war with a toy pistol while a group of PAVN soldiers looks on in the background.

and the affection and the support of our people is the eternal source for our army to successfully fulfill its mission."

To cement the bonds between military and civilians, the government announced in November 1964 that "Military-Civilian Unity Days" would be celebrated annually. The objective, it stated, was "to propagate the tradition of military-civilian unity, with the goal of strengthening brotherhood between the army and the people ... to build and protect the North and to defeat the American imperialists and their lackeys, who plot to invade and destroy the North." Preparation for "Unity Days" lasted about a month. The military disseminated leaflets urging cooperation between soldiers and civilians. Troops and villagers met at social gatherings. Former guerrilla fighters gave speeches about how civilians and troops had worked so closely together during the resistance against the French. Community officials even chaired grievance sessions where civilian representatives could voice their criticism of military behavior.

Unity Day itself featured cultural events, but the highlight was a series of joint military-civilian defense exercises for educational purposes. "During these exercises," the government commented, "the army has come to believe more firmly in the local people's ability in the local armed forces role. ... Everyone has become more attached to the main army, has seen clearly the importance of military preparedness, of unity, and of serving the fighting army."

In a further effort to consolidate military–civilian relations, the party placed wounded, demobilized army veterans in community and party positions. In 1965, for example, Hai Duong Province appointed 103 military veterans to be secretaries of township party committees, over 40 percent of the total number of secretaries. Veterans also comprised half of the province's 113 township chairmen and 487 of its cooperative managers. The party believed that through their military experience and discipline, ex-soldiers could better coordinate the community's national defense activities. "In townships where there are many wounded soldiers and demobilized troops participating in the work," *Nhan Dan* stated in July 1965, "generally speaking one can see very clearcut progress, not only because these people are very capable but because they have prestige, enjoying the love and faith of the people because they have braved death before; thus they are capable of mobilizing others to participate in every task."

Even as North Vietnam's mobilization involved the military in traditionally civilian affairs, it involved the civilian population in military ones. In 1965 the government revived its militia and self-defense forces, which had been deactivated after the defeat of the French in 1954. Their rallying cry: "A rifle in one hand, a plow in the other." General Vo Nguyen Giap was one of the principal proponents of the militia system. "The people's war line is the line of mobilizing all the people," he asserted, "driving all the people, and leading all the people to fight the aggressors. ... With regard to the self-defense and militia forces in particular, our party has asserted that they are a strategic force throughout the armed revolutionary struggle in our country."

North Vietnam mustered almost every able-bodied person not in the regular army into self-defense militia units. By mid-1966 the militia had grown to 200,000. In an average village of 3,000 to 4,000, the militia took as many as 300 to 400 men. In 1968, nearly 10 percent of all the people remaining in Hanoi were members. Most militia recruits were drawn from factories and farm cooperatives and served near their place of employment. They ranged in age from seventeen to thirty-nine. The core of the militia units was made up of military veterans recently discharged from the army, but the Lao Dong party maintained a controlling presence. In Hanoi, for example, 27 percent of the militia were party members.

As the war progressed, the militia increasingly depended on women to fill its ranks. In 1965 the percentage of women in the military was 22. By 1970, women accounted for 40 percent of the militia and 32 percent of militia commanders. Kurt Stern, an East German, talked to a young woman who worked at a machine factory and led its militia unit of thirty women. "Surely you would prefer to work without having to shoot?" he asked her. She crisply replied, "Until the Americans have withdrawn I shall work so that we can shoot, and shoot so that we can work." The women's militia unit training at a Nam Dinh fruit-canning plant regularly conducted bayonet drills. One line of women with bayoneted rifles in hand lunged at another line of women who, with their bare hands, tried to parry the thrusts and to wrest the weapons from their opponents.

The militia's mission was "to protect local areas" by providing crews for AAA batteries, supplying them with ammunition, and giving them rifle and machine-gun cover. At a Nam Dinh factory, for instance, the militia group manned permanent AAA positions nearby. At an AAA battery near the DMZ, Marceline Loridan met "two young girls mending uniforms who were members of the people's militia in a neighboring village. A little apart, there are a dozen militiamen and women in a military training class being taught by two battery gunners. Each of the people must be able, if needed, to replace an artilleryman put out of action. There are daily training courses."

Militia units also patrolled coastal areas to watch for American amphibious landings and were responsible for sighting downed U.S. planes and capturing the pilots. The military gave them specific instructions for best locating and seizing American fliers. "When you are pursuing bandit pilots," a directive stated, "and you see aircraft circling in the area, you know immediately that a bandit pilot landing there has marked his location for his friends.

The People's Militia

North Vietnam's national militia encompassed nearly all of the country's population not serving in PAVN, including women, children, and elderly men. While doing their regular jobs, militia members also performed a variety of civil defense tasks ranging from manning antiaircraft batteries to patrolling border and coastal areas to capturing downed U.S. pilots.

Right. An air defense militiaman (left) and a hospital worker (right) join in rescue efforts after a 1967 air attack on Nam Dinh, the DRV's third largest city.

Above. An antiaircraft gunner. Men over forty-five years old, who were exempt from military service, participated in North Vietnam's self-defense units.

Left. A loom operator remains at a textile plant in Hanoi, most of whose employees were evacuated to the countryside. About 20 percent of all workers in rural factories were equipped with rifles and machine guns.

You must act quickly. If not, enemy helicopters will come down and drop a rope ladder to pick up the bandit pilot." "In cases when the bandit pilot has gotten on the rope ladder," it cautioned, "you must resolutely concentrate your firepower to shoot down the aircraft and kill the bandit pilots."

One of the militia's chief tasks was training young men for possible service in the regular army. It taught engineering, signal techniques, chemical warfare, and intelligence. Some militia units prepped for infiltration to the South with long night marches and by carrying heavy loads. They also dug trenches and bomb shelters, transported troops and materials, maintained boats and docking facilities, and repaired dikes.

The militia was supplemented by another paramilitary force known as Youth Shock Brigades. Formed in early 1965, these brigades put more than 100,000 young people to work maintaining and repairing roads and bridges. Brigade members, aged fifteen to thirty, served a three-year enlistment. Sixty percent of them were girls and women. They got five dong ($1.50) per month, as well as clothes, sandals, and soap. In return, the government assured them of career advancement after their enlistment. The brigades made extra provision for women by supplying portable bathhouses. Health specialists accompanied the brigades, which were usually mobile. Wherever they deployed, the brigades had to secure their own food and lodgings.

In his travels around the North, David Schoenbrun encountered numerous companies of the Youth Brigade. "They camp out in the paddies or in the forests all night long to be available in case of an emergency road repair," he said. One of the brigades' most dubious assignments was the detonating or defusing, if possible, of delayed-action bombs. In 1967 brigade member Nguyen Thi Kim was decorated for her bomb-clearance record. "The most essential thing," she said, "is to grasp the characteristics of the bombs. There are bombs which give out smoke, others a blue flame, others heat. The lookout, who stands barefoot at the very place the bomb has fallen, can feel all these things. . . . He has a few seconds to warn his comrades who work nearby. Everybody must then lie down. When the bomb is detonated, to protect our heads against flying stones we cover them with our shovels." "For this," Kim said, "many have given their lives."

"Bombing brains"

North Vietnam's strict regimentation reflected the Lao Dong party's intent to harness, and control, the energies of the people. Yet party leaders recognized that control alone, without the people's emotional support, was not enough to achieve their war aims. So they organized an intensive propaganda campaign to appeal to the people's nationalism and will to resist the U.S. bombing attacks.

On August 5, 1964, the party's Central Information Bureau started a two-year training program for propaganda specialists called "news and information cadres." The curriculum for the first class of 365 students included courses on Marxism-Leninism, party policies, and "interpretation of news events." The party also established a central government agency to coordinate the activities of the several hundred thousand cadres directly or indirectly involved in propaganda. According to the party Central Committee, the agency's function was "to broadly disseminate . . . policies of the party . . . enabling every citizen in any place and at any time to clearly realize his own situation and his duty to follow."

The Lao Dong party dominated all forms of mass communication, a network of media propaganda specialists exploited to the fullest. A 1966 party pamphlet defined the press as "propagandist, an agitator and an organizer, guiding the people in socialist construction in the North and the fight to achieve peaceful national reunification." All newspapers—like the party organs *Hoc Tap, Nhan Dan,* and *Quan Doi Nhan Dan*—were state owned and operated. Propaganda workers directed dozens of similar publications dealing with culture, economics, youth, and social affairs.

Since television was virtually nonexistent in North Vietnam, the party focused on national outlets such as radio and motion pictures. Only one of every thirty-two Vietnamese families owned a radio. The government regulated private ownership of radios by limiting the number available for purchase, requiring party approval, and placing restrictions on how they could be used. The general public received radio programming over a national system of 225,000 public loudspeakers connected by land lines. The government numbered the loudspeakers in Hanoi alone at 33,000, connected by 470 miles of transmission lines. Radio Hanoi made no pretense about its purpose: "Propaganda operations for carrying out the political mission of the Party and government."

Radio Hanoi provided farmers and workers with news, music, commentary, and entertainment during the morning and evening hours. It also greeted them—whether they wanted to hear or not—when they returned home at night. "There is nothing more pleasant," one of the broadcasters said, "as to return home to rest after production hours and listen to the station broadcasting one's life, religion and one's resistance against America and accomplishments for national salvation." For many North Vietnamese the blare of the loudspeakers for two or three hours at a time, four times a day, proved a source of irritation. "It's difficult to talk to each other," complained one citizen. "They get used to having to shout."

Party propagandists used films as well as radio for mass indoctrination. In 1964, seventeen mobile film units showed more than 7,000 films in Ha Bac Province north of Hanoi. By 1965, according to Minister of Culture Hoang

Minh Giam, "hundreds" of film teams were operating in remote provinces. Furthermore, he asserted, "every North Vietnamese viewed at least five motion pictures a year—an overall attendance totaling 352 million." Then there were books. In 1965 North Vietnam published more than 25 million books. Among the twenty-one new titles that year, six dealt with the war in South Vietnam, two with the "correct" ideology of the Lao Dong party, three with the Vietnamese national revolution, and five with the "economic and social progress of the Democratic Republic of Vietnam." By far the best selling books were the collected writings of President Ho Chi Minh and General Vo Nguyen Giap.

Besides the mass media, propagandists made use of meetings, parades, lectures, demonstrations, art exhibits, and sports rallies to promulgate the party's ideology and war policies. Song writers put their talents to work composing uplifting revolutionary lyrics. Musical groups toured facilities all over the country. During a visit to North Vietnam in 1967 John Brown observed, "Much war effort we discovered goes into transporting talented musical groups to the DMZ and elsewhere. Each factory or agricultural cooperative we visited had its composer, accordionist, and singers—ready to hold forth, for instance, on the shooting down of American planes. 'Our songs,' said one troupe leader, 'teach us how to hate correctly—that is very important.'"

In delivering its propaganda messages, the party believed the personal touch was all-important. A 1965 directive apprised "information cell" propagandists that "direct exchanges and talks with each person, each household, each group constitute the main form of work of the propaganda workers." It also encouraged them to make use of other forms of "mass culture" such as folk songs, work songs, books, magazines, posters, and pictures. In Nhuc Ho cooperative in Quang Binh Province, propagandists read party newspaper articles aloud to groups of workers and their families. They also searched out the villagers' concerns and addressed them in local news broadcasts. Sometimes party workers held question-and-answer sessions. *The People's Army* selected propaganda cadre Nguyen Manh Thuan as 1968's "emulation warrior of the year." It lauded his efforts at a village cooperative "to build a system of bulletin boards and broadcasting towers to propagandize and disseminate news of victories and describe the examples of good people and good works of the cooperative members in the village."

Party propaganda themes were as varied as the issues of the war itself. Information cadres endlessly cranked out "fact sheets" accusing the United States of imperialist intervention in the South; making war against the legitimate representatives of the people, that is the National Liberation Front; blocking peace negotiations; and bankrolling a "corrupt" South Vietnamese regime. North Vietnamese propaganda also depicted the United States, along with

its "lackeys," as cruel aggressors who regularly committed war crimes—using chemical and biological warfare, committing wanton brutality and atrocities, and enslaving and impoverishing the people.

The North Vietnamese portrayed their enemies as "barbarians." Newspapers and wall posters offered graphic depictions and accounts of alleged American atrocities—a grisly array of torturings, mass rapes, and grotesque disfigurations of men, women, and children. According to this propaganda, American and South Vietnamese troops often turned on each other. One lurid tale spoke of three captured South Vietnamese soldiers who ran out of food while on a spy mission across the DMZ. After one soldier had "piggishly" eaten all their remaining rations, his two comrades cried, "Eat all the rations, will you! Now we'll eat you!" Having said that, the tale continued, "they leapt upon him and tore into his body. They were fighting over his gall bladder when they noticed the muzzles of the border defense forces aimed at their chests."

Anti-American propaganda insinuated itself into every aspect of North Vietnamese life. The party frequently proclaimed "Hate America" days. In 1965 the party Central Committee passed a resolution that everything possible "must be turned into aids in the teaching of hatred toward the American gang ... like a bullet shot directly at the enemy." Schoolchildren who wrote letters of inspiration to soldiers at the front won the distinction of being named "kill-Americans and save the nation heroes." A standard mathematics lesson in North Vietnamese schools was, "In a battle in which the gallant National Liberation Front forces defeated the army of the American imperialists and their Vietnamese puppet troops, 840 enemy soldiers were killed. If one-fourth of the dead were puppet troops and the rest of the dead were American imperialists, how many American imperialists were killed in the battle?"

Defiance to the end

Operation Rolling Thunder provided North Vietnamese propagandists a focal point for arousing anti-U.S. feelings. In a grim way, the relatively modest number of civilian casualties inflicted by the bombing worked against the United States. The bombing killed just enough people to instill in the North Vietnamese a fierce desire for vengeance but not enough to incite panic and defeatism. "We'll keep on fighting," avowed a laborer, "if all we have left is an undershirt for clothing." Standing next to his wrecked home near the DMZ, a peasant was quoted as saying, "I don't care about my home. I will rebuild it and it will be better. The Americans are wrong if they think they are terrorizing us."

In their hatred for the bombing, the people commonly referred to American pilots as "air pirates" or "bandits." All along the streets popular graffiti carried the slogan, "Down with Johnson the American pirate." In the bomb-

The Other Psywar

Amid the flurry of bombs, planes, antiaircraft fire, and missiles, the air over North Vietnam also buzzed with the verbal weapons of the propaganda war. While the bulk of Radio Hanoi's "Voice of Vietnam" programming was directed toward boosting Communist morale, by 1972 as many as 32 out of a total of 728 broadcasting hours each week were in English. Radio Liberation, the clandestine mouthpiece of the Vietcong, supplied an additional 12 hours of English-language programming. The objective: eroding the confidence of the American servicemen stationed in South Vietnam.

Strangers in the strange surroundings of South Vietnam, many bemused American soldiers tuned in to their favorite Communist disc jockey, Thu Huong, better known as "Hanoi Hannah." In the notorious tradition of Axis Sally, Lord Haw Haw, and Seoul City Sue, Hanoi Hannah would alternately harangue and cajole the Americans between plays of the latest pop tunes. She would, recalled one serviceman, denounce alleged U.S. atrocities in the South and point out "that the proletarian sons of American society were forced to carry the guns while the sons of the bourgeosie carried the briefcases" to win GI sympathy for their proletarian counterparts in the Vietcong. Broadcasts such as this one oftentimes urged the Americans to defect or to at least lay down their arms:

Put yourself in the place of the South Vietnamese.

How would you react if half a million foreign troops were in your homeland, freely killing, bombing, d[e]stroying day after day? Think hard, GI Joe. Vietnam is not American soil and you have no business here.

The South Vietnamese People's Committee for Solidarity with the American People does not like to see you die in Vietnam only because Johnson sent you here. So it tells you to resolutely demand your withdrawal from Vietnam now. The committee also calls on you to refuse to go to battle and avoid a useless death, not to encroach upon the life and property of the South Vietnamese people.

Radio Hanoi frequently aired tapes featuring Americans whom the Communists deemed friendly to their cause. Ronald Ramsey, a member of the Student Nonviolent Coordinating Committee who used the noms des guerres of "Joe 'Libre' Epstein" and "Granny Goose," sent Hanoi "Radio Stateside" recordings urging servicemen to defect. On a visit to North Vietnam in 1967, Stokeley Carmi-

An announcer for Radio Hanoi broadcasts out of a mountain cave near Thanh Hoa in September 1967.

chael taped a message encouraging black GIs to leave the war to "the white man . . . it's his war. Let him fight it." North Vietnamese broadcasters also highlighted American newspaper and journal articles critical of the war. Sometimes they quoted writings or speeches from obscure American sources. This piece, attributed to a U.S. "compatriot" identified only as Ed Anderson, was read to American servicemen on November 7, 1966:

Nobody has to tell the pilots in Vietnam that every time a bomb is dropped or a plane goes down somebody is making money. Heavy spending for the war in Vietnam means increased sales and earnings for the

wide variety of aircraft, missile, and electronics firms.

While Radio Hanoi and its honey-voiced broadcaster took their propagandizing seriously, American GIs regarded their efforts as simply comic relief. If anything, Radio Hanoi's lavish praise of antiwar demonstrators in the United States only angered the troops who saw the protesters as reinforcing the enemy. The same was true of broadcasts seeking to inflame racial tensions among U.S. troops. Black GIs, who were courted as "brothers" against white Americans, were not flattered by the attentions of the DRV. In response to Radio Hanoi's broadcasts in 1968 urging black soldiers to "cross over to the [North Vietnamese] people's side," black Specialist 4 Gerald Walker commented, "Where was all this brotherhood crap when my friends got killed?"

For American POWs, Hannah was the primary link to the outside world and often an inadvertent source of good tidings. They received news of the unsuccessful November 1970 raid on the POW camp at Son Tay, for example, when an indignant Hanoi Hannah declared at the end of a broadcast, "How dare [the Americans] say that America could land airplanes on the streets of Hanoi and pick up prisoners." Her ire brought joy to the imprisoned Americans of the Hanoi Hilton.

Radio Hanoi irritated U.S. military commanders into making it a bombing target. U.S. warplanes struck the Hanoi Radio station for the first time on February 22, 1968, but the transmitter continued working. During the Christmas bombings of 1972, American B-52s blasted the station again. Despite the destruction of its main power supply (the Vietnamese had brought in diesel generators), the station stayed on the air.

Following the peace accords in 1973, Hanoi Hannah's audience had left and the show was canceled. But that was not the end of her career: in 1976, Thu Huong resurfaced in what was once South Vietnam. There, as described by former antiwar activist Cora Weiss, she became "the Barbara Walters of Saigon TV, minus, of course, the high salary."

battered farming village of Phu Xa, embittered relatives of the twenty-four slain villagers erected a memorial that read: "In hatred toward the American aggressors who massacred our compatriots of Phu Xa, hamlet of Nhat Tan, on August 13, 1966."

The already vengeful attitude of the people toward the bombing was heated by the North Vietnamese propaganda machine to a fever pitch. In cities around the country huge billboards, like gruesome baseball scoreboards, recorded the number of U.S. planes brought down. When the total reached 500, the government issued commemorative stamps. As part of the "Drown Out the Bombs' Noise With Singing Movement," schoolchildren began their day singing songs like this:

> Girl with rounded arms of such pure whiteness,
> would you dare to fire on the aircraft?
> But yes, at this very moment, for if
> you failed to fire on them,
> the cruelty of the Yankees would not wait.

Bombing exhibits were everywhere. The Official War Crimes Museum displayed an assortment of bombs and explosives dropped by U.S. planes. A similar display at Hanoi in 1965 drew 300,000 people before going on tour of the provinces. Movies with such titles as *Shooting Down Enemy Planes with Rifles* and *At the Gate of the Wind*, which featured fishermen shooting down American planes, played to large audiences.

Thanks to its propagandists, North Vietnam resounded with accounts of valiant deeds against the enemy. Early in 1967, at a "Congress of Heroes and Outstanding Fighters," Pham Van Dong and Ho Chi Minh honored, among others, militiawoman Ngo Thi Tuyen, who "under a rain of bombs carried on her shoulders cases of ammunition to supply the ack-ack guns"; Tran Thi Ve, a seventeen-year-old boy who "saved from death comrade victims of a bombing raid"; and pilot Nguyen Van Bay, who "brought down four enemy planes in four dogfights." Vietcong guerrillas also gained reknown in the North for their exploits. The most famous was Nguyen Van Troi, a Saigon teen-ager who tried to assassinate Secretary of Defense Robert McNamara during a visit to South Vietnam in 1965. After a court found him guilty and sentenced him to death, South Vietnamese authorities executed Nguyen, who was promptly acclaimed a hero in the North. Numerous films told his life story. A biography of Nguyen Van Troi, published in Hanoi in 1965, was translated into four languages, and North Vietnamese admirers bought almost 500,000 copies in one month. Many youths, in Nguyen Van Troi's memory, renamed their youth brigades "determined to die" units.

Another aim of North Vietnamese propaganda was to

Propaganda posters fill the room of a student boarding in a peasant's home. One (right top) translates "Women of the South determined to defeat American aggressors."

A propaganda billboard atop the government shopping center on Hanoi's Tran Hung Dao Street depicts the deeds of Communist forces on the Southern battlefield. The words (right) read "Arm for the victory against American aggressors."

insulate the people from outside influences. Between 1965 and 1967 American planes dropped 300 million leaflets over North Vietnam. Some warned people to stay away from military targets, others urged Northerners to refrain from "attacking their southern brothers." Sometimes U.S. planes scattered "gift kits" containing candy and toys for children and such things as fishhooks and cigarette lighters.

North Vietnam denounced U.S. efforts to "bomb the brains" of its people. The deputy propaganda chief of Quang Binh Province, for example, called them a "dark plot and wicked scheme." Party cadres tried to combat U.S. propaganda by telling villagers that the gifts were infested with smallpox and tetanus germs. They ordered villagers to turn the packages in to the police and periodically held bonfires to burn them. Because Hanoi jammed foreign radio broadcasts by the Voice of America, Radio Free Asia, and the British Broadcasting Corporation, the United States dropped small transistor radios in the North. The North Vietnamese neutralized many of them by barring the sale of batteries to anyone whose radio was not registered with the security police.

North Vietnamese authorities feared more than U.S. propaganda. They sought to alert the people to infiltration by U.S. and South Vietnamese commandos, spies, and saboteurs. In 1965 the newspaper *Chingh-Nghia* published a story about a thirteen-year-old boy who saw a young man emerging from the forest one night. When the boy asked where he was going, the youth replied that he was running away from home. "They walked together," *Chingh-Nghia* reported. "The stranger youth asked many questions: Is your post office near here? How many bridges are there? Are there anti-aircraft units in your village? The thirteen-year-old boy became suspicious and instead of leading him to his home brought him to a security post where he was found to be a spy."

While crying foul at U.S. propaganda, the North Vietnamese conducted a similar campaign against South Vietnam. The North's Voice of Vietnam broadcasted approximately seventy hours a week of news and propaganda into the South. On the international front, North Vietnam published a number of periodicals intended for foreign readers. In addition to *Vietnamese Studies*, articles on socialism in French and English, North Vietnam's Foreign Languages Publishing House distributed *Facts and Events*, which featured accounts of "Viet Cong victories" and "U.S. atrocities." Propaganda films for foreign distribution included such titles as *Fighting Vietnam* and *Kim Dong*, about a boy hero in the Communist guerrilla movement.

During the 1960s the North Vietnamese did what they could to manipulate American opinion and stir up the antiwar movement. Hanoi frequently applauded the U.S. protesters and their demonstrations. It annually appealed to American peace organizations to support the North's stand on the war. When American war protester Norman Morrison committed suicide outside the Pentagon in Washington, D.C., by self-immolation in 1965, he was all but canonized in North Vietnam. Billboards carried his picture, and a song, "Norman Morrison Will Never Die," immortalized his sacrifice.

To push their case in the United States, North Vietnam invited numerous Americans—journalists, clergymen, pacifists, and antiwar leaders—to visit their country. In December 1965 Herbert Aptheker of the American Communist party, Professor Staughton Lynd of Yale University, and Tom Hayden of Students for a Democratic Society toured the North in order, in their words, to "achieve understanding with the North Vietnamese." Afterward, in two books, *The Other Side* by Lynd and Hayden, and *Mission to Hanoi* by Aptheker, they expressed their conviction that "the Hanoi government and the National Liberation Front are competent, even representative of Vietnam." Dave Dellinger, a pacifist and editor of *Liberation* magazine, brought back from his 1966 trip to the North graphic photographs and stories of death and destruction from the bombing. Said Dellinger, "I argued to North Vietnamese officials that when the American people found out about the nature and effect of the bombings, they would put an end to them."

From 1965 to 1975 Hanoi played host to a parade of selected Americans. They included leading antiwar spokesmen like Father Daniel Berrigan and Professor Howard Zinn of Boston University, writers Susan Sontag and Mary McCarthy, journalists Harrison Salisbury, Seymour Hersh, and Anthony Lewis. In 1966 Salisbury drew attacks from some who complained that he allowed North Vietnamese propaganda to seep into his firsthand reports of civilian bomb damage in the city of Nam Dinh. In American terms, the most controversial—some say infamous—visitor to North Vietnam was actress Jane Fonda. Fonda enraged many Americans in 1972 by making a broadcast over Voice of Vietnam Radio in Hanoi in which she told U.S. pilots to halt their raids on North Vietnam: "I implore you, I beg you to consider what you are doing. . . . In the area where I went it was easy to see that there are no military targets, there is no important highway, there is no communication network."

Statements by peace activists who went to North Vietnam heightened the antiwar fervor of the protest groups they represented. There were angry charges that the North Vietnamese had somehow infiltrated the American antiwar movement, but FBI, CIA, and Congressional investigations uncovered no direct connection between Americans and Communists. Nevertheless, by courting sympathetic American visitors who might disseminate its views in the United States, Hanoi did succeed in influencing the tone and substance of the Vietnam War debate.

After President Johnson called off air strikes above the

nineteenth parallel in April 1968 and then halted all U.S. bombing raids against North Vietnam the following October, the North Vietnamese people heaved a collective sigh of relief. Evacuees began trickling back to their homes in the cities, and in the most heavily bombarded areas of the southern panhandle men, women, and children, for the first time in years, emerged unafraid from their bunkers and other underground havens. What happened in Hanoi was typical of the renewal of life taking place around the country. In a city that once moved only at night, thousands of cyclists jammed the midday streets, darting in and out among the overcrowded streetcars. Along formerly quiet boulevards thousands of people strolled, peering into nearby shops and store windows. Hanoi's shady parks once more teemed with young

Top. New York Times *reporter Harrison Salisbury tours Pho Nguyen Thiep Street in Hanoi after it was struck during a U.S. air attack on December 13, 1966. Above. American actress Jane Fonda converses with a group of North Vietnamese during her 1972 visit.*

couples walking hand in hand, laughing children, and ice cream and soft drink vendors. A British diplomat remarked, "You sense the same letup now in Hanoi that we felt in England after the heavy Luftwaffe attacks were broken off in England."

No longer tensed for the bombing, the North Vietnamese began feeling more acutely the constraints imposed upon them: severe shortages of food, consumer goods, and housing. Evacuees returning to their towns and cities waited in long lines to buy food and other essential goods. What's more, when they reached the store counters, they did not find much to purchase. One visitor to Hanoi in 1969 recalled that the only nonessential goods he saw for sale were "some Chinese-made ping pong balls." In 1968, the monthly ration of rice, which previously averaged from twenty to fifty pounds per month depending on one's age and occupation, was cut in half. In place of the rice, people received rice substitutes of imported Russian wheat flour and Rumanian corn meal, both distasteful to the Vietnamese palate. In addition to food, other items, from bicycles to cigarettes to clothing, were in very short supply. The annual ration of cloth was just enough for a person to make two suits or smocks. In a 1968 newspaper article, tobacco factory workers apologized for having to make cigarettes "half full of tobacco." Chronic shortages prompted one fourteen-year-old boy to write an irate letter to his father fighting in the South: "I eat rice mixed with wheat. The shirt I wear is full of patches. The paper I write on has many lumps. I have only rubber sandals to ward off the winter cold."

Because of insufficient raw materials and skilled workers, the goods that were available often broke down or became quickly unusable. *Nhan Dan* wrote that "many metal goods such as kerosene lamps are not durable. From the items produced by the factories to things made out of tin, it is as if they were made out of paper." Peasants grumbled about their government-issue farm equipment. They renamed the latest model plow "*Mot Nam*," meaning "one season."

The only recourse for most consumers, if they had the cash, was a ubiquitous black, or what the Vietnamese called, "sneak," market. In 1970 a North Vietnamese soldier said those "who wanted to buy things on the black market did not have difficulty doing so because marketeers were not likely to be arrested. Some believed it possible to buy anything on the black market." A farmer, for instance, could get four times as much for his rice if he sold it on the black market rather than to the state. In Hanoi one would find black-market bicycle-repair shops, where for three times the official price a bike could be fixed without the usual delay at the state-run stores. A 1967 U.S. intelligence analysis stated that, "Trade in the black market was usually confined to friends of the employees in the state-owned stores. The employees gave extra rations of meat and sugar to their friends who sold them on the black market."

Government efforts to clamp down on the black market were ineffective. In 1970, Phan Van Binh, president of the Supreme People's Court, explained why: "North Vietnamese warehouses are clogged with goods of such poor quality that corruption, waste, speculation, and smuggling leading to inflation and market upheavals are rampant." *Nhan Dan* called for "a more efficient system of state marketing. This situation is having a bad effect on production, on the social order, and on the morale of cadres, workers, employees, and the population."

North Vietnam's security forces sought and prosecuted government employees in league with black marketeers. In 1970 the police announced that they had arrested and jailed twice as many "economic criminals" as the year before (no specific figures were given). The same year the newspapers reported the cases of several factory managers prosecuted for "selling part of their products for personal gain and living like princes in dachas." *Hanoi Moi* subsequently carried the story of the chairman of a state cooperative who had dismantled three locomotives and "reassembled the parts to make vehicles to sell for money."

The black market survived the government's sporadic crackdowns in part because party leaders grudgingly tolerated its existence. While the black market violated the Lao Dong party's socialist principles, it had the virtue of enabling people to obtain basic commodities that party cadres and policies were not able to supply through the official state system. So the party closed its eyes to all but the most blatant black market schemes.

The thriving black market dramatized for some party leaders that, now that the bombing had ended, it was time to begin rebuilding the North's badly bruised economy. Until 1969 the North Vietnamese had been eking out a living in a "resistance" or subsistence economy. Military production and expenditures had taken priority over consumer items. In 1969 the party formulated plans for economic reconstruction and revivification. Instead of the usual five-year plans based on pie-in-the-sky projections, party leaders opted for improving the economy through careful planning and setting realistic goals.

Guns and butter

The search for priorities for economic reconstruction provoked a vigorous debate in the Political Bureau. Party First Secretary Le Duan took the lead by calling for a guns-and-butter approach. He felt that economic deprivation since 1965 had exacted too heavy a toll from the North Vietnamese people and threatened to undermine morale and long-term support for party war aims in the South. Accordingly, he decreed that "leading cadres should visit every locality and every cooperative to assess the situation, recommend bold measures, build a national economic structure, and carry out a redivision of labor." Furthermore, he advocated more pragmatic than ideologically oriented economic policies such as material incentives, bonuses, and a modest free-market system to ease the consumers' plight and reinvigorate production.

Truong Chinh expressed stern opposition to Le Duan's relaxation of strict socialist policies. He had long decried the extent to which prosecuting the war in the South had diverted the party from advancing revolutionary socialism in the North. In 1969, for example, he vociferously attacked "rightist" or revisionist tendencies in the party's management of the economy. "In many places, the management of co-op production means is far from good," he declared. "The co-op land is not yet tightly managed. Specifically, co-op members are allowed to occupy collectively owned land to develop it for themselves, turn it into living areas, dig ponds for fish raising, or divert collectively owned land for private use." Truong Chinh also condemned the rise of the black market and Le Duan's suggestions for a limited free market as setting the stage for a revival of capitalistic ways. "The strength of the customs of millions of small producers is a terrible strength," he maintained. "The struggle between the two lines in North Vietnam should be waged with vigor."

In the state's reconstruction plans for the early 1970s, Le Duan's pragmatic approach prevailed. "If we think we can build socialism with proletarian enthusiasm alone," he responded to his critics at the party's fortieth anniversary celebration in June 1970, "while disregarding all objective economic laws, we are grossly mistaken." State economic plans granted peasants and industrial workers various incentives to boost production and raise their income. The government offered peasants higher prices for their farm produce and permitted them to retain a larger portion of their crops for sale on the free market. It also froze the farmers' production quotas for five years and stimulated individual performance with a "self-suffi-

ciency" policy based on the principle "he who works not eats not." For industrial workers the government introduced a similar policy of "salary according to production." "At the Tran Phu machinery shop where this system was first tried," according to *Hanoi Moi*, there quickly developed "an atmosphere of seething competition."

Like economic dispersal and evacuation, economic rehabilitation confronted the Lao Dong party with a major organizational challenge. Restructuring the economy demanded more leader-types with technical and managerial skills than the party possessed. In 1970 Le Duan kicked off a new "emulation" campaign to promote the party's image and recruit suitable cadres for the tasks ahead. The campaign exhorted potential party workers to emulate the recently deceased Ho Chi Minh's example of devotion to party and country. While in the past the party had molded cadres after the dictum "more red than professional," the new emphasis was for members "both red and professional."

A worker rolls out reams of freshly dyed black cloth to dry on a Hanoi boulevard in 1968. The cotton material was used for the "pajamas" worn by so many Vietnamese peasants.

Leaders took the opportunity of reorganization to purge the party of corrupt, inefficient, and lackadaisical members. The Lao Dong Political Bureau took aim at members who "displayed very inferior political standards and work performance and have failed to fulfill the tasks entrusted to them by the party and the state." It sought to rid the party especially of "bad elements, of opportunists whose aims are to sabotage the party or satisfy personal ambitions."

Reconstruction brought many tangible benefits to North Vietnam's war-beleaguered population. In the Hanoi area foreign journalists reported significant improvements in living conditions. In January 1971, journalist Michael Maclear was struck by the change since his previous trip in mid-1968. Everywhere he noticed "the bright red of brick and tile. . . . New homes, schools, offices and factories stand out against the straw roofs of the collectives." In Hanoi, a new housing complex was under construction, and the Polytechnic Institute and Central Market, both shut down during the bombing, were reopened. Reconstruction of roads and railroads progressed rapidly. By 1971 the North's electrical generating capacity had been restored to 60 percent of its prebomb level. All of this activity bettered the average citizen's immediate economic lot and lifted the standard of living above the subsistence level.

In the long run, however, party leaders were disappointed by the results of their rebuilding schemes. Although state plans called for 16.4 percent growth in industrial production, it rose by less than half. Light industry increased by 2.1 percent instead of the hoped-for 26 percent. In agriculture the rice harvest edged up from 3.7 million tons in 1965 to only 4 million tons in 1971, far below the 5.9 million necessary to feed the population. Continuing scarcity of fertilizers and agricultural implements exacerbated the situation. While it took only 14 hours of labor in Chile or only ninety minutes in the United States to produce 220 pounds of rice, it still required 120 hours of work in North Vietnam.

As under the bombing, North Vietnam's reconstruction goals mandated a full-blown mobilization campaign to galvanize the energies of the people. This time, the zeal of North Vietnam's population did not quite rise to party expectations. In the summer of 1970 the government chided the dockworkers at Haiphong for leaving "tons of cargo to rot and rust on the piers." A 1970 British government study revealed that in North Vietnam's factories "some machines were found to be in use only two or three hours a day, and workers were taking off early after four to six hours on the job." This contrasted markedly with the labor discipline and productivity during Rolling Thunder.

One group singled out for special criticism was Vietnamese youth. Lieutenant General Song Hao of North Vietnam's Political Directorate berated a "small number" of young people "for romantic and soft sentiments and too

much love of life, too much fear of death and hardship." Although North Vietnam saw no organized outbursts of youth antiwar feeling, General Song prated about U.S. propaganda efforts to "sow doubt in the party's leadership and doubt in the victory of the revolution, create the illusion of peace, and lower their fighting spirit."

North Vietnam did endure something of a generation gap. Government officials blamed the several thousand Vietnamese youths educated abroad each year for popularizing Western music and clothing styles forbidden in the North. Party propagandists derided these "hippies" for their longish hair, tight trousers, and fondness for "yellow," or rock 'n' roll, music. They complained of "girls who wear sheer and provocative nylon dresses." In 1971 the state even sentenced a young musician named Phang Thang Toan to fifteen years in prison for forming a rock group that played "yellow, heartrending music." The regime organized a youth union to "combat violations of party lines and policies." Unofficially, it sponsored "patriotic" youth groups that roamed the streets of Hanoi and other cities to harass "degenerates."

Party frustration over signs of public laxity vented itself in the form of paranoia about internal spies and "counterrevolutionaries" bent on sabotaging the war effort. Minister of Public Security Tran Quoc Hoan, the J. Edgar Hoover of North Vietnam, frequently ranted about plots by "elements of the former exploiting classes, reactionary elements under the cover of religion, and armed bandits who refuse to be reeducated." The government cast particular suspicion on Catholics, whom they distrusted because of their former colonial associations with the French. Party security cadres also bore down on writers and educators who evinced the slightest "romanticism" or "softness" about the war or the socialist revolution. Despite all this ballyhoo about internal enemies, the Lao Dong party remained in firm control.

Ironically, the biggest boost to Hanoi's mobilization drive came in November of 1970 when President Richard Nixon resumed bombing operations against North Vietnam. The roar of U.S. jets and the thunder of their bombs jolted the North Vietnamese people out of their brief lapse into sleepy security. By December, posters plastered the walls of buildings urging, "Fight the enemy wherever and whenever and with whatever form he comes." Antiaircraft guns were hoisted back onto roofs, and air-raid shelters were made ready again. The bombing was a jarring reminder to the people that so long as the Lao Dong party pursued the war in the South, peace in the North was not yet at hand.

Captured USAF pilot Captain Charles Boyd is paraded before the public during an anti-U.S. propaganda campaign in 1966.

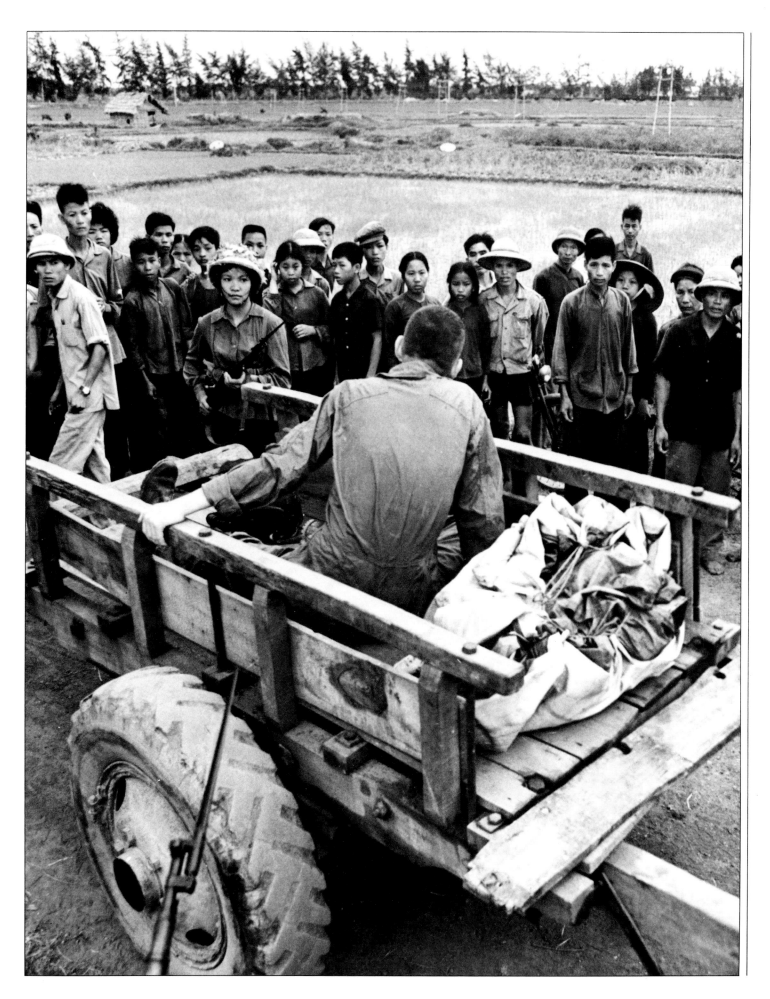

The North Takes Over

In February and March 1968, reports reaching Hanoi from the Southern battlefields turned bleak. Following the initial success of attacks against population centers—provincial capitals, district towns, and five of six major cities, including a daring and highly visible sapper raid against the United States Embassy in Saigon— the People's Liberation Armed Forces had been beaten back. The general offensive and uprising of Tet Mau Than, phase two of the winter-spring campaign, had faltered. Losses in men and materiel were staggering.

The gambit at Khe Sanh alone cost some 10,000 lives. Around the encircled Marine base in the northwest corner of South Vietnam, some units suffered as much as 90 percent losses to a relentless downpour of American bombs and artillery; by U.S. admission, the bombardment exceeded anything that had ever been seen before in history. And yet the siege, launched ten days before the Tet offensive, had been intended as a diver-

sion, according to Chief of Staff Senior General Van Tien Dung. "The attack at Khe Sanh was aimed only at pulling in the United States Marines and the U.S. Cavalry," he said after the war. "Encircling them ... keeping them there as a diversion ... we never intended to take the base ... it was merely a tactic."

But it had not succeeded as a classic military diversion, for the U.S. and South Vietnamese response throughout the South, after the early surprise of the widespread attacks, had been ample and furious. Two months of fighting, by U.S. estimates, had cost the Communists some 57,000 lives.

The offensive had mainly been carried out by Southerners, the PLAF forces, and the losses proved devastating to this once formidable army. As a military force, the PLAF had been virtually destroyed, and the role played by the Southerners in their own cause declined sharply thereafter. Lieutenant General Tran Van Tra, a Lao Dong party Central Committee member and military commander of COSVN, admitted, "We suffered large sacrifices and losses with regard to manpower and materiel, especially cadres at the various echelons, which clearly weakened us." Nguyen Tuong Lai, a PLAF regimental commander whose troops had attacked the U.S. base at Bien Hoa, explained the changes that took place after Tet. "The southern forces were decimated," he said, "and from that time on served mostly in intelligence, logistics and [as] saboteurs for the northerners."

In vicious street fighting, U.S. Marines finally retook Hue, ending twenty-five days of Communist occupation. Here a Marine leads off a PAVN prisoner.

Although PLAF units remained in the field and maintained their unit designations, they were increasingly reconstituted with "filler packets" of Northern soldiers. Between February and May, as PLAF units were carrying out the Tet offensive, an estimated 50,000 PAVN soldiers infiltrated into South Vietnam. In June 1968, U.S. intelligence estimated that 70 percent of all Communist forces in the South were Northerners. More and more of the combat burden fell to PAVN as opposed to NLF units.

By 1972 PAVN was to account for about 90 percent of daily combat.

During Tet, main force PAVN units had remained in reserve throughout most of South Vietnam. But PAVN units of the Tri-Thien-Hue front did mount attacks against Khe Sanh and Hue. The gracious imperial city of Hue remained in the hands of PAVN for twenty-five days before the Northern soldiers were dislodged by U.S. Marines in street fighting that reduced much of the city to rubble.

During those twenty-five days the only activity connected to the principle of *Khoi Nghia*—the General Uprising—that the Communists hoped for had taken place in Hue. A North Vietnamese history of the battle in that citadel city described the event in positive, even glowing, terms: "The population ... turned out into the streets and, together with the guerrillas, broke down the apparatus of oppression." But the true story was a grisly one.

The underground NLF cadres who surfaced, along with NLF sympathizers and young PAVN soldiers, plunged into an orgy of killing. Parading through the streets with bullhorns, they rounded up suspected "counter-revolutionaries"—civil servants, military personnel, and "whoever works for the Americans." They dragged people out of their houses and shops. In one sweep they arrested several hundred Roman Catholics huddled in Phu Cam Cathedral, bound their hands behind their backs, and marched them out of sight of the general population to be killed. The Communist cadres ultimately massacred at least 2,800 civilians and dropped their bodies into large common graves.

The Communists denied committing the atrocities and variously blamed American bombings or South Vietnamese troops for the carnage. But their arguments were pure sophistry. "We were the people," a Communist officer named Nguyen Minh Ky who fought at Hue said after the war. "How could we kill ourselves? ... A few criminals may have been spontaneously eliminated by the people,

---

Preceding page. A Communist soldier pours down machine-gun fire on enemy positions at Hue during the Tet offensive in February 1968.

The body of a Vietcong sapper, one of a team that carried out a daring raid against the United States Embassy in Saigon, lies in the compound courtyard.

like stepping on a snake. But most of those bodies—if there were any—were probably patriots who helped us and were murdered by the puppets after we left." General Tran Do, deputy commander of COSVN, used the same jargon in rationalizing events at Hue. Some citizens of Hue may have liquidated "despots," he said, in the same way that "they would get rid of poisonous snakes who, if allowed to live, would commit further crimes."

Truong Nhu Tang, a founder of the NLF, later questioned front leader Huynh Tan Phat about Hue. According to Tang, Phat denied that the front had planned a massacre. Instead, frantic young soldiers had killed indiscriminately, and local citizens had taken justice into their own hands. Tang later wrote, in paraphrasing Phat, "It had simply been one of those terrible spontaneous tragedies that inevitably accompany war."

COSVN planners had expected popular uprisings to occur all over South Vietnam. They believed their solid supporters among the Southern people would welcome the Communist forces and instigate *Khoi Nghia.* But it never happened. "In all honesty, we didn't achieve our main objective, which was to spur uprisings throughout the South," said General Tran Do.

In anticipation of uprisings, many underground cadres and NLF sympathizers had indeed surfaced during the attacks on the cities. They went about their assigned tasks, trying to rally friends and neighbors to welcome the Communist troops. But the city residents recoiled from the horror of the attacks. And as the tide turned against the Communists, these cadres found themselves isolated and exposed. When the PLAF forces were driven out of the cities, the NLF sympathizers were standing alone. They had to flee.

Some of them took to the jungle and found their way to the area where COSVN was located. In April 1968 they formed the nucleus of the Alliance of National, Democratic and Peace Forces, a nationalist organization whose function was to provide a public counterweight to the Communists in the NLF and in COSVN. The ANDPF was to be the forerunner of the Provisional Revolutionary Government. One of the PRG's tasks, ironically, would be to assuage fears among Southerners—arising from the Hue massacre—about the brand of "revolutionary justice" that might follow a Communist victory.

Political reverberations

At precisely 4:00 A.M. on May 5, 1968, a barrage of rockets and mortars slammed into the heart of Saigon, and the equivalent of two PAVN divisions launched an attack against the city. At 119 other locations throughout South

Marines leveled the house in background when Communist troops were discovered there during the battle of Hue. Communist casualties lie atop the wall in the foreground.

Vietnam, PAVN forces fired on provincial and district capitals and allied military installations, and in several places the Communist infantry followed up with attacks. The People's Army of Vietnam units had commenced phase three of the winter-spring campaign.

According to their plan, the North Vietnamese had intended it to be the climax of the winter-spring offensive—independent attacks nationwide with one psychologically shattering blow against a major target, perhaps Saigon. Since so much of the PLAF forces had been decimated in phase two, phase three had to be carried out by PAVN. Some analysts have suggested that PAVN was designated all along to execute phase three, and that is why those troops were held in reserve during the Tet offensive.

In any case, the two PAVN divisions attacking Saigon drove almost to the heart of the city. In a week of vicious fighting, ARVN and U.S. troops drove most of the invaders out, only to have the Communists reappear two weeks later in a second surge of attacks. The allied forces eventually cleared the city, but the tactical air support called in by the defenders, as well as the shelling and street fighting, left much of the city in a shambles.

When phase three was over, PAVN was shown to have paid dearly, in Saigon and throughout South Vietnam. U.S. and ARVN forces had not been caught by surprise. The Tet II (phase three) wave of attacks had been predicted by intelligence, and allied forces this time were on the alert. U.S. and ARVN troops had intercepted many PAVN units as they maneuvered into position close to the cities, thus preempting many of the planned attacks. During the month of May, PAVN/PLAF lost an average of 4,000 per week. Overall the nine-month winter-spring campaign—comprising the late 1967 border battles at Con Thien, Loc Ninh, and Dak To; the offensive of Tet Mau Than; and the so-called Tet II—had cost General Giap 85,000 of his best soldiers, and he had little military gain to show for the sacrifice.

This military failure, especially the maiming of the PLAF, altered the strategic balance in the South against the Communists. For the two years that followed, U.S. and ARVN forces conducted a nationwide counteroffensive. PLAF and PAVN troops were forced to recede from the cities and villages. A history of the war published in Hanoi in 1982 provides a glimpse into the strategic realignment:

In the rural areas we were vulnerable and were strongly counterattacked by the enemy, so our forces were depleted and in some places the liberated area was reduced. The revolutionary movement in the Nam Bo lowlands [Mekong Delta] encountered many difficulties and our offensive posture weakened. When the enemy launched a fierce counteroffensive our weaknesses and deficiencies caused the situation to undergo complicated changes after Tet Mau Than.

If the Vietnam War had been conventional, it might well have been winding down toward its conclusion after the 1968 Tet offensive. Having killed so many enemy troops, the U.S./ARVN forces would have been on the verge of victory. But the *dau tranh* strategy employed by the Lao Dong party, with its military and political components, precluded such a conventional conclusion. For the Americans and South Vietnamese to achieve victory, they had to defeat both *armed* and *political dau tranh*, and in fact they had defeated neither. Communist forces were able to retreat to their sanctuaries to refit and prepare for future battles. Their military setbacks at Tet produced not defeat for the Communists but military stalemate. Political *dau tranh* meanwhile suffered no such setback; and its *dich van* aspect—action among the enemy—produced dramatic results 10,000 miles away in Washington.

Only months before, Americans had been told by their leaders—General Westmoreland and other officials—of great progress being made against the Communists. Coming as it did on the heels of that orchestrated "success offensive" by the White House, the Tet offensive, while militarily devastating to the Communists, was psychologically catastrophic to the United States. It widened the credibility gap between the American people and their government. The attacks and their psychological impact on American public opinion so shook President Lyndon Johnson that on March 31 he announced he would not seek reelection. In order to remove his office from the "partisan divisions" of the 1968 electoral campaign while the United States sought peace talks, he was quitting the race for the presidency.

This sensational development the Communists had not anticipated, but they welcomed it as a by-product of *dau tranh*. "As for making an impact in the United States," said General Tran Do, "it had not been our intention—but it turned out to be a fortunate result." In an article in *Foreign Affairs* published just before he joined President Richard Nixon's government as national security adviser, Henry Kissinger wryly acknowledged: "The Tet Offensive brought to a head the compounded weaknesses—or, as the North Vietnamese say, the internal contradictions—of the American position."

Faction bashing

The Communists were not without contradictions in their own camp. May 5, the day the phase three offensive burst in Saigon, also marked the 150th anniversary of the birth of Karl Marx. In the Northern capital, Truong Chinh, the third-ranking member of the Political Bureau, rose before a congress of middle- and senior-level party leaders to present what at first seemed to be a routine commemorative speech. But the *eminence grise* of the Lao Dong party, one of the original quadrumvirate that included Pham Van Dong, Ho Chi Minh, and Vo Nguyen Giap, had a stern message to deliver.

He quickly plunged into a scathing criticism of the war

Hue Massacre

A year and a half following the 1968 Tet offensive, the South Vietnamese found mass graves containing the bodies of Hue residents the Communists, calling them "hooligan lackeys," singled out and killed during their twenty–six–day occupation. The well–concealed burial sites were discovered at various locations a distance from the city. The exhumed remains of some 2,800 victims, whose identification often proved difficult, were reburied in simple pine coffins.

Above. *Family members pay their last respects to the victims of the Hue massacre.* Left. *A woman grieves for a loved one before reinterment.*

effort, especially the "quick victory" policy embraced by Le Duan and the Southern-first faction and their costly winter-spring campaign. Exaggerated importance had been paid to military *dau tranh*, he argued, while political *dau tranh* had been neglected. "We must grasp the slogan 'protracted war and reliance mainly upon oneself,'" Chinh declared. He was calling for a return to orthodox revolutionary warfare. By this he meant military retrenchment coupled with renewed political struggle—a new emphasis on political over military *dau tranh*. In Chinh's analysis, President Johnson's abdication had proven the validity of political *dau tranh*. "We are currently taking advantage of the contradictions between the hawks and the doves in the American ruling class," he said.

Truong Chinh also applied his rigorous ideology to North Vietnam, where he felt the building of orthodox socialism had to take priority over liberating the South. Le Duan had relaxed the standards of socialism by proposing material incentives for production and allowing private agricultural plots to weaken collectivization. These were ideological drifts Truong Chinh deplored. To implement true socialism, he said, the party had to adhere to orthodoxy and purify itself by enrolling zealous new members while expelling "provocative elements who oppose the Party, are partisans, and are depraved in their politics as well as in their virtues and qualities." Without a firm basis of socialist construction, he warned, the strain of war might give rise to counterrevolution.

At the upper levels of the party, Truong Chinh's "faction-bashing" broadside provoked, as Hanoi Radio later admitted in a decided understatement, "several sessions of heated debate." To admit to debate in the Political Bureau was rare indeed for Hanoi—particularly on such a sensitive issue as overall strategy. Those prolonged sessions stretched over four months as the senior party officials reexamined their strategy in the light of Truong Chinh's corrective analysis. Though it is not certain, they must also have debated Le Duan's leadership of the party, for Truong Chinh's report was a challenge to the authority of Le Duan as apostle of the flawed strategy.

Truong Chinh
Hanoi's Hard-Liner

Truong Chinh, the Lao Dong party's leading theoretician, was a man for whom the term hard-liner was written. The choice of his nom de guerre "Truong Chinh"—meaning "long march"—was typical of the man born Dang Xuan Ku. His open admiration for the Long March—Mao's famous military campaign—might have proven a political liability in Vietnam, a country with long-standing enmity to the Chinese. Yet, Truong Chinh's alignment with Maoism derived from his obsession with doctrine rather than favoritism toward China. Even among the xenophobic Vietnamese, his personal prestige and dedication to Vietnam placed him beyond suspicion.

His involvement with communism dates to 1925, when at seventeen he joined the Revolutionary Youth League. After participating in student strikes at high school, Dang Xuan Ku was expelled by the French colonial authorities. In 1930 he joined the Indo-Chinese Communist party (ICP) as a founding member and began to edit the party's newspaper, *Sickle and Hammer*. A year later the French police arrested Ku for propaganda activities and sent him to Son-La, a mosquito-infested labor camp in Thailand reknowned, ironically, as a breeding ground for hardened revolutionaries. At Son-La he met hundreds of other members of the ICP and gained valuable experience converting and indoctrinating newcomers to the cause. When he was paroled in 1936 with the proclamation in France of the Popular Front, he was known to be a first-rate organizer and theorist.

The French banned the Communist party in 1939, provoking an exodus of Communists to China, Dang Xuan Ku among them. His incisive articles on agrarian problems and international affairs had already brought him to the attention of the ICP leadership. In May 1941 at the Eighth Party Conference, Ho Chi Minh appointed him secretary-general of the banished party. By this time Dang had taken Truong Chinh as his pseudonym.

Shortly thereafter, Truong Chinh infiltrated into Vietnam and established underground party headquarters in the Red River Delta. While Chairman Ho Chi Minh, General Vo Nguyen Giap, and Pham Van Dong busied themselves training the Vietminh army in the mountainous hinterland of Vietnam, Truong Chinh took

In August, Truong Chinh's report was accepted by the party. Published in Hanoi and broadcast by Hanoi Radio, it was praised as "a new contribution to the treasury of theoretical works on the Vietnamese revolution." The report, it seemed, had been accepted in its entirety. Chinh had effected a wholesale shift in strategy and at the same time had restored himself to prominence as a leading revolutionary war strategist and the party's ideological conscience.

Meeting the enemy in Paris

As the debate raged in the Political Bureau following Truong Chinh's speech, a significant element of political *dau tranh* was taking shape in Paris. There, on May 13, 1968, delegations from North Vietnam and the United States met to begin peace talks. The event held such promise that 1,300 expectant news reporters from thirty-nine nations covered the opening. The American negotiators, headed by Ambassador-at-Large W. Averell Harriman, had high hopes that an agreement might be concluded in a matter of months, perhaps before the November presidential elections.

The North Vietnamese entertained no such illusions. They considered negotiation a technique of *dau tranh*, not a method of resolving conflict. Peace talks fit into a scheme they called Talk/Fight, which was neatly summarized by the Central Committee's Thirteenth Plenum in 1967: "We can only win at the conference table what we have won on the battlefield." (After he became U.S. negotiator, Henry Kissinger expressed his frustration in confronting that attitude: "Acts of goodwill [by the United States] that did not reflect the existing balance of forces were treated as signs of moral weakness, even as they scorned them.")

Led by Xuan Thuy, a Central Committee member and veteran propagandist, the delegation from Hanoi included newspapermen such as Nguyen Thanh Le, editor of the party daily *Nhan Dan*. Their purpose was to conduct a propaganda offensive against the United States and South Vietnam.

---

on the arduous task of proselytizing and organizing the peasantry in the Hanoi region. This was the formative experience of his revolutionary career. Working among the people convinced Truong Chinh of the primary importance of political mobilization; not incidentally, it allowed him to construct a personal power base that ensured him a position in the future of the party.

After the Second World War, Truong Chinh published two theoretical works that solidified his reputation as the party's leading intellectual. Both were bluntly critical of the party. In *The August Revolution* (1946), a blueprint for revolution, he analyzed his experiences engineering the 1945 Communist resistance against the Japanese. Then after the Japanese relinquished Vietnam to the Vietminh at the end of World War II, he wrote, the party had been "conciliatory to the point of weakness," ignoring Lenin's dictum that "a victorious party must always be dictatorial."

Truong Chinh published *The Resistance Will Win*, a program for guerrilla warfare, in 1947, when the Vietminh struggle against the French was at a low ebb. In this tract Truong Chinh reviewed the importance of his political experiences among the people and excoriated party leaders who believed "everything can be settled by armed forces." In these two works Truong Chinh showed himself to be more concerned with the correct interpretation and application of Marxist theory than with any short-term expedient.

Following the Communists' consolidation of power in North Vietnam in 1954, Truong Chinh was given the responsibility for agrarian reform, considered to be the first step in the socialization of agriculture. He threw himself into the task, although as the realities of land reform took shape, thousands of people classified as "feudal elements" were executed. Popular opinion turned against the Communists, and by 1956 peasant revolts had broken out all over North Vietnam.

To restore the party's credibility, Ho Chi Minh instigated a "rectification of errors" campaign. Truong Chinh admitted publicly to shortcomings, including "leftist deviationism," and as a result lost his post as secretary-general.

His eclipse was, however, short-lived. In 1958 Truong Chinh was appointed vice-premier and in 1960 was elected chairman of the National Assembly. His speedy rehabilitation was primarily brought about by his supporters on the Central Committee, who had worked with him during the resistance.

As the outspoken leader of the left wing of the Lao Dong party, Truong Chinh often clashed with the pragmatic party members led by Le Duan. On every major issue the two leaders found themselves at odds. While Truong Chinh thundered against PAVN involvement in the South, Le Duan argued for stepped-up Northern involvement. Truong Chinh insisted that the war in the South be fought by indigenous guerrillas; Le Duan advocated conventional war. Truong Chinh demanded that industry and agriculture be collectivized, but Le Duan pushed for individual production.

Though the vote often went against him, Truong Chinh never compromised. Since revolutionaries rely heavily on theory to legitimize their regimes, Truong Chinh, as the party's foremost theoretician, proved indispensable; throughout the vicissitudes of war and postwar reconstruction, he performed the role of watchdog, signaling the Communists whenever their hard line softened.

A central disagreement at the outset concerned the legitimacy of the Saigon regime and the National Liberation Front and whether either should be included in the talks. The public talks quickly reached impasse as the spokesmen for both sides repeated the same arguments, though couched in diplomatic niceties. "Never have I heard two nations call each other sons of bitches so politely," remarked one seasoned U.S. diplomat. Neither side budged.

In June, Le Duc Tho arrived in Paris as a special adviser to the North Vietnamese delegation, bringing the authority of the Political Bureau to the peace talks. He held no government post—the only Political Bureau member without one—and therefore was little known in the West. Yet Le Duc Tho (a nom de guerre meaning virtue and longevity chosen by the man born Phan Dinh Khai) wielded considerable power in the party.

A Northerner by birth, Le Duc Tho had been a deputy to Le Duan in COSVN during the French Indochina War. He returned to the North in 1955 and joined the Political Bureau. A close ally of his former COSVN patron, Le Duc Tho joined Le Duan's Southern-first faction in urging armed struggle in the South.

Appointed head of the Lao Dong party's important Organization Department, Le Duc Tho gained control over appointments and promotions; he thus also shouldered responsibility for the quality and performance of the party's cadres. Another of his roles seemed to be that of party trouble-shooter. For example, he had carried out several diplomatic missions to other Communist capitals. Although Le Duc Tho customarily worked in obscurity, his presence in Paris was soon to make him the most visible of North Vietnam's leaders.

After his arrival, a series of private meetings began between the North Vietnamese and Americans. Away from the public posturing of the weekly meetings, the tough North Vietnamese negotiators seemed to the Americans to be more accommodating and flexible. The adversaries shared tea and made pointed small talk. Progress made in private, although limited, encouraged the Americans and provoked an exaggeration of the normal diplomatic exigency of interpretative analysis—contrasting public and private behaviors and statements. Each North Vietnamese gesture, inflection, or action was carefully scrutinized for meaning.

A major question of interpretation soon intruded. In July and August 1968, Communist attacks in South Vietnam decreased sharply. In September, a number of main force PAVN units began pulling back from South Vietnam into sanctuaries in Cambodia, Laos, and across the demilitarized zone into North Vietnam. Hanoi's action was interpreted by hopeful United States officials as restraint, a gesture of good will in return for Lyndon Johnson's partial bombing halt. Then on October 9, Le Duc Tho placed an important item on the table: he asked whether the United States would agree to a total bombing halt if the North Vietnamese admitted the South Vietnamese as a party to the talks.

Coming after months of diplomatic wrangling, Tho's question precipitated a burst of activity. "The lights went on throughout the government," said one U.S. official. But it also induced misplaced optimism. From Saigon, U.S. Ambassador Ellsworth Bunker cabled Washington that he believed the initiative to be a "fairly clear indication that Hanoi is ready for a tactical shift from the battlefield to the conference table."

By October 27 a compromise agreement had been hammered out to the satisfaction of Washington. But the South Vietnamese, now to be admitted to the peace talks along with the National Liberation Front, raised objections. A major difficulty was Saigon's demand for guarantees from the North that a bombing halt would be matched by a de-escalation of military activity in South Vietnam. Hanoi would give no written guarantees but agreed verbally to respect the demilitarized zone and to refrain from attacking South Vietnam's cities. Despite the absence of a written agreement, Ambassador Harriman assured Washington that the North Vietnamese understood that to violate the terms risked a resumption of the bombing. Saigon remained unsatisfied, but Washington threatened to act alone, so the South Vietnamese relented.

On October 31, President Johnson announced an end to "all air, naval, and artillery bombardment of North Vietnam," effective the following day. He had ordered the halt in the hope that "this action can lead to progress toward a peaceful settlement of the Vietnamese war." Although Johnson threatened to resume bombing if North Vietnam took advantage of the halt, the prospect was unlikely so long as the talks in Paris continued.

The North Vietnamese were delighted, for in a relatively short time their diplomatic offensive had reaped tremendous results. By pitting the United States and South Vietnamese governments against each other, and by appealing to Johnson's hunger for peace before the end of his term, they had sown suspicion between the allies and exploited the contradictions between them. Henceforth, Saigon had to be wary of Washington's tendency to act unilaterally and in its own interests.

Hanoi had been forced to recognize the legitimacy of the South Vietnamese government by allowing its participation in the talks, but that had always seemed inevitable, and now the National Liberation Front was included as well. Most important, Hanoi had obtained an end to the bombing.

Dau tranh strategy had brought surprising results in 1968, in a kind of payout of inverse dividends. Military *dau tranh*, in the form of the failed Tet offensive, had been

translated into political capital with the downfall of the American president and an invitation to peace talks. Then political *dau tranh* had scored a strategic military victory by securing a total bombing halt in return for an inevitable concession and other vague promises.

In an appeal issued November 3, after the skies over North Vietnam had been quiet for two days, President Ho Chi Minh called the bombing halt only an initial victory. He continued unequivocally:

> A sacred mission of our entire population at present is to manifest a spirit of determination to fight and win, and of determination to liberate the South, defend the North, and advance to the peaceful unification of the homeland. As long as there are aggressors in our country we must continue to fight and sweep them out.

Neorevolutionary warfare

The shift in emphasis to political *dau tranh*, and the beginning of Talk/Fight, did not mean an end to armed *dau tranh*, only an adaptation. From the very first moments that peace talks became likely, COSVN issued a situation report that cautioned the battered PLAF forces against "deviationist thoughts." They should not think, for example, that the bombing halt indicated a United States desire for peace. The document warned, "We should absolutely not entertain peace illusions, wait-and-see attitudes, or lower our fighting will."

After a period of doctrinal argument among members of the PAVN High Command, a new form of military *dau tranh* emerged. American analysts called it neorevolutionary warfare. A compromise between proponents of guerrilla and big-unit warfare, it combined a sophisticated form of guerrilla war by highly trained sappers with occasional assaults by massed forces, either single attacks or a coordinated series over a wide area. The Americans came to label these surges "military high points," presumably because of the way they appeared on their graphs of Communist activity.

The objective of neorevolutionary war was to buy time for Hanoi while keeping the enemy on the strategic defensive. Although no documents have emerged from these discussions, it is clear the Political Bureau realized that its only alternative after the decimation of the Southern PLAF forces was to send more and more Northern soldiers to fight in the South. PAVN would carry the burden of combat.

Freed now from the merciless pounding of Rolling Thunder attacks, the North Vietnamese could re-form and refit their main forces, battered in the winter-spring offensive, in Quang Binh, the southernmost province, just above the DMZ. The Northerners could also set about extending lines of communication to the DMZ, reconstructing their bomb-shattered country, and building socialism in the "great rear base."

The tactics of neorevolutionary warfare called for sappers, armed with the latest weapons and explosive devices from the Soviet Union, to strike into the heart of enemy installations, causing extensive damage and demoralizing enemy troops. But sapper attacks alone, while conserving manpower and reducing the Communists' risks, could not defeat the enemy. Intermittent large-unit attacks were planned to inflict significant casualties on the enemy.

As if to initiate the new U.S. President Richard M. Nixon to the war, the first major attacks came in February 1969. Just after the Tet holiday, PAVN launched a coordinated offensive throughout South Vietnam. But this time, unlike the Tet 1968 attacks, the Communists moved conservatively, seldom using units larger than companies. The targets were mostly U.S. installations rather than South Vietnamese military bases or population centers.

The new tactics succeeded admirably. In three weeks the Communists killed 1,140 American soldiers, while enduring, comparatively, only a third of the losses they had suffered the previous year. But the numbers were still high. In February 1968, the Communists lost 40,000 men, by U.S. count; in February 1969, 14,000.

A sequence of three policy decisions made by the United States in the early summer of 1969 underscored the wisdom of Hanoi's neorevolutionary war strategy. After meeting on Midway Island on June 8 with South Vietnam President Nguyen Van Thieu, President Nixon announced the beginning of U.S. troop withdrawals, the first an increment of 25,000 troops. The decision was posited on the negotiating progress in Paris, the tapering of Communist military activity, and improved South Vietnamese military capability.

This was the start of what became the Nixon policy of "Vietnamization" of the war. A three-phase program without time limit, Vietnamization was supposed to upgrade South Vietnamese ground forces, develop Vietnamese combat support capabilities, and gradually reduce the American presence to a military advisory mission.

Nixon's third policy decision emerged from his chat with reporters on Guam during a tour of Asia. He suggested that although the United States would honor its existing treaties, in the future military defense in Asia "will be increasingly handled by, and responsibility for it taken by, the Asian nations themselves." Although the Nixon Doctrine, as the pronouncement came to be called, did not bear specifically on the situation in Vietnam, it raised the principle of the Vietnamization program to the level of foreign policy doctrine. Frustrated by Vietnam, the United States would no longer risk its manpower in another nation's fight. For the United States in Vietnam, Hanoi might have assumed, there would likely be no reversal of its military retrenchment. Time was on the side of Hanoi.

COSVN analyzed Nixon's troop withdrawal announcement and Vietnamization policy in a document entitled Resolution 9, disseminated in July. Vietnamization, said

COSVN analysts, was an insidious attempt to appease American public opinion by slowly withdrawing troops. The Communists intended to foil such a plan by increasing U.S. and South Vietnamese casualties so as to raise anti-war fervor in the United States and thereby force Nixon to accelerate withdrawal. (Henry Kissinger later wrote: "The withdrawal increased the demoralization of those families whose sons remained at risk, and it brought no respite from the critics, the majority of whom believed that since their pressure had produced the initial decision to with-draw, more pressure could speed up the process.") The United States might then consent to a neutralist, coalition government that the Communists could come to dominate.

To prepare for that eventuality, the NLF on June 10, shortly after the Nixon–Thieu Midway meeting, had an-nounced the creation of the Provisional Revolutionary Government. An ostensibly nationalist government-in-waiting, the PRG superseded the NLF as a political entity and competed with Saigon's claim that it was the autono-mous and legitimate representative of the South Vietnam-ese people. The PRG, according to one of its founders, Jus-tice Minister Truong Nhu Tang, was soon "fighting hard in every international forum to establish its own claim to le-gitimacy."

In fact, the PRG was little more than another front directly answerable to COSVN and dependent upon the Communist military for its sustenance in the jungle. But the PRG, under President Huynh Tan Phat, was nonetheless soon recognized by fifteen Communist-bloc nations and allies as the legitimate government of South Vietnam. Armed with a twelve-point "Action Program" quite similar to that of the NLF, the PRG supplanted the NLF delegation at the Paris peace talks. Led by the shrewd but charming foreign minister, Madame Nguyen Thi Binh, the PRG em-barked on what Justice Minister Tang called "full-scale diplomatic warfare."

Death of a president

Throughout America's involvement in the war, Ho Chi Minh had played a central, though largely misunderstood, role in North Vietnamese politics. To most westerners, es-pecially Americans, Ho Chi Minh was the personification of the war, and his resilience in spite of bombing and pun-ishing defeats of his troops in the field proved mad-deningly frustrating, and not a little awe-inspiring. In the words of a respectful South Vietnamese newspaper, he was "a legendary, almost mythological figure" who had founded a nation and who had led that nation to victory over one great power and to stalemate with another. Even as his health declined in 1969 and he dropped out of sight for months at a time, Ho remained the symbol of the North Vietnamese war effort, a revolutionary Wizard of Oz ma-nipulating all the levers of resistance in the private coun-cils of the Lao Dong party. "Until his [final] illness," com-

mented the *New York Times*, "he held the reins of state firmly."

But in holding the reins of state, he exerted the gentlest of pulls. As founder and symbol of the country, Ho Chi Minh towered above his colleagues, and as such he re-mained above the mechanics of governing or even of run-ning the war. Ho had set the party agenda, on which all were unanimously agreed, even if they disagreed, some-times vociferously, on the means to achieve those goals. They argued along the lines of Marxist-Leninist dialectics, exposing the flaws, or the contradictions, in the opposing position. Their arguments, by and large, were fraternal, certainly not fratricidal. Ho once calculated that the thirty-one members of the pre-1960 Central Committee had been imprisoned a cumulative total of 222 years by a com-mon enemy, and their experiences had undoubtedly vis-ited on them the importance of group solidarity and party discipline. For this revolutionary band, Ho Chi Minh served as visionary, adviser, counselor, and, ultimately, as arbiter, one who could tip debates one way or the other.

Ho Chi Minh's immense presence came to its physical end on September 3, 1969, when, twenty-four years and one day after proclaiming the birth of the nation, he died at the age of seventy-nine of an apparent heart attack. While the khaki-clad body of "Bac Ho" (Uncle Ho) lay in state in Ba Dinh Congress Hall, and tributes poured in from around the world and foreign delegations arrived for the September 10 funeral, many wondered what his death would mean to the war effort. And who would succeed him? The answer was: no one person.

In Hanoi the succession proceeded smoothly. Ton Duc Thang, the obscure eighty-one-year-old vice president, ascended to the presidency of the Democratic Republic, a largely ceremonial post. And on September 6, Radio Hanoi announced Ho's successor in the Lao Dong party, and hence in the rule of the nation:

A collective leadership of officials and fighters, who have been selected and well trained by our beloved President Ho Chi Minh, will continue to battle for freedom and independence of all our people and all our nation until the last American aggressor is driven from our land, the South is completely liberated, and our fatherland united once again.

Although the broadcast mentioned no names, the rank-ing members of the Political Bureau were First Secretary Le Duan, Truong Chinh, Premier Pham Van Dong, De-fense Minister Vo Nguyen Giap, and Le Duc Tho. Another ranking member, Pham Hung, had been away from Hanoi for two years, dispatched to the South to run COSVN. With the exception of two deaths—of General Nguyen Chi Thanh and now Ho Chi Minh—the party lead-ership remained essentially the same in 1969 as it was in 1950. The eleven-man Political Bureau had been reduced to nine men, who despite their differences of opinion, were joined in what Confucians called a unity of opposites. (The remaining three members were Foreign Minister Nguyen

Duy Trinh; Le Thanh Nghi, chairman of the State Planning Commission; and Hoang Van Hoan, vice chairman of the National Assembly.) The Political Bureau had decided unanimously not to replace Ho Chi Minh but to elevate him to the status of chairman emeritus. His memory sustained an inspirational cult, making Ho Chi Minh useful even in death.

To American analysts familiar with Soviet battles of succession in which Stalin, Khrushchev, and Brezhnev all emerged victorious from leadership troikas, the prospect of collective leadership in Hanoi promised intraparty strife, if not outright power struggles. "It would be most unusual if [Hanoi's leaders] were devoid of personal ambition," noted an official U.S. government assessment. But Hanoi's leaders moved quickly to dispel any hint of disunity. Two weeks after Ho's funeral, Truong Chinh appeared before the National Assembly, of which he was chairman, and addressed the matter squarely: "Our enemies fancy that after President Ho Chi Minh's death we will be bewildered and divided, or will depart from his revolutionary line. But they are grossly mistaken." Coming from Truong Chinh, who had publicly rebuked Le Duan for his handling of the war, such a declaration was particularly significant.

As party first secretary, Le Duan became the first among equals; if he had been personally ambitious, he might have been in a position to consolidate power. But in a February 1970 paper commemorating the fortieth anniversary of the founding of the Indochinese Communist party, Le Duan first praised Truong Chinh, his erstwhile political opponent, and then affirmed his own adherence to the new status quo. Citing the benefits of a collective intellect in making collective decisions, Le Duan reiterated, "The Party's leadership rests upon *the principle of collective leadership.*" An enemy awaiting a sign of weakness or listening for the rumble of a power struggle in Hanoi was going to be disappointed.

Modernizing PAVN

In his exhaustive February disquisition on the Vietnamese revolution, Le Duan stressed the need for flexibility and pragmatism in prosecuting the war. "There has never been nor will there ever be a single formula for carrying out the revolution that is appropriate to all circumstances and times," he wrote. His remarks reflected the influence of a series of three articles by North Vietnam's three leading military strategists—Vo Nguyen Giap, Chief of Staff General Van Tien Dung, and Lieutenant General Song Hao, head of the General Political Directorate—that had appeared in *Nhan Dan* in December. They had argued for

Somber textile workers in Hanoi listen to a reading of Ho Chi Minh's last will and testament published in the party newspaper Nhan Dan.

technological improvement of PAVN as a means of confronting the Americans or, after their withdrawal, an ARVN force strengthened by Vietnamization. People's War, such as that espoused by Truong Chinh, had to be modified.

The scenario for modernizing PAVN came in North Vietnam's 1970 state plan, which emphasized technical development. Such advances, along with economic and industrial improvements and the purification of the Lao Dong party by creation of the ''Ho Chi Minh class'' of dedicated cadres, would lay the groundwork for the upgrading of PAVN as a conventional force. Mobilization of the North could be counted on to expand the army and bring in men with more technical experience. The actual expansion of combat capability would take place with the acquisition of more sophisticated weaponry and training from the Soviet Union and China.

In late 1969, DRV engineers had completed construction of a four-inch pipeline from the Mu Gia Pass to the A Shau Valley in Thua Thien Province. This extended logisti-

cal nose protruding into South Vietnam permitted an improved transportation network along the Ho Chi Minh Trail. Gone were the days of porters pushing supplies forward on bicycles and of oil traveling downstream in fifty-five-gallon drums. Truck convoys carrying war materiel and soldiers soon moved to the front faster and in greater quantities, pausing to refuel at jungle filling stations. Tanks, armored personnel carriers, and soon 130MM long-range artillery, mostly supplied by the Soviet Union, cruised toward the Southern battlefields. By 1972 some 25,000 Vietnamese had received training abroad, most of them in the Soviet Union and Eastern Europe. More than 3,000 North Vietnamese tank crews trained for up to five months at the Soviet armor school in Odessa.

General Giap, noted especially for his logistical abilities and his preparation of the battlefield, patiently moved this improved war machine into position in Laos and Cambodia. Main force PAVN and PLAF units withdrew into sanctuaries to rest and refit, saved for the larger battles to come. In South Vietnam Giap employed the tactics

With Communist-bloc-supplied heavy equipment, the People's Army developed in the 1970s into a conventional, mechanized force. Above. Tank crews demonstrate enthusiasm for their Soviet T54 tanks. Right. PAVN infantry engage in training exercises with T34s.

of neorevolutionary warfare, sending his remaining troops sparingly into battle. In all of 1970 and 1971, U.S. and ARVN forces recorded only fifteen battalion-sized attacks against them; sapper raids were the norm of Communist military activity.

War of the sanctuaries

In March 1970, Hanoi's planners faced a crisis in Cambodia when right-wing Defense Minister Lon Nol ousted Prince Norodom Sihanouk in a coup d'état. Lon Nol closed the port of Sihanoukville to the Soviet, Chinese, and East European ships that carried materiel destined for the Cambodian sanctuaries. In response, Hanoi hurriedly put into effect a plan called "Campaign X." It combined military with political goals. Four divisions from South Vietnam—the PLAF 5th and 9th and the PAVN 1st and 7th—entered Cambodia to protect supply lines while political cadres worked with the Khmer Communists to expand the revolutionary force formally named FUNK (Front Uni National du Kampuchea) but known as the Khmer Rouge.

Hanoi did not permit its intervention in Cambodia to detract from its strategy in South Vietnam. It viewed the Communist insurgency in Cambodia as secondary to the liberation of South Vietnam. The Vietnamese Communists had paid fraternal lip service to the Khmer Rouge struggle against Sihanouk, but Hanoi never endorsed the Cambodians' strategy or tactics and provided precious few arms or other aid to the insurgency. Even now, as the Vietnamese Communists allied themselves with the Khmer Rouge, they did so to protect their own supply lines and to keep the U.S.-supported Lon Nol regime on the defensive. Policy was to guard resources for the war in Vietnam. As one internal party document stressed, "We will not let ourselves get into trouble" in Cambodia.

General Giap's logistical build-up in the sanctuaries had not gone unnoticed by the Americans and South Vietnamese. Following the overthrow of Sihanouk, ARVN forces made several forays into Cambodia to destroy Communist supply caches. One of those helicopter as-

saults landed virtually atop the PRG's jungle encampment and near COSVN headquarters. While soldiers from the PLAF 7th Division held off the South Vietnamese attackers, COSVN and PRG members fled west along prearranged escape routes. After weeks on the run they regrouped near Kratie, deep inside Cambodia. PRG Justice Minister Truong Nhu Tang, who had joined the exodus, later described his and his comrades' relief at their near miss. "With an opportunity to relax and begin recuperating from this ordeal, spirits began to revive," he wrote. "COSVN's Pham Hung and General [Tran Nam] Trung joked that 'Even though we ran like hell, still we'll win.'"

On April 30, U.S. and South Vietnamese forces poured across the Cambodian border in an invasion designed, according to President Nixon, "to guarantee the continued success of the withdrawal and Vietnamization programs." Operating for two months within a self-imposed limit of thirty kilometers, the combined U.S./ARVN forces, 78,000 strong, seized sufficient weapons and ammunition to equip an estimated fifty-five main force battalions and perhaps ninety artillery battalions. They also killed some 10,000 Communist troops, even though most Communist troops had retreated west beyond the thirty-kilometer limit.

The tactical military success of the Cambodian invasion translated, in the terminology of *dau tranh*, into a strategic defeat for President Nixon. This came about because the Cambodian invasion provoked a whirlwind of protest and student strikes in the United States, culminating in the killing of four students by National Guardsmen at Kent State University in Ohio. The contradictions between the American government and the governed had widened to an unbridgeable distance.

An indignant Congress soon passed the Cooper-Church amendment, barring any further use of U.S. ground forces beyond the borders of South Vietnam. Moreover, the incursion contributed to the passage in 1973 of the Church–Case amendment, barring any form of U.S. military action in Indochina. Later the same year, the War Powers Act became law. This prevented an American president from committing troops to action anywhere for more than sixty days without approval from Congress.

President Nixon hailed the Cambodian incursion as a victory that set back Communist offensive plans for a year. But as Truong Nhu Tang later wrote:

This "victory" arguably did more to undermine American unity than any other event of the war. . . . [H]ow does one judge the cumulative effects on one's own body politic of ingrained distrust and ill will? To achieve a year or so of battlefield grace, Nixon and Kissinger incurred a propaganda defeat. . . . Whatever the facts of who first infringed on Cambodian neutrality, the significance of that engagement was that it helped separate the American leadership from its internal support and instilled among many Americans a lasting skepticism about their government's morality. It was—to Vietnam's revolution and to the revolutions that have followed Vietnam—an enduring gift.

Half a year later, the North Vietnamese base areas in Laos, stocked with conventional war materiel and petroleum, became inviting targets. For the Americans, the same rationales that held for Laos held for Cambodia. Disruption of the Communist supply system might interfere with North Vietnam's ability to launch a dry-season offensive for another year, and that, in turn, would permit the continuing withdrawal of U.S. troops. But there was an added factor. With U.S. ground troops barred from Laos by the Cooper-Church amendment, U.S. participation was restricted to air and helicopter support. The policy of Vietnamization came to a dramatic test with Operation Lam Son 719, carried out in February and March 1971 entirely by South Vietnamese ground troops.

In Lam Son 719, the stakes for the North were different. The rupture of Cambodian supply lines in 1970 had enhanced the strategic importance of the Ho Chi Minh Trail through Laos, and Hanoi had chosen to upgrade its defenses against a preemptive attack. There would be no retreat in Laos as there had been in Cambodia. PAVN would stand and fight.

When the South Vietnamese invaded, Hanoi responded with what it termed "counter-punch warfare" and brought its tanks to bear against ARVN firebases. Although accustomed to meticulous planning and even rehearsals before an attack, PAVN performed well in unaccustomed reaction. Its artillery, infantry, and armor forced ARVN first into a retreat, then into headlong flight.

For North Vietnam, the results of Lam Son 719 were gratifying. Using fundamental conventional principles of mass maneuver, PAVN had driven the South's best troops from Laos. PAVN now seemed more than a match for South Vietnam's forces in conventional battle. Its tank attacks against ARVN firebases verified PAVN's progress toward conventional war—and demonstrated ARVN's susceptibility. Lam Son 719 identified a major flaw of Vietnamization's phase one: though ARVN troops were well trained, their officers performed poorly without American advisers by their sides.

When caught under fire with their Vietnamese units, impatient American advisers had often grabbed the telephone to orchestrate supporting artillery fire. Their Vietnamese counterparts had not gained experience in that essential skill. So when stripped of the reassuring presence of the Americans, ARVN leaders in Lam Son 719 lost their poise; when confronted with mass enemy formations, they failed to coordinate fire properly against the attackers. The battle dramatized that ARVN was not an army ready to stand on its own.

PAVN soldiers overrun South Vietnamese positions during the 1971 ARVN invasion of Laos, Operation Lam Son 719. North Vietnam's triumph paved the way for the next year's Easter offensive.

Easter Offensive:

The View From the North

On Easter Weekend, 1972, following a long-range bombardment with new Soviet-made 130MM artillery, North Vietnamese troops invaded South Vietnam across the demilitarized zone. To Hanoi it was the 1972 strategic offensive. South Vietnam called it the Easter offensive. With subsequent attacks against the central highlands towns of Dak To and Kontum, and against the provincial capital of An Loc 100 kilometers north of Saigon, PAVN ultimately threw fourteen divisions into the greatest military offensive the world had seen since the Korean War.

Using long-range artillery and more than 200 tanks, PAVN raised the Vietnam War to the level of full-scale conventional warfare. Against such military might, ARVN troops fell back. Only the employment of U.S. air power could stem the Communist advance. The pictures on these pages show the offensive from the attackers' perspective.

As North Vietnam's tanks and armored carriers rumbled south, bridges became important military objectives. Here, PAVN infantry in northern Quang Tri Province capture a bridge that retreating ARVN forces failed to destroy.

Surrender

The 1,500 soldiers remaining in the green 56th ARVN Regiment dug in at Camp Carroll just south of the DMZ after retreating under the PAVN onslaught. The sprawling American-built firebase in Quang Tri Province contained huge 175mm guns that offered the only response to PAVN's long-range artillery. But ARVN regimental commander Lieutenant Colonel Pham Van Dinh and his executive officer, Lieutenant Colonel Vinh Phuong, had no intention of fighting.

Talking to PAVN officers on the radio, the pair negotiated the surrender of the regiment and firebase, complete with artillery and ammunition. "The soldiers did not want to resist the liberation forces anymore," Col. Dinh said in a radio address the next day. It was the only instance during the war when an entire unit crossed to the other side.

On Easter Sunday a North Vietnamese officer accepts the surrender of 1,500 men of the 56th ARVN Regiment from Lt. Cols. Pham Van Dinh (shaking hands) and Vinh Phuong (to his right).

Loc Ninh
Under Attack

A week after the invasion of Quang Tri Province, the Easter offensive entered its second phase when a PAVN infantry division supported by a tank regiment moved out of Cambodia and attacked the ARVN outpost of Loc Ninh. The 9th ARVN Regiment and a Ranger battalion beat back five separate waves of tanks but finally gave ground before the relentless attacks.

PAVN forces then closed on An Loc, capital of Binh Long Province and the last major obstacle on the road to Saigon. President Thieu ordered the city defended "at all costs" and ARVN complied. Supported by intensive U.S. air strikes, ARVN held An Loc during a ninety-five-day siege in what may have been the most important battle of the war for the South Vietnamese.

PAVN tanks roll across the airstrip at Loc Ninh on Highway 13. The fall of the ARVN outpost led to the epic siege of An Loc.

142

Battle for the Highlands

The third phase of the offensive began when North Vietnamese troops attacked ARVN outposts near Dak To in the central highlands, locales familiar to Americans who fought in pitched battles there in late 1967. First Rocket Ridge fell, then Ben Het, then Dak To itself. PAVN troops then swung South down Highway 14 to attack the provincial capital of Kontum.

In breaking through ARVN lines, Northern troops introduced a new weapon from the Soviet arsenal—the AT-3 "Sagger," a wire-guided antitank rocket. But the U.S. advisers also unveiled a new weapon. Theirs was the TOW (tube-launched, optically tracked, wire-guided) missile, which was fired from helicopters. With TOW missiles knocking out PAVN tanks, ARVN managed to stall the highlands offensive at Kontum.

Northern troops overrun an ARVN firebase in the highlands region of Dak To.

The Road to Saigon

Buoyed by their success against ARVN's Operation Lam Son 719, Hanoi's leaders began in the spring of 1971 to smell the possibility of victory. In the three years since the Tet offensive had savaged the Communist military, North Vietnam's fortunes had shifted dramatically. The United States was now in the process of disengaging from Vietnam, and PAVN had shown its superiority over the South Vietnamese army—the major obstacle left standing between the Communists and their long-sought goals of victory and reunification. In the spring of 1971, both party journals, *Nhan Dan* and *Hoc Tap*, reflecting the mood of the party leadership, were calling for "battles of annihilation" as the next stage of war.

In May the members of the Political Bureau and the Central Military Party Committee began planning for a new offensive. With PAVN's new-found conventional war capability, the campaign was designed to "win a decisive victory in 1972, and force the U.S. imperialists to end the war by

negotiating from a position of defeat." But to mount an offensive required a new infusion of military aid from Hanoi's Soviet and Chinese suppliers. In the Cambodian and Laotian campaigns PAVN had lost or consumed vast quantities of war materiel.

Hanoi's relationship with Peking, however, was chilling. China's Mao Tse-tung, Prime Minister Chou En-lai, and Defense Minister Lin Piao had all applauded the North Vietnamese victory in Laos. But China, a consistent opponent of main force warfare, drew quite a different lesson from the United States's "catastrophic defeat" than the one drawn in Hanoi.

That the United States was continuing its withdrawal in spite of the Lam Son 719 debacle indicated to China a U.S. retrenchment. America's days in Vietnam, concluded China's leaders, were numbered. Thus North Vietnam's escalation to main force warfare was needless; South Vietnam could be defeated by continued guerrilla war. Moreover, the U.S. action confirmed Mao's belief that the United States, while still dangerous, was an ever-lessening menace. For Mao, the Soviet Union had replaced the United States as China's principal threat.

Prior to the invasion of Laos, Peking had privately informed the United States of its desire for improved relations. Lam Son 719 interrupted communications, but they resumed shortly afterward. Peking issued a surprising invitation to an American Ping-Pong team touring Asia to visit China, and Washington reciprocated with several actions, including relaxing travel restrictions to China and permitting export of nonstrategic goods. This diplomatic courtship became known as "Ping-Pong diplomacy." Then early in July 1971, presidential envoy Henry Kissinger secretly visited Peking to make arrangements for a presidential trip. On July 15, President Nixon, a stalwart anti-Communist, irrevocably shifted the balance of superpower affairs when he announced that he would journey to China in early 1972.

Hanoi was stunned by the impending China-U.S. rapprochement, and the growing rift between Hanoi and Peking provided an opportunity that Moscow sought to exploit. Soviet President Nikolai V. Podgorny came to Hanoi in October 1971 to deliver news of Moscow's own summit with President Nixon, scheduled for the following May. But to reassure Hanoi about Soviet intentions, Podgorny offered Moscow's backing for the upcoming offensive and promised an increase in aid. In December the Kremlin announced an agreement with Hanoi guaranteeing "additional aid without reimbursement." That aid took the form of medium and light tanks, track-mounted cannons, 130MM cannons, and antiaircraft and antitank missiles. Added to

the flow of materiel still arriving from China, the Soviet aid completed the transformation of PAVN to a modern army capable of launching a conventional offensive.

An honorable exit

In late 1971 and early 1972, the signs of a Communist offensive build-up were unmistakable, and the Americans and South Vietnamese steeled themselves for an attack, as in 1968, during the holidays of Tet Nham Ty. Hanoi delayed the offensive until the last weekend in March.

On Holy Thursday the equivalent of three divisions, supported by some 200 tanks, poured across the demilitarized zone and rapidly broke through the green ARVN 3d Division, positioned there precisely because the South Vietnamese, thinking there would be no breach of the DMZ, assumed the inexperienced troops would be safe. On Easter Sunday, three days after the start of the offensive, 1,500 men of the 56th ARVN Regiment, defending the former American base at Camp Carroll with its huge 175MM guns, stacked their rifles and turned themselves over to the North Vietnamese. It was the only wholesale surrender of the war. Other ARVN units fell back in disarray, but ultimately they regrouped and managed to stall the North Vietnamese onslaught at the My Chanh River, some twenty kilometers south of Quang Tri City.

The second phase of the offensive began on April 5, when a three-division force swept out of Cambodian base areas, quickly captured Loc Ninh, then surrounded An Loc, preventing the arrival of overland reinforcements. PAVN laid siege to An Loc, expecting it to fall within two weeks. But ARVN units, backed by American advisers and resupplied by air drops, fought heroically in perhaps the most important battle of the war, for the fall of An Loc would open the road to Saigon to PAVN armor.

B-52 strikes against the massed PAVN formations, with bombs dropping occasionally to within 500 meters of ARVN lines, enabled the South Vietnamese and the Americans to hold out. PAVN armored commanders, in their first sustained action of the war, allowed tanks to get ahead of the infantry, and the South Vietnamese knocked them out one by one. The siege endured for ninety-five days before the U.S./ARVN firepower forced a withdrawal. In the process An Loc was reduced to rubble.

As PAVN was besieging An Loc, and as phase three of the offensive began with an attack on the highlands city of Kontum, Premier Pham Van Dong explained Hanoi's strategic thinking about the offensive to a French interviewer:

We have never believed in the success of Vietnamization, but it was necessary to show that it was failing. Nixon appears to believe that the war will end one day without combat. That is why until now he has always refused to negotiate seriously, but the war will end only when Nixon perceives that it brings him nothing. He has everything to lose except the honorable exit we are determined to let him make.

After a battle near Quang Tri City during the 1972 Easter offensive, soldiers of the 1st ARVN Division check to be sure that PAVN dead are not booby trapped. The campaign cost PAVN as many as 100,000 killed.

But Richard Nixon was not interested in the sort of exit proffered by Pham Van Dong. He was actively pursuing "peace with honor" in Vietnam, but his notion of what was honorable did not include being forced to the negotiating table by the guns of the North Vietnamese Army. On April 6, just over a week after the offensive began, the president initiated a bombing campaign called Operation Linebacker in which U.S. aircraft struck PAVN forces and supply lines north of the DMZ. As the weeks passed, Linebacker expanded until B–52s and fighter–bombers were flying close to Hanoi and Haiphong.

The bombing seemed to take the North Vietnamese by surprise. They had not counted on such a bold response. Hanoi's historians of the war expressed disapproval of the unpredictable president: "Nixon proved to be extremely obstinate and reckless, and did things Johnson never dared to do." But if surprised, the North Vietnamese were hardly unprepared; their air defenses took a significant toll on U.S. aircraft, and they grudgingly carried out a limited evacuation of their major cities.

Early in May, with the offensive showing no letup, President Nixon took perhaps his boldest gamble of the war: he ordered the mining of Haiphong Harbor and of the North's coastal waterways. Nixon wagered that rapprochement with China, culminating in his recently concluded February visit, and the Moscow summit, scheduled for later in May, had softened the attitudes of Hanoi's benefactors toward the United States. The gamble paid off. Not wishing to endanger the upcoming summit, Moscow let the mining pass without comment. Peking issued a statement conveying "utmost indignation" but did little else.

Backstopped by U.S. air power, the stubborn South Vietnamese defense finally ground the 1972 strategic offensive to a halt. In Quang Tri Province, South Vietnamese forces began a counterattack that over four months pushed back PAVN units and in September 1972 recaptured Quang Tri City in a fiercely destructive battle.

Militarily, the offensive took a tremendous toll on PAVN; as many as 100,000 soldiers were killed. Moreover, PAVN had demonstrated that its conventional war managers required more training before PAVN could become a fully capable mechanized force. Still, the offensive failed only because of the extraordinary application of U.S. air power, an asset that was being withdrawn from the Indochina theater. If the U.S. will to use air power diminished in the future, PAVN would be unstoppable.

Strategically, PAVN captured about 10 percent of South Vietnam's land area along the spine of the Annamite Mountains and much of Quang Tri Province. The battle lines had been pushed inside the country. Base areas in Cambodia and Laos were now safeguarded, and North Vietnam immediately began material improvements. Before long, PAVN trucks were able to complete the journey from North Vietnam to the bottom of the Ho Chi Minh Trail, due north of Saigon, in less than a month. PAVN also began to ship war materiel through Dong Ha, the captured South Vietnamese port just below the DMZ. Equally important, the seizure of territory inside South Vietnam permitted political cadres to renew their political proselytizing among the people and reverse some of the successes of pacification. The Southern Liberation Radio commented, "These liberated zones can serve as very favorable springboards from which to launch offensives and to advance the resistance toward complete victory."

Politically, the offensive created a favorable climate for negotiations. Hanoi's demands crystallized into the following: withdrawal of all U.S. troops, replacement of President Thieu with a coalition government, or, failing that, recognition of the PRG as a legitimate political entity. If negotiations now faltered, the North Vietnamese were prepared to be obdurate. As the offensive raged in May, Premier Pham Van Dong told his French interviewer:

Believe me. If we could by negotiation end this war in twenty-four hours, we would do it. But we are ready to continue for years with passion because we know that, whatever our sacrifices, we have time on our side.

The Christmas bombings

At the instigation of the Soviets, negotiations resumed between Hanoi and Washington as the spring offensive was taking place. On May 2, with PAVN forces rolling through ARVN defenses, Le Duc Tho and Henry Kissinger had met in Paris. In what Kissinger later described as a "brutal" meeting, Le Duc Tho, adhering to the principle that only what is won on the battlefield can be obtained at the negotiating table, merely recited PAVN's triumphs. His intransigence persuaded Kissinger of the need for a firm military response to the offensive, and on his return to Washington, he and President Nixon decided to expand the bombing and to mine Haiphong Harbor. By the time Tho and Kissinger resumed their meetings, on three occasions in July and August, the tide on the battlefield was shifting in favor of the South Vietnamese.

The U.S. position in negotiations had softened considerably, with Kissinger having dropped the demand, in May 1971, for a mutual withdrawal of troops. This major concession meant that PAVN would be permitted to remain in the South. The Americans' demands were reduced to three—a cease-fire, the return of prisoners of war, and a guarantee that Thieu's government would endure. On May 8, the day that Nixon publicly announced the mining of Haiphong Harbor, he reiterated that the United States would remove all military personnel in four months in return for a prisoner exchange and a cease-fire.

In a secret meeting between Kissinger and Le Duc Tho on September 26, the North Vietnamese dropped what had previously been a nonnegotiable demand for a coalition government. The two sides were so close to an agreement that Le Duc Tho suggested a treaty be signed on October 30, a week prior to Nixon's anticipated reelection. On October 8, he presented Kissinger with a list of nine points that became the basis of the Paris agreement.

Hanoi's major concession called for the establishment of an "Administration of National Concord," an advisory body that would recognize the existence of both the Thieu government and the PRG and that would supervise future elections. Tho told Kissinger, "This new proposal is exactly what President Nixon has himself proposed: ceasefire, end of the war, release of the prisoners, and troop withdrawal. . . . And we shall leave to the South Vietnamese parties the settlement of these [political] questions."

After four years of fruitless negotiations, the breakthrough had come. In order to ensure an American withdrawal, Le Duc Tho had, in effect, separated the indissoluble tenets of dau tranh into quite disparate military and political issues. Henry Kissinger later wrote admiringly of Tho: "He had stonewalled ingeniously for three years. And when the occasion to settle had been imposed by Hanoi's defeats in 1972, he did so with flexibility and speed."

All that remained was for Kissinger to gain the assent of President Thieu. In the interim, Hanoi ordered its soldiers and cadres in the South to seize as many hamlets as possible prior to a cease-fire in place. In a brief flurry of fighting in the latter part of October, as many as 5,000 Communist soldiers and cadres were killed or captured by the South Vietnamese.

When the terms were laid before him, Thieu balked. He could not abide the continued presence of PAVN in South Vietnam, the composition and functions of the proposed supervisory body—renamed the National Council of National Reconciliation and Concord—or the failure to define the DMZ as a political boundary separating two sovereign states. Thieu proposed so many textual changes as to render the negotiated instrument meaningless and thereby scuttled the agreement.

When Kissinger and Le Duc Tho met again in Paris on

November 20, the latter admitted that support for the treaty had eroded among his fellow Political Bureau members. The more hard-line among them thought they had been tricked by Kissinger into exposing their Southern forces only to have them battered by ARVN forces. The talks continued into December, but the two nations were again at an impasse.

After talks broke off in Paris, Kissinger threatened "grave consequences" if Hanoi did not engage in serious negotiations. By then Nixon had been overwhelmingly re-elected to the presidency. Although the American people, and much of Congress, opposed continuing the war, the electoral mandate provided Nixon with a certain degree of freedom of action. He was impatient to end the war before his January 20, 1973, inauguration.

The consequences threatened by Kissinger came to pass on December 18, when President Nixon launched what came to be called the Christmas bombings. For twelve days, with a pause for Christmas itself, U.S. B-52s and fighter-bombers struck targets in Hanoi, Haiphong, and Thai Nguyen in the largest single bombing campaign of the war. At first the waves of bombers came in straight lines along the same route, presenting easily tracked targets for the surface-to-air missiles that the North Vietnamese fired profligately. They threw up salvos of three or more at a time, the first night sending up more than 200 SAMs to bring down three B-52s.

Soon the Americans varied their tactics and flight paths, approaching targets at different altitudes and along diverse paths. North Vietnam's store of SAMs was limited, its supply from the Soviet Union having been cut off by the mining of Haiphong Harbor. The North Vietnamese, firing a total—by U.S. count—of up to 1,242 surface-to-air missiles, ultimately claimed fifteen of the giant strato-fortresses. But by the final two days of the campaign, December 28 and 29, North Vietnam was virtually out of ammunition. The B-52s encountered only a handful of missiles, which detonated harmlessly.

Though normally stolid in the face of tactical raids by U.S. fighter-bombers, North Vietnam's citizens had not seen strategic bombing by what the North derided as the B-52 "trump card." According to the Northern history of the war, residents of Hanoi "calmly and actively" carried out an evacuation. Of those who remained, it said: "Our soldiers and people, especially those in Hanoi, deservingly punished the enemy for their escalated, barbarous attacks."

But U.S. prisoners of war reported dramatically different reactions. As the ground shook and plaster fell from the ceilings, their Hanoi guards dove into concrete manholes or cowered in the lee of prison walls. When the bombers kept coming day after day, their guards' faces, navy Captain James B. Stockdale later wrote, "telegraphed accommodation, hopelessness, remorse, fear." They knew that "all that separated Hanoi from doomsday was an American national order to keep the bombs out on the hard targets. We prisoners knew this was the end of North Vietnamese resistance, and the North Vietnamese knew it too."

Cease-fire

Uncharacteristically for Richard Nixon, he had initiated the bombings without any fanfare or ponderous speeches to the American people. To the mind of the American public, the bombing began abruptly. But to the North Vietnamese, Kissinger had communicated the ultimatum of "grave consequences" unless the Communists returned to the table. After eight days of air attacks, Hanoi responded that it would not return to Paris until the bombing ceased. Two days later, President Nixon grounded the bombers, and ten days after that, talks resumed in Paris. Kissinger credited Nixon's silence with permitting Hanoi to return to Paris without loss of face. Asked later whether the bombing had thus been a form of coercion, Kissinger answered this way: "I will say there was a deadlock in the middle of December and there was rapid movement when the negotiations resumed on January 8. These facts have to be analyzed by each person for himself."

According to North Vietnam's analysis, a resumption of talks did not indicate capitulation. In its cable of December 26, North Vietnam denied that it had "walked out" of the peace talks, adding that it maintained a "constantly serious negotiating position." That simple message prompted an end to the bombing.

On its return to Paris, North Vietnam felt it held a position of strength. It had survived Nixon's desperate bombing ploy (what one American historian called the "penultimate sanction") and left Nixon, buffeted by a whirlwind of domestic and worldwide condemnation, without another trump card to play. Furthermore, Hanoi's rejection of all the proposed treaty changes belatedly put forth by President Thieu had made adversaries of the South Vietnamese and Americans. Unknown to Hanoi, President Nixon had threatened Thieu with a rupture of the Saigon-Washington alliance and with a separate Hanoi-Washington peace if Thieu failed to assent to the treaty negotiated by Kissinger. Nixon's letter to Thieu had driven an unremovable wedge between the allies. From Hanoi's point of view, another contradiction between the allies had been exposed.

Armed with these strengths, Le Duc Tho fell back on the treaty draft that he had negotiated with Kissinger in October. The military pressure of the Christmas bombing may have stimulated a resumption of talks, but it exacted no concessions from the North Vietnamese. President Nixon, said Le Duc Tho, could either "resolve the Vietnamese problem and sign the treaty that was agreed upon or else continue the war. The American administration must make a definite choice."

The bell tower of this Catholic church in Phat Diem Province was destroyed during Linebacker I bombing in September 1972. The North Vietnamese often clustered antiaircraft artillery near such nonmilitary locations.

A Year of Bombing

The year 1972 brought the resumption of regular bombing of North Vietnam by the United States after a four year lull. Operation Linebacker I, prompted by Hanoi's Easter offensive, attempted to cut the supply lines feeding the North's troops in South Vietnam. President Nixon initiated the twelve-day campaign of strategic bombing called Linebacker II, the so-called Christmas bombings, soon after peace talks broke down in Paris in December.

Right. Workers pick through the rubble of a Hanoi textile factory leveled during the Christmas bombings.

Progress came rapidly. Within two days of renewed Le Duc Tho–Kissinger talks, the cease-fire agreement had been approved along lines of the October document. The outstanding roadblocks erected by Thieu—the status of the demilitarized zone, the Provisional Revolutionary Government, and the National Council—were all essentially decided in favor of the North Vietnamese. Once again President Thieu declined to go along, but President Nixon bluntly told him that he had "irrevocably decided" to sign the treaty and that if Thieu demurred, it would mean an end to the South Vietnam–United States relationship. Thieu could do nothing but acquiesce.

The Agreement on Ending the War and Restoring Peace in Vietnam was signed in Paris on January 27, 1973, and an immediate cease-fire was supposed to go into effect. The Communists in the Lao Dong party greeted the event not with relief at the end of a war but with a continued sense of mission. First Secretary Le Duan later summarized Hanoi's view of the accord this way:

The Party Central Committee has pointed out that the purposes of signing the Paris Agreement were to drive the United States from the South, win a fundamental victory over the enemy and lay the groundwork for eventually completing the people's national, democratic revolution throughout the country.

Between the wars

The agreement signed by the Americans and the Vietnamese in Paris fell far short of its earnest promise. It neither ended the war nor restored peace in Vietnam. The period of cease-fire began not with the hoped-for silence over the battlefields but with renewed skirmishing as both the Saigon regime and the Communists strove to bring more territory under their control. Henry Kissinger had foreseen this fighting as a time when the two sides would test each other before settling into the political reality of the end of the war. But Kissinger had anticipated the truer reality when, four years earlier, he wrote of the negotiations, "It is beyond imagination that parties that have been murdering and betraying each other for 25 years could work together as a

team giving joint instructions to the entire country."

In the period of relative calm following the Paris agreement, both North and South Vietnam refitted militarily and vied politically while building toward an ultimate confrontation. At the urging of Truong Chinh, Pham Van Dong, and Le Duc Tho, and with the support of Le Duan, the Lao Dong party Political Bureau hoped to complete the revolution by emphasizing political *dau tranh*. They favored building up their political structure in Communist-held territory, which they called "The Third Vietnam." From a strong political base in those areas, the Commu-

nists believed they could send cadres out to South Vietnamese-controlled territory to undermine the Saigon regime. To that end Hanoi dispatched some 30,000 civilian technicians and political cadres to the South with orders "to build roads, farm communes and cities, and to organize and run a governmental structure."

Another faction in the Political Bureau, reflecting the views of Pham Hung and Vo Nguyen Giap, doubted the efficacy of political *dau tranh* and favored a military resolution of the war. Even before the cease-fire, North Vietnam had increased the tempo of its infiltration to the South. Tanks and armored personnel carriers came down the Ho Chi Minh Trail. PAVN engineers installed surface-to-air missiles in Communist-held territory, especially in Quang Tri Province, to defend against the possible reintroduction of U.S. air power, the factor that had proved so decisive during the 1972 offensive.

But in early 1973 the People's Army of Vietnam was in no condition to mount a decisive military challenge. It was an army bloodied and battered after a decade of war that culminated in the destructive 1972 offensive. Its logistical system had also been weakened by prolonged strain and more than a year later was still the object of criticism by the PAVN High Command. PAVN desperately needed the respite the cease-fire provided.

By the fall of 1973, the Lao Dong party's political approach was clearly failing in South Vietnam. In direct violation of the Paris agreement, President Nguyen Van Thieu stood fast to his program of "Four No's," in which he ruled out negotiations with the enemy, a coalition government, any Communist activity in South Vietnam, and any surrender of territory to enemy attack. With Thieu thus sabotaging Hanoi's strategy, the party necessarily fell back on its military options.

At the Central Committee's Twenty-first Plenum, held in Hanoi October 13, 1973, the party acknowledged the weakness of political *dau tranh* in the South. After reviewing the history of the war in the South since 1955, in which military *dau tranh* had, except for the post-Tet period, constantly expanded, the Central Committee reaffirmed, "The revolutionary path of the South is the path of revolutionary violence. No matter what the situation, we must maintain the offensive strategy line."

But the Communist position in the

Cease-fire. Members of the North Vietnamese government attend a diplomatic reception in Hanoi on January 24, 1973, to celebrate the Paris agreement. Second from left is Truong Chinh. Behind him are Prime Minister Pham Van Dong; Tien Hoan, head of the National Assembly; and General Vo Nguyen Giap.

South was not yet conducive to a major offensive. The Military Committee admitted to a host of problems: the slow logistical build-up, poor relations between main force troops and local guerrillas, and a lack of coordination between the military and political struggles. In an example of self-criticism, the Military Committee admitted where the problems originated: "The principal reason is that we have deficiencies, not that the enemy is strong."

The Communists nevertheless embarked on a series of "strategic raids" designed to bleed South Vietnamese units and improve the Communists' strategic position. The campaign began on November 4 with a division-sized attack on ARVN outposts in Quang Duc Province, and as the battles developed, members of the Political Bureau anxiously awaited the U.S. response. Earlier in the year, Le Duan had declared in a Political Bureau meeting that the United States had left Vietnam "never to return." Now events seemed to prove him right: U.S. planes remained on the ground in Thailand and Guam.

Moreover, on November 7, Congress reduced the likelihood of their ever taking to the skies over Vietnam by passing the War Powers Act. The Church-Case amendment, which took effect on August 15, 1973, prohibited any U.S. military action in Indochina. The War Powers Act raised that prohibition to the level of national policy by severely restricting a president's authority to commit the U.S. military anywhere on his own authority. For Hanoi both these actions fell under the rubric of *dich van*—action among the enemy. PRG Justice Minister Truong Nhu Tang cited the War Powers Act as "proof of the truly pervasive victory we had gained on the American domestic battlefield." It was perhaps the final exploitation of contradictions in the alliance between the South Vietnamese and Americans; the South Vietnamese were now isolated militarily. Although President Nixon still brandished the threat of U.S. warplanes as a means of backstopping the South Vietnamese, and hence enforcing the Paris agreement, the War Powers Act robbed his threat of its menace.

Planning the final offensive

Throughout 1974 Communist and South Vietnamese forces battled back and forth, with the Communists achieving their dual purpose of gradually improving their strategic position while bleeding ARVN. South Vietnam lost 20,000 soldiers killed in the first eight months of 1974. Even worse, its armed forces in the year's last quarter suffered a desertion rate that, if prorated for one year, would have amounted to nearly a fourth of its entire strength. To the extent that it had ever existed, the esprit de corps so necessary to an army was clearly eroding in ARVN. In addition, South Vietnam's economic woes, compounded by declining aid from the United States, heightened its vulnerability to Hanoi's strategy.

As the party's men in the South, COSVN chairman Pham Hung and his military commander Lieutenant General Tran Van Tra recognized South Vietnam's weaknesses, especially the thinness of its defenses and its inadequate reserves. A concerted attack in one area that required ARVN reinforcements would of necessity leave other areas very lightly defended. But when they journeyed to Hanoi in late 1974 to join in the planning for a new offensive, they failed at first to get much of a hearing. Tra's recommendations may have been suspect because, as the South's leading military commander, he still bore a large measure of responsibility for the disastrous attack against Saigon during Tet Mau Than and for the failure of a general uprising to occur. In fact Tet had cost Tra an opportunity to leap from the party Central Committee to the Political Bureau.

For the party leadership, logic dictated a conservative approach. Having spent two years rebuilding PAVN and its logistical systems, the General Staff under Senior General Van Tien Dung and the Political Bureau were chary of launching a major offensive that risked ghastly losses on the scale of the 1968 and 1972 offensives. Instead, their plans for the upcoming winter-spring campaign called for probing attacks in the central highlands and in Quang Tri Province. The plan anticipated that it would take a second phase in the year 1976 to win final victory over the South. "We must fight in such a way as to conserve our strength" for the following year, said Le Duan.

But Hung and Tra persisted in lobbying for an immediate major offensive against the border province of Phuoc Long, north of Saigon. They believed it to be a significant weak point for the South Vietnamese, and they finally managed to enlist Le Duan in their cause. In a meeting in Le Duan's Hanoi living room, Hung and Tra persuaded the first secretary, the originator of COSVN and the primary Southern-firster, that Phuoc Long Province could be taken without employing Communist reserve forces, thus preserving COSVN's strength for a later offensive role. That seemed to be what Le Duan wanted to hear. "If that is so, then go ahead and attack," he said. "There's no problem. . . . But you must be certain of victory and not use large forces."

When the Political Bureau and the Military Committee convened for an expanded meeting on December 18, unanimity had been reached on the two-year offensive. Even Northern-firster Truong Chinh agreed that the time had come for a military push. Rising from his seat, Truong Chinh put on his glasses and glanced down at the notebook in his hand. According to Tra, Truong Chinh "was always careful, as if not wanting to make even a small mistake. He paid attention to each word and comma." Truong Chinh analyzed the weaknesses of the South Vietnamese and drew attention to their tendency to retreat into defensive enclaves, especially in cities, which were difficult to attack. To prevent their retreat, he said, "We must create conditions for striking a strategic annihilating blow, but we must not limit ourselves to just one annihilating blow."

Truong Chinh also raised the question of intervention by the United States but suggested that even its use of air power would be limited. Pham Van Dong, pacing back and forth, predicted that the United States would not possibly introduce infantry. As for U.S. air power and naval support, the prime minister predicted that neither would greatly influence the coming battle. He added with a laugh, "I'm kidding, but also telling the truth, when I say that the Americans would not come back even if you offered them candy."

The expanded Political Bureau conference to plan the offensive dragged on until January 8, and as deliberations continued, Communist troops were battling the South Vietnamese in Phuoc Long Province. Progress was closely monitored in Hanoi, not least by Pham Hung and General Tra, who had guaranteed victory. Tra kept in touch with his commanders by wire.

A week before the main attack toward Phuoc Long's provincial capital of Phuoc Binh, COSVN troops moved against Tay Ninh City, far to the southwest. To reinforce Tay Ninh, ARVN shifted the bulk of its local reserves there, leaving the remainder of the military region with only a small reserve force. When the attack came in Phuoc Long, ARVN initially sent only one battalion as reinforcement.

The noose tightened quickly around the city of Phuoc Binh. One North Vietnamese division captured the outlying town of Duc Phong, while another laid siege to Don Luan. After a thousand-round artillery barrage on December 26, the Communists overran stubbornly defended Don Luan. With the North Vietnamese now closing on Phuoc Long, Le Duan and the Political Bureau gave Gen. Tra permission to commit to battle more of the heavy T54 tanks and 130mm field guns. Led by tanks, the North Vietnamese troops, who held a four-to-one advantage in manpower, took the capital city within days, even though the ARVN defenders knocked out at least sixteen tanks. Despite his declaration that he would never surrender territory to the enemy, President Thieu, caught without reinforcements, was forced to cede the province.

The news arrived in Hanoi on January 6 while the Communist party leaders were in session. When a messenger read from the dispatch that Hanoi's soldiers "had killed or captured all of the enemy troops and completely liberated Phuoc Long province," the men burst into applause. For the first time PAVN had liberated an entire province of South Vietnam. Addressing the group, Le Duan pointed out the lack of "reaction of the [South Vietnamese], and especially the United States." The South Vietnamese had little capacity for counterattacks, while the United States, led by Gerald R. Ford since President Nixon's August resignation, had by inaction shown its reluctance to rejoin the fight.

Emboldened by the fall of Phuoc Long, the Political Bu-

reau ordered the General Staff to draw up plans to attack the highlands city of Ban Me Thuot. Previous North Vietnamese offensives—in 1965, 1968, 1972—had made Kontum or Pleiku their targets, so South Vietnam had arrayed its defenses there. Ban Me Thuot was more lightly defended. Furthermore, the North had learned from a spy in the South Vietnamese president's circle that Thieu intended not to reinforce the western highlands if an attack should materialize there but to begin forming a strategic reserve for the defense of the Saigon area.

The signs augured well for the Communist offensive. Chief of Staff Van Tien Dung, who had commanded the 1971 counterattack against Lam Son 719 and the 1972 strategic offensive, traveled to the South in early February to take command. Several measures were taken to conceal his absence from Hanoi from foreign diplomats who might pass the ominous word to Saigon that PAVN's senior general had taken to the field. His limousine continued to make daily round trips between his house and office, for example, and the army volleyball team still showed up at his house for regular afternoon matches.

As he journeyed south, General Dung formulated his plans for the attack against Ban Me Thuot. Dung had refined a tactic he called the "blossoming lotus," in which his troops skirted enemy perimeter defenses to strike at the heart of a city. After destroying enemy headquarters and communications centers, they fanned out to attack enemy defenses from the rear, "like a flower bud slowly opening its petals." Dung now planned to apply the blossoming lotus against Ban Me Thuot. And with its senior general in the field, PAVN could react quickly to exploit any advantages that arose.

The conquest of South Vietnam

To thwart electronic eavesdropping by the South Vietnamese, PAVN units had maintained strict wireless silence while moving into position. Instead they communicated over radios connected by telephone wire. But the 320th PAVN Division, whose whereabouts had been a mystery to the South Vietnamese, finally broke radio silence, and its location was pinpointed west of Pleiku. The radio signals were a ruse designed to focus ARVN's attention on Pleiku, and the ploy drew the expected South Vietnamese response: deployment of reserve forces to Pleiku.

On March 1 the 968th PAVN Division launched a diversionary attack against Pleiku, more than 100 kilometers north of Ban Me Thuot. Other PAVN units attacked Route 19 east of Pleiku, severing the main artery between the provincial capital and the coast. Pleiku appeared to be PAVN's main target. But as the battle developed, the 9th Regiment of the 320th PAVN Division moved well south of Pleiku to sever Route 14, the north-south road connecting Pleiku to Ban Me Thuot. The effect was to isolate Ban Me Thuot, preventing any possible reinforcement by convoy.

Then on March 10, a corps of PAVN troops—three divisions and an independent regiment—attacked Ban Me Thuot from three directions. With long-range artillery barrages falling on the town, the infantry advanced rapidly behind tanks. A key battle soon developed for the airfield east of the town, where the ARVN 53d Regiment, conscious of the importance of the airfield if ARVN was to have any hope of reinforcement, held off a ferocious PAVN assault. But as darkness approached, an air force bombing mission fell short of its target, hitting the ARVN tactical operations center and knocking out its radios. Communication with the battlefield commanders was lost, inhibiting further artillery and air support.

By noon of the following day, Ban Me Thuot had fallen. The ARVN defenders were driven east, along with the civilian population fleeing the fighting. In Saigon, President Thieu issued the order that had previously been decided upon. Hoping to trade land for time, he ordered a retreat from the highlands. With civilians and soldiers rushing frantically to escape, the withdrawal turned into chaos.

General Dung recognized the strategic importance of the South Vietnamese abandonment of the highlands. Destruction of the entire South Vietnamese II Corps, according to Dung, "would cause a military and political chain reaction that would reach even to America." To hasten that reaction, Dung, ignoring any distinction between civilians and soldiers, launched devastating attacks against the flanks of the South Vietnamese columns in which retreating troops and fleeing civilians were hopelessly mixed. The exodus became known as the "Convoy of Tears." Some 60,000 civilians completed the journey to the coast, about a third of the number who set out. As for the

military, South Vietnam's Joint General Staff grimly concluded that up to three-fourths of the II Corps combat strength had been destroyed.

The Ho Chi Minh Campaign

The final offensive progressed with an inexorable finality, as the South Vietnamese forces disintegrated. From the attack on Ban Me Thuot to the fall of Saigon, the chain reaction took just fifty-five days. PAVN divisions attacked Hue from the north on March 21, while other PAVN troops severed Route 1 south of the city, thus isolating the ancient capital. The sea presented the only possible evacuation route, and several thousand residents and soldiers managed to escape on a ragged flotilla of jam-packed boats before the city fell on March 25.

Da Nang was next. Swarming with refugees who camped in the streets and squatted in every building, the city proved impossible for the ARVN military to control, or to defend. As the North Vietnamese pounded Da Nang with artillery and advanced with infantry, pandemonium set in as refugees and soldiers besieged the airfield and docks searching for an escape. When they reached the outskirts on March 30, the PAVN troops paused for a day. Then the Northerners marched into the city, capturing it on March 31.

The same day Le Duan sent a cable to General Dung at his jungle headquarters in the western highlands. Having monitored the astonishing ARVN collapse in the highlands and in Military Region I, the Political Bureau had decided to move swiftly against Saigon. On behalf of the Political Bureau, the first secretary ordered Dung to swing

Left. *PAVN troops advance through the litter of ARVN tanks, armored cars, and other vehicles abandoned at Hue in March 1975. Top. Bien Hoa, north of Saigon, falls on April 28. Above. The capture of Tan Son Nhut airport seals the fate of Saigon.*

his divisions south and liberate South Vietnam's capital before the onset of the monsoon season at the end of May. The careful plan for a two-year offensive formalized less than three months earlier had been abandoned. PAVN must seize this "once-in-a-thousand years" opportunity in a final offensive to be called the "Ho Chi Minh Campaign."

As Dung, COSVN leader Pham Hung, and General Tra mapped out the offensive, Le Duc Tho arrived at their headquarters, riding casually on a motorcycle. The coauthor of the Paris agreement, for which he won a share of the Nobel Peace Prize, an honor he declined, Le Duc Tho had come to make certain the field commanders explicitly understood Hanoi's wishes. He joined his fellow Political Bureau members Dung and Pham Hung in orchestrating the offensive.

The Saigon regime had centered its defenses in the town of Xuan Loc, northeast of the capital, and PAVN troops attacked on April 9. ARVN forces put up a stubborn fight, but the 25,000 available troops, about one-third of what remained of the 500,000-man army, could not hold out. After a frontal assault by PAVN forces failed to take the town, Dung swung some of his troops around Xuan Loc in a flanking maneuver. ARVN troops gave up Xuan Loc on April 20.

The road to Saigon now lay virtually open to the PAVN forces. With the outcome of the offensive no longer in doubt, President Nguyen Van Thieu resigned his office and left the country. Dung spent several days regrouping his forces and positioning his divisions for the final assault—a strike into the heart of Saigon.

With five corps of PAVN divisions arrayed against the capital, the Ho Chi Minh Campaign began on April 26 and concluded in a startling four days. ARVN had completely crumbled. Soviet-made tanks rolled virtually unopposed into the city of Saigon, and the T54 tank in the lead rammed into the iron gate of Independence Palace. The flag of the Provisional Revolutionary Government appeared on the flagpole at 11:30 A.M.

At their headquarters in Ben Cat, the Communist leaders in the South greeted the news with jubilation. As General Tra recorded, "Le Duc Tho, Pham Hung and Van Tien Dung, who were very moved, hugged and kissed one another and firmly shook hands. There are few moments in life when one is so happy that they want to cry." General Tra's personal reaction typified the euphoria experienced by the Communist victors. "I suddenly felt as if my soul was translucent and light," he wrote, "as if everything had sunk to the bottom." The thirty-year war waged by the Communists for control of their country had come to an end.

North Vietnamese T54 tanks roll across the lawn of Saigon's Independence Palace on April 30, 1975, completing the conquest of South Vietnam.

The Fruits of Victory

The flags flying from North Vietnamese tanks as they rolled into Saigon were red and blue with a gold star, the banner of the Southern PRG. But this was an irony, for victory had been achieved not by the PRG and its Southern forces but by the People's Army from the North and by the Lao Dong party. "To the Party goes credit for victory," wrote American analyst Douglas Pike after the war. "It was able, in ten years of all-out struggle, to hone communism to perfection, both as creed and mechanism. The creed became national salvation, saving the country through proper application of Marxism-Leninism. The mechanism was control of events, established by a compact leadership and maintained by a corps of experienced revolutionaries."

One of the events controlled, or at least expertly manipulated, by the party during the war was the activity of the Provisional Revolutionary Government. The party needed the PRG in the South as a broadly based political entity to compete

with the Saigon regime and to gain sympathy and support overseas that would not have been accorded the Northern government. To help court foreign diplomats, most PRG embassies, although financed by Hanoi, were relatively more luxurious than those of North Vietnam. The buildings were larger, the cars newer, the furniture finer.

But with liberation, the PRG was no longer needed. As the party asserted control over the South, the PRG maintained the façade of authority; many of its members believed that they were creating the government that would rule South Vietnam. But Hanoi quickly placed a military management committee over the PRG to maintain order. Colonel General Tran Van Tra, a native Saigonese, became its head; another Southerner, Vo Van Kiet, a COSVN veteran and party boss for the Saigon region, became the leading political officer. Like Tra, Kiet was a Central Committee member and a Saigon native; he kept in close contact with the Political Bureau, which he was to join in a year.

Northern party officials and technicians soon flooded the South and took over the mechanisms of government. The party ultimately subsumed the PRG, although it existed in name for another year, until the National Assembly of a reunified Vietnam assumed functional control. At the same time, in the summer of 1976, the South's PLAF was abolished, and its full military units, consisting mostly of Northern soldiers, joined the People's Army of Vietnam.

The PRG policy of national concord and reconciliation after the war, to which Le Duan himself had agreed, had been a potent political weapon that, like many elements of political *dau tranh*, had paid a military dividend. According to Truong Nhu Tang, the PRG justice minister, the policy had attracted individuals of integrity to the side of the PRG, and in 1975 it "had helped to generate among the Saigonese (and Southerners in general) a reluctance to put up a die-hard battle as the Thieu regime began to crumble."

When the Military Management Committee, in its very first directive, ordered all ARVN soldiers to report for reeducation, bringing with them enough supplies and personal effects for ten to thirty days, many construed it as evidence of the party's leniency. Perhaps 250,000 men, the majority of them ARVN officers, left Saigon in this first deportation.

But when the men failed to return after ten or thirty days or more, the Southerners realized that "reconciliation" was going to mean bending to the party's terms. The Southern leaders were to remain imprisoned in reeducation camps. Hindsight suggests that the Southerners should have foreseen this glum prospect. As one party analyst wrote in 1980, "To free the former leaders of the

army and of the puppet political-administrative apparatus would simply facilitate an eventual reconstitution of their forces and invite them to launch civil war against the revolutionary power."

Reeducation camps allowed the party to deal with the "class enemies" who had worked for or supported the Saigon regime. By party count, that amounted to 1.3 million soldiers and civil servants, plus their family members—a total of about 6.5 million people—who were considered to be "compromised," and of that number, more than 1 million people were destined for reeducation over the following decade.

A ravaged country

Among the material spoils of war the North acquired in the South was the remainder of a huge U.S./ARVN arsenal and the complex of U.S.-built installations, ports, and airfields. When the U.S. withdrew its troops in 1973 the Pentagon estimated the value of the equipment left behind at $5 billion. The acquisition of this arsenal catapulted the 615,000-man PAVN into a major regional force, although many of the larger weapons and airplanes would not remain serviceable for long without spare parts. Hanoi sold some equipment on the open market. (For example, ten C-130 cargo planes went to Libya.)

Perhaps the most significant acquisition in the South was the rice bowl of the Mekong Delta. South Vietnam was nearly self-sufficient in rice production, whereas the North had been importing rice for fifteen years to feed its growing population. In 1975 the population of unified Vietnam was 49 million, with a high growth rate of 2 percent per year. Feeding these millions of new mouths required greater agricultural productivity and the conversion of millions of acres of new and war-ravaged land to production.

In addition to the food crisis and a runaway birthrate, war damage had crippled the country. Hanoi estimated that in the South the war had left behind 362,000 invalids, 800,000 orphans, and 2 million widows. In the North, six industrial cities and thirty-two towns had suffered heavy damage, while roads, railways, bridges, and ports had all been heavily damaged or destroyed.

Damage to the transportation network impeded economic reconstruction. To raise agricultural productivity, Vietnam needed to manufacture tractors and tools as well as the chemicals required for fertilizer. But raw materials had to be transported to the factories and finished products to the countryside.

The enormous task of reconstruction required a vast infusion of aid. During the war both Vietnams had had dependent economies, the South relying on the United States and the North on Peking and Moscow, much of it "aid without reimbursement." But as of April 30, 1975, Vietnam found the gift pipeline closed down. The Soviet Union and

Preceding page. Right after the war reconstruction begins in Vinh, one of the most heavily bombed cities, located in the panhandle region of North Vietnam.

164

A North Vietnamese soldier stands guard over a fleet of U.S. helicopters abandoned in Da Nang. Vietnam acquired an enormous modern arsenal with its capture of the South.

China were no longer willing to grant nonrefundable aid. They now offered only interest-bearing loans that Vietnam, with no appreciable export industry to earn capital, would find impossible to repay. Vietnam thus found itself plunging heavily into debt to its two benefactors.

This dismal scenario confronted the Lao Dong party Central Committee at its Twenty-Fourth Plenum in July 1975, at the South Vietnam mountain resort town of Da Lat. Among other items on the agenda were formal reunification of Vietnam and the economy, specifically the formulation of a five-year economic plan. But flushed with triumph, the party leaders failed to appreciate the parlous state of the economy. "In the euphoria of victory ... ," wrote party historian Nguyen Khac Vien, "we somewhat lost sight of realities."

In fact only some of the leaders had lost sight of reality. Balancing the ideologues were the party pragmatists. Le Duan headed a faction that favored a gradual socialization of the economy with incentives. He was joined by Le Duc Tho, Pham Van Dong, and others with Southern experience such as Vo Van Kiet and Nguyen Van Linh.

The ideologues, dominated by Truong Chinh and the powerful PAVN leadership, disdained a gradual approach, advocating instead rapid socialization of the South and of the Southern economy, and they won this critical argument. Their views were to be incorporated into the 1976 to 1980 five-year economic plan being prepared for the next party Congress.

Almost immediately, as it had during the war, the party in peacetime applied the techniques of *dau tranh* to the problems of the economy. "This is our Third Resistance," a Radio Hanoi commentator asserted that summer. "The economy is our new battlefield." A party publication declared the strategic task of the revolution to be completing reunification and "rapidly, strongly and steadily advanc[ing] the entire country to socialism." The old party slogan, "All for the Frontlines, All for Victory," was replaced by a new and cumbersome one, "All for Production, All for Construction of Socialism, All for the Fatherland's Strength and Prosperity and People's Happiness."

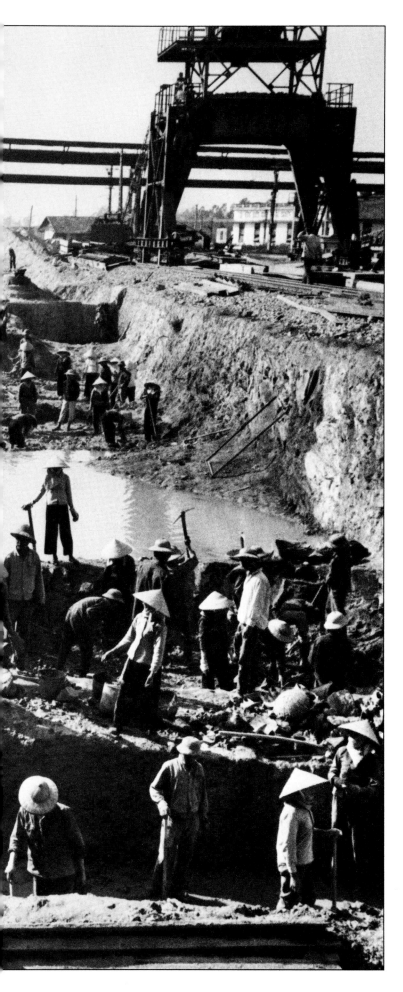

In a rare departure from the collective leadership stance of the Lao Dong party, Truong Chinh put his personal prestige behind the party's economic direction. At a November conference held in Saigon to discuss reunification, Chinh analyzed the state of the two Vietnams in Marxist terms. The North was actively building socialism, he said, while the South had not yet achieved the earlier stage of national democratic revolution. "Does this mean that reunification should wait until the South has caught up?" he asked rhetorically. "I think that is not necessary." The use of the first person singular not only identified Chinh personally with the program but also indicated that division existed in the Political Bureau over these crucial economic decisions.

The Fourth Party Congress

In the spring of 1976, it was time for the creation of a new National Assembly, an act that would ratify the party's creation over all Vietnam. The election was Communist style: citizens who did not vote would lose their ration cards; there was a single slate of 605 candidates from which voters were to select 492 delegates; there was no campaigning. Most of the candidates were known for their participation in one way or another in the Communist war effort. Meeting in June, the new assembly formally proclaimed the unification of the two Vietnams into one country and baptized it the Socialist Republic of Vietnam.

A more significant event took place December 14 to 20, 1976, when 1,008 delegates, representing 1.6 million Lao Dong party members, convened in Hanoi for the Fourth Party Congress. Because of the war, there had not been a party congress since the third in 1960. The major business of the congress was to reorganize the party leadership and approve the already-in-place economic five-year plan.

Workers in Hanoi planted some 300,000 flowering trees and spruced up the city for the party's gathering, a celebration of self-congratulation. "We have come to summarize the experience of victory," one speaker told party delegates and observers from twenty-nine foreign Communist parties.

Reflecting the absorption of the party in the South, the congress enlarged both the party's ruling organs. The Central Committee, which included members of the Political Bureau, grew from 77 members and alternates to a total of 133. At least 30 of the former members disappeared from the list. New members included some who had experience in economics. Several generals also joined the Central Committee, which meant that six of the top eleven PAVN generals now held seats on the Central Committee and Political Bureau.

Vietnamese workers rebuild the Thai Nguyen steel plant, a favorite target of U.S. bombers during the war.

The Political Bureau itself expanded to seventeen seats (fourteen full members and three alternates) from the original thirteen. Two key COSVN officials joined the Political Bureau, political officer Nguyen Van Linh becoming a full member and Vo Van Kiet joining as an alternate. Another key promotion to full member was that of Colonel General Chu Huy Man, wartime commander of Military Region 5. A protégé of Le Duc Tho and a strong supporter of Le Duan, Man provided the pragmatist Le Duan faction with a counterweight to PAVN generals Vo Nguyen Giap and Van Tien Dung. With such powerful patrons, Man was to rise in PAVN to the second most powerful post, that of chief of the Political Directorate. This gave him authority to recommend the appointment, transfer, or removal of officers from the rank of lieutenant colonel up. Le Duc Tho's organization department then passed on such recommendations.

Long-time member Hoang Van Hoan, a founder with Ho Chi Minh of the Communist party in 1930, was dropped from the Political Bureau. A former ambassador to China, Hoan expounded the Chinese line in the Political Bureau and even urged that Vietnam emulate Mao's Cultural Revolution. "Although he remained a member of our Party, his soul and heart became Chinese," one party official later explained. The removal of a venerable pro-Chinese figure from Hanoi's ruling circle reflected the deterioration in relations between Vietnam and China.

As a tribute to Ho Chi Minh, the party reassumed the name Vietnam Communist party, as Ho had designated it in 1930. The title of chairman was also retired in deference to Ho. The party's leader, in this case Le Duan, was henceforth to be called secretary-general.

The five-year plan

The 1976 to 1980 five-year economic plan the Fourth Party Congress was asked to approve had been under way for nearly a year. It was a wish list more than a realistic economic program. There was a program called "Leap Forward in Agriculture" calling for a 7.8 percent annual increase in rice production that would make Vietnam self-sufficient by 1980. To open up new lands, the party planned New Economic Zones to be cleared and tilled by people relocated from the overcrowded Red River Delta and the cities. Millions of people were to be moved to New Economic Zones in the central highlands, while peasants in the Mekong Delta were to turn over their holdings to NEZs established there. An irrigation campaign, increased use of fertilizers, and the introduction of double-cropping were supposed to increase production.

The New Economic Zone program faltered from the start. It failed to attract sufficient settlers, and many who did inhabit the often primitive sites did not stay for long. Most "volunteers" were former South Vietnamese soldiers or officials, some of them recently released from reeduca-

tion camps, or other "unreliables" who were relocated from the cities, either forcibly or because they had no other alternatives for supporting their families. To lure Northern peasants to the Southern NEZs, the government offered the adventure of an airplane ride.

As early as the end of 1976, however, word had spread that New Economic Zones were a kind of Siberia. Of the 400,000 people relocated from Saigon, about 60 percent had already returned to the city. Even without ration coupons or a place to live, for many people life in the city was preferable to life in a New Economic Zone.

The five-year plan also contemplated improvement of heavy and light industry, but unrealistic forecasts calling for a 16 to 18 percent annual increase were patently impossible goals for a war-ravaged country with a ruined infrastructure. The country needed reconstruction of roads and pipelines, improvement of port facilities, and creation of maritime cargo and commercial air fleets.

The ambitious five-year plan carried a huge price tag, approximately $7.5 billion. Vietnam's primary exports, coal and seafood, could do little to finance such an enormous expenditure. The Soviet Union agreed to finance $2.5 billion of the five-year plan in the form of interest-bearing loans, but China made available only a disappointing $300 million for the first year, with subsequent loans to be approved on a yearly review basis.

An essential element in the expansion of light industry and production of consumer goods was control of distribution, which meant severely restricting the capitalist free trade in the South. The government nationalized the banks in South Vietnam in 1975 as a first step toward controlling trade. To socialize the markets without substituting a workable system of distribution would have been too drastic so, in obvious deference to the pragmatists, the party decided to allow pockets of free trade to remain during the transition to socialism. The party attempted to exercise a degree of control by assigning to private business economic cadres who were supposed to work side by side with the capitalists.

Two years of this gradualist approach to limiting private trade failed miserably. By early 1978 private factories and small businesses still accounted for 65 percent of total industrial production in the South. Several thousand economic officials from the North had taken over administrative and managerial jobs from incumbents believed to be incompetent or corrupt. Nguyen Van Linh, who headed the Committee for the Transformation of Private Industry and Trade, was held responsible for the sluggish performance and was fired. He was replaced by an alternate Political Bureau member, Do Muoi, who had been minister of construction in Hanoi.

The party then launched a drastic attack on the merchant class, many of whom were ethnic Chinese, or *Hoa*, as the Vietnamese called them. On March 23 thousands of boys and girls drawn principally from the Ho Chi Minh

Youth Brigades, and accompanied by PAVN soldiers, descended on shops in Saigon's Chinese district, Cholon. In pairs they made inventories of every item. Stocks were then seized, with payment offered at cost plus a profit of 20 percent if a shopkeeper could show a receipt for his goods. Most businessmen, having acquired their commodities on the black market, had no receipts and therefore had their goods confiscated without any payment. Eight days later, on March 31, Do Muoi, acting on authority of Prime Minister Pham Van Dong, outlawed trading altogether.

These draconian edicts had brutal results. They wiped out most businessmen, except those who had concealed gold. Soon hordes of *Hoa* were fleeing Vietnam in the notorious exodus of the "Boat People." Refugees had been slipping away from Vietnam in ever-increasing numbers since 1975. In 1976, according to the United Nations High Commissioner on Refugees, 5,619 Vietnamese refugees turned up on the shores of neighboring countries such as Thailand, Malaysia, and Indonesia. In 1977, the number grew to 15,657. But with the flight of the *Hoa*, the "Boat People" problem reached crisis proportions. In 1978 some 88,736 refugees, the majority of them ethnic Chinese, reached those so-called countries of first asylum, and in 1979 the number shot up to nearly 100,000. Thousands more never made it. United Nations officials estimated that between 15 and 33 percent of refugees who left the country died at sea, victims of weather, starvation, or piracy.

In angry reaction to Vietnam's treatment of the *Hoa*, China abruptly canceled all aid and recalled its advisers who had been overseeing seventy-two projects, including the construction of a bridge over the Red River and modernization of a major coal mine. For years Vietnam had performed an agile balancing act between the two Communist superpowers, but now it had come to a sudden end. Vietnam was squarely in the Soviet camp.

The loss of Chinese aid required Hanoi to importune the Soviets for more funding. In June 1978 Vietnam joined COMECON, the Soviet economic bloc, and in November signed a treaty of friendship and mutual cooperation with the Soviet Union. The alliance with Moscow was bound to bring repercussions from China, which had reason to oppose the spreading influence of Moscow into Southeast Asia. A return of the historic confrontation between China and Vietnam began to seem inevitable.

The role of PAVN

The end of the war found most of the People's Army of Vietnam positioned in the South and about to carry out a task for which it was not ready—that of military government. Radio Hanoi, echoing Lenin's exhortation to the Red Army after the Bolshevik revolution, told the soldiers that they were midwives at the birth of a new society. Their midwifery tasks were security—tracking down ARVN sol-

diers still in hiding, defending installations, maintaining public order—and mass motivation—that is, stabilizing the party's political base and indoctrinating the population. PAVN also was charged with administering the reeducation camp and New Economic Zone programs.

Fighting was not over for all PAVN units, however. Early in May some units moved to the Cambodian border and to Phu Quoc Island to defend against attacks by Khmer Rouge soldiers. An animosity that dated back centuries separated the Cambodians and Vietnamese, and the Communists who now prevailed in Cambodia were profoundly anti-Vietnam. Soon after taking over Cambodia, they sent troops to fortify their border with Vietnam. Units from each side fell to fighting that summer, but bilateral talks between Phnom Penh and Hanoi brought a temporary end to it. Still the hostility between the two Communist neighbors was to continue for more than three years, eventually escalating into full-scale warfare.

Once the war for the South was over, the fighter-combatants (enlisted men), and many of their revolutionary cadres (officers), expected to return to their homes in the North to exchange their weapons for the modern equivalents of plowshares. But demobilization was not so easy to achieve. A factional dispute developed in the Political Bureau over the future of PAVN. For almost two years it pitted Truong Chinh and his advocates of social reconstruction against Vo Nguyen Giap and the army's hierarchy.

The party leadership was agreed that Vietnam should become a major regional power with a substantial army, but beyond that there was little agreement on major strategic, ideological, and institutional questions such as the need to root out any resistance forces in the South, what to do about the bellicose Cambodian neighbors, and the potential for conflict with China. The PAVN generals understandably wanted to preserve their military force empire and to assure the army's modernization.

Starting in 1970, PAVN had made great strides in its modernization campaign, principally under the guidance of General Giap. By the end of the war, Giap's political strength was waning, and he had handed over control of PAVN to Chief of Staff Van Tien Dung. But Giap still wielded considerable influence as a strategic planner, arguing convincingly that PAVN had to be molded into a modern armed force capable of fixed defense. "Now that the Fatherland is unified, all territory, airspace, territorial waters, the vast continental shelf, all are ours," he said in an October 1975 speech. "Our coast is long and beautiful. We must know how to defend it."

Giap's position conflicted with Truong Chinh's socialist ideology. As Truong Chinh argued, a large standing army contributed little to the economy. The Chinh faction wanted PAVN military units transferred more or less intact to civilian labor markets to work on reconstructing the economy. PAVN's security duties in the South would transfer to the newly formed paramilitary Armed Youth Assault Force. The Chinh faction also saw other ideological considerations, in what some analysts have called the "red" versus "expert" debate, that militated against PAVN's modernization. Party doctrine and the theory of *dau tranh* held that indomitable Vietnamese will, more so than military might and materiel, was the key element in warfare. In the dictates of Mao Tse-tung, men were more important than weapons.

As in so many Political Bureau disputes, the result was a compromise that offered something to each side, although in this case the generals seemed to have won more than half the argument. The party agreed to a limited demobilization, the use of some PAVN troops for some economic duties, an increased budget for PAVN's modernization, and a continued military draft. The result of all this was not a smaller standing army but a larger one. PAVN expanded from its 1975 total of 650,000 men to more than 1 million a decade later, with a reserve force of some 2.5 million and a general staff numbering more than 450. Thus Vietnam, with the largest per capita armed force, would achieve the dubious distinction of being the world's most militant society.

Demobilization of PAVN veterans, called revolutionary retirees, was therefore quite selective. Most of those first released from service had been students who were drafted out of colleges and technical schools; they were free to resume their studies. This amounted to but a few thousand soldiers. A year later, the Central Military Party Committee ordered the demobilization of those fifty years of age or older and those disabled soldiers who had not yet been discharged. From the generals' point of view, this was not a great sacrifice.

PAVN threw itself into both modernization and its economic tasks with the rationale that Vietnam could be successfully defended only if it became a powerful country and that economic development was the route to that power. In the summer of 1976 the number of PAVN infantry divisions had increased from twenty-seven to fifty-one, but of those, thirty-eight were regular infantry while thirteen were smaller economic construction divisions composed mainly of older soldiers, including many who had gained experience fighting in the South. Each unit,

Vietnamese soldiers march off two Khmer Rouge caught near the village of Thuong Phuoc, Vietnam.

fully armed, had both military and economic duties; many of them were stationed in northern Vietnam along the sensitive China border. With their combat experience, especially in guerrilla war tactics, they provided security against border infringements by China.

In 1976 the Political Bureau issued policy guidelines for the economic units:

An important task of the armed forces now ... is building the economy and building the nation. ... We must inculcate cadres and combatants with an awareness that both combat and labor are glorious so they uphold revolutionary heroism in productive labor, develop responsibility and revolutionary spirit.

PAVN economic units undertook a host of tasks, including land reclamation, water conservation, road and railline construction, and construction of harbors and port facilities. To ease the strain on the country's agricultural system, troops were expected to feed themselves six months of the year, and some units showed remarkable success growing rice and vegetables and raising fish and livestock. Articles and statistics in the Vietnamese press extolled what one called "the strong and active troop advances [that] have been no less difficult or arduous than the combat operations of former years."

Modernization remained a priority for the army's high command. In addition to the increase in infantry units, including one airborne brigade, the Vietnamese air force grew from three to five air divisions, one of them a helicopter division. The leadership increasingly emphasized military technology and relied on Soviet materiel and tactics, including the concept of combined arms—the coordination of infantry, artillery, and armor. PAVN's military journals carried numerous articles on subjects such as air power, massed artillery, and vertical envelopment. Reflecting the views of the high command, Senior General Hoang Van Thai, vice minister of National Defense, declared, "Either we will acquire the needed technological knowledge or we will be exterminated."

The Cambodian quagmire

While all these internal struggles to build a viable nation were taking place, Vietnam was bedeviled by its Cambodian neighbors. By late 1978 border trouble had festered for more than three years as Cambodian leader Pol Pot continued to heat up the anti-Vietnam passion that was a hallmark of the Khmer Rouge's xenophobic revolution. Hanoi finally decided its diplomacy, and its patience, was exhausted.

The Political Bureau chose to solve the problem Moscow style—with an invasion of Cambodia. Hanoi assumed that the Treaty of Friendship and Cooperation signed with the Soviet Union in November 1978, which contained provisions for mutual defense, posed sufficient threat to Peking, Cambodia's principal benefactor, to forestall any potential retaliation from China.

Vietnamese armored columns struck into Cambodia in late December 1978. Moving along four fronts, 200,000 Vietnamese invaders routed the Cambodian units and

around Lao Cai, severely damaging Vietnam's ability to produce fertilizer for its sagging agriculture. The Chinese devastated tin, chromium, and coal mines and thus diminished outright Vietnam's small export earnings.*

Paying the price

One of the immediate effects of Hanoi's invasion and occupation of Cambodia was to rob Vietnam of whatever tenuous support it had gained either in Asia or in the rest of the non-Communist world. In the late summer and fall of 1978, after the decision to invade Cambodia had already been made in the Political Bureau, Premier Pham Van Dong made a good will tour of regional capitals to preach cooperation and peace. Following the invasion,

captured Phnom Penh on January 7, 1979. But the advance moved slowly, giving the bulk of the Khmer Rouge, including all the top leaders, time to flee with trucks and equipment to the western mountains. From there Pol Pot promised to carry on a resistance war.

For China the invasion of Cambodia was a final provocation. Calculating that the treaty between Vietnam and the Soviet Union would not bring down Soviet retaliation, China mounted an invasion of its own, one designed, said Chinese leader Deng Xiaoping, "to teach a lesson" to the Vietnamese. During the seventeen-day invasion of northern Vietnam that began on February 17, 1979, both sides suffered greatly.

After penetrating a few miles inside Vietnam, Chinese troops withdrew, scorching the earth as they went. They razed farms and villages and seized livestock. They blew up power stations and destroyed the phosphate mines

PAVN soldiers resume patrol past Khmer Rouge casualties after a skirmish. The border war between Vietnam and Cambodia festered for three years before Hanoi decided to "settle" the problem with the invasion of December 1978.

Vietnam found itself condemned as an aggressor and rebuffed by the governments it had courted.

As a result, Vietnam was forced into ever-increasing dependency on the Soviet Union. Vietnam had no arms industry, so all military hardware had to come directly from the Soviets, though apparently at no cost. "Arms and ammunition don't cost us a penny," party propagandist Hoang Tung told foreign correspondents in early 1980. "Our Soviet friends supply all that."

* For a more complete account of Vietnam's invasion of Cambodia, and the Chinese invasion of Vietnam, see Chapter Three of *The Aftermath,* another volume of THE VIETNAM EXPERIENCE.

The break with China heightened Vietnam's hostility toward its pro-Chinese party members and toward ethnic Chinese. The best-known victim of this hostility was former Political Bureau member Hoang Van Hoan. Three years after he had been removed from the party's ruling circles, Hoan felt so ill treated that in July 1979, without informing his wife or son, a party official, he defected to China. En route to East Berlin for treatment of an illness, Hoan deplaned during a refueling stop in Pakistan and traveled to Peking. He had planned his defection carefully; authorities who searched his house in Hanoi found all his papers missing. In Peking, during an interview with Nayan Chanda, a reporter for the *Far Eastern Economic Review*, the bitter Hoan criticized the pro-Soviet policies of "Le Duan and Company." Le Duan had usurped the party leadership and ruled by "dictatorial and police methods." In spite of its national democratic struggle against the French and Americans, Hoan said, Vietnam was neither independent nor democratic. Thus the revolution should continue.

Hoan's defection was a propaganda embarrassment for Hanoi, tearing away the mask of solidarity the party had so carefully nurtured. Hanoi responded by sentencing Hoan to death for treason and purged other party figures considered to have ties to China. Four former envoys to China lost their seats on the Central Committee. Some other officials, among them General Chu Van Tan, a founder of PAVN, and General Le Quang Ba, former chairman of the Minorities Commission, were placed under house arrest. "We have to be vigilant," said one party official. "Chu Van Tan and Le Quang Ba are basically good communists, but we cannot ignore the fact that they have family ties in China. The Chinese might make an attempt to kidnap them to use their names in an anti-Vietnamese front."

Economic realism

In addition to these military and political woes, Vietnam's economy, drained by defense expenditures, was in a shambles. The five-year plan had failed disastrously. Even the weather seemed to conspire against Vietnam. In 1978, typhoon Lola had burst dikes in the Red River Delta and transformed the Mekong Delta into a vast, muddy paddy. One million hectares of planted rice and another 3 million tons of dry crop were lost. Since the harvest for 1978 already represented a 2 million ton drop from the previous year, Vietnam faced possible famine. Millions of tons of grain had to be imported, further dwindling Vietnam's currency reserves. Moreover, loans contracted between 1975 and 1977 were maturing and, according to a study by the International Monetary Fund, "Already in 1978 the service of the debt in convertible currencies [$150 million] had exceeded Vietnamese export receipts."

Even as Secretary-General Le Duan tended toward the Soviets, however, he remained a pragmatist, and pragmatism was required to deal with the abysmally weak economy. In 1979 extreme poverty was commonplace. Food rations, which had declined steadily since 1975, dropped further, to thirteen kilograms per person per month, six kilograms being rice and the remainder potatoes, wheat, and cassava. To supplement their diets, Vietnamese bought food on the black market at prices ten times those of the state price. The average Vietnamese spent 85 percent of his salary on food.

Out of a working population of 23 million, almost 3 million people had no jobs. (A 1979 census pegged Vietnam's population at 52.7 million.) Vietnam's low productivity was very likely attributable in part to the tiredness of the workers. "If you don't have enough food, you can't work," said Vo Van Kiet, who in 1983 was to become Vietnam's chief economic planner.

In mid-1979 the pragmatists in the Political Bureau beat a gradual retreat from the unyielding socialist concepts of the failed 1976 to 1980 five-year plan. Enterprises exporting goods were accorded most favorable industry status in the form of priority supplies of raw materials. Prime Minister Pham Van Dong ordered an end to all checkpoints on the roads in the South, permitting freer exchange of goods between the cities and the countryside. Formerly guards at those checkpoints had examined cargo and even measured gas tanks; vehicles with more than a half tank of gas had the excess siphoned off and confiscated.

The Sixth Plenum of the Central Committee, held in September 1979, endorsed a plan encouraging peasants to reclaim virgin lands and exempting all crops grown on that land from taxes for three to five years. The Central Committee also debated a series of liberalizing measures to offer incentives for production, under which any output exceeding quotas could be kept by the industry or collective for sale either to the state or on the open market. The pragmatists promised the ideologues that such suspensions of socialist ideology would be permitted only until Vietnam's economy was strong enough to resume all-out socialization.

It took until 1980, at the Ninth Plenum, for the pragmatists to win that debate. The Central Committee issued sweeping directives, instituting contract systems for agriculture, fishing, and industry. In many state-run enterprises, piecework wages replaced fixed salaries. There were quick results. In fishing, for example, the catch more than doubled. Plants were allowed to be run by their own directors, using any system they chose so long as they met state quotas. Import/export companies were established in Saigon (renamed Ho Chi Minh City), Can Tho, Da Nang, and Hanoi. Except for rice, petroleum products, rubber, and coffee, these companies were permitted to export any commodities and retain for their own use the hard currencies earned. With their earnings, companies began to import raw materials and spare parts.

The contract system brought especially dramatic results in agriculture. In 1980, the year before the system was introduced, total grain production was about 14 million tons. By 1982, grain output had risen to more than 16 million tons, and in 1983, with a harvest of just under 17 million tons, Vietnam had achieved the barest level of self-sufficiency in rice, a per capita standard of 1,800 calories per day. Agricultural goals called for increases of 1 million tons of rice per year, and if these goals were met, Vietnam's hunger would be eased even more.

A somber congress

Where the Fourth Party Congress in 1976 had been a celebration of victory and a paean to the might of the Vietnamese Communist party, the Fifth Congress in March 1982 opened under a cloud. There were reasons to fear that the Vietnamese might rise up in dissatisfaction. They had done so before. According to *Far Eastern Economic Review* correspondent Nayan Chanda, there had been food riots in 1980 in Nghe Tinh Province and in Haiphong. These had been easily put down, but the fear of recur-

rence hung heavy over the party leaders. So instead of ordering flowering trees planted for this congress, as they had done for the one in 1976, officials canceled all leaves for the armed forces and placed the country on security alert before the congress assembled.

In addition to nourishing the possibility of rebellion in Vietnam's people, seven years of authoritarian rule and economic mismanagement had fostered disunity in the party ranks. At provincial meetings held prior to the congress, government journals reported "heated discussions" among the delegates and the tabling of "tens of thousands of resolutions" to be considered at the congress. The party hierarchy was at the same time thrashing out divisions in its own ranks. The Central Committee met three times in four months, and the Tenth Plenum lasted a record twenty-five days in October and November 1981.

When after the acrimonious internal debate the congress convened on March 25, the leaders were ready to

A Vietnamese soldier guards a member of a Chinese tank crew captured in Cao Bang during China's punitive invasion of northern Vietnam in March 1979.

acknowledge errors committed at every level of the party—except at the top, the Political Bureau. Le Duan, in ill health and appearing worn-out from the strain of the political infighting, accepted the party's full responsibility for the disastrous 1976 to 1980 five-year plan. "The Party's Central Committee sternly criticizes itself before the Congress," he said. "Following the congress we propose to move to deepen criticism and self-criticism in the party, in the state bodies at all levels, and to devise effective means to correct these very grave shortcomings and errors." His voice grew weak and faltered, and Le Duan could not finish reading the political report. An aide finished for him.

As head of the party's Organization Department, Le Duc Tho delivered the political report, and he spoke with unusual candor on the state of the party. He blamed the Central Committee, as well as the Council of Ministers and the rank and file, for the party's "very serious shortcomings" in economic management. The general quality of party officials was troubling to Le Duc Tho, who charged that "no small number" had abandoned discipline and succumbed to bourgeois lifestyles. Those officials, including some who were prominent but unnamed, had to be purged, he said. (According to official publications, some 86,000 people had been expelled from the party over the previous five years for "corrupt and degenerate" practices.) Whereas in 1976 Le Duc Tho had celebrated the "high degree of unanimity" within the party, he now decried the "lack of a high degree of agreement" on party policies.

Pham Van Dong's economic report continued the same tone of self-criticism. Employing the rarely used first person singular, the premier said, "I feel I must emphasize the direct responsibility for these shortcomings and errors—especially in the elaboration and implementation of the [five-year] plan—that belongs directly to the Council of Ministers." The goals of the plan, he admitted, had been "too great in scale, too high and beyond the capacities" of Vietnam.

The party shakeup

In his report the premier unveiled the next five-year plan, which affirmed the party's new liberal economic orientation. It set realistic goals for increases in agricultural productivity of 3 to 4 percent per year and emphasized the manufacture of clothing and consumer goods along with improvement of the transportation system and production of electricity. Dong also announced that the controversial contract system, which had brought dramatic improvements in agricultural productivity, would be continued. Even after the transition to socialism was completed in the future, he said, some pockets of the "individual economy" would remain.

On the last day of the congress, the line-up of party figures who would lead Vietnam was announced. At the pin-nacle of power nothing had changed. Aging leaders Le Duan, Truong Chinh, Le Duc Tho, Pham Hung, and Pham Van Dong all retained their party and government positions, a development some foreign observers found surprising. British analyst P.J. Honey commented about Le Duan:

This old man, his health failing, with a record of unrelieved failure since the military victory of 1975 and nothing new to offer the country, bitterly criticized by his Party colleagues and most Vietnamese people, has been reappointed Secretary General of the VCP. ... His aged colleagues in the oligarchy of Communist leadership are so fearful of what might happen if they displace him that they prefer to retain him in office. That is the dilemma of Vietnam.

But below that handful of oligarchs, the party reshuffled the leadership, reflecting the economic, political, and foreign policy crises of the three previous years and reflecting as well the aging process. Six lower-ranking officials left the Political Bureau, including Foreign Minister Nguyen Duy Trinh, who was removed for senility, and former State Planning Chief Le Thanh Nghi, fired for mismanaging the five-year plan. The most prominent member to depart was the internationally known General Vo Nguyen Giap. In 1980, while remaining a Political Bureau member, Giap had already turned over his defense portfolio to General Van Tien Dung. Now he obligingly retired to head the Science and Technology Commission. These retirements brought promotions to Generals Dung and Chu Huy Man and also to former alternate members Vo Van Kiet, named head of state planning, and Do Muoi. Three of four new Political Bureau members owed some allegiance to Le Duc Tho, indicating his consolidation of power within the party and the possibility that he would eventually succeed the ailing Le Duan.

More extensive purges took place in the Central Committee, which lost 39 members, among them Colonel General Tran Van Tra, whose forthright memoir of the final 1975 offensive had exposed political wrangling among the party's elite. The committee was expanded to 152 full and alternate members. The combination of the purge and expansion brought 70 new officials, mostly technocrats and local party officials, to the party's ruling circles.

The Soviet alliance

Corruption, inefficiency, and incompetence were given as the reasons for these dismissals, but another, unstated, cause was the continuing purge of pro-Chinese party members. Le Duc Tho had sharply criticized "certain Maoist elements who have betrayed the Party and put themselves on the payroll of the enemy." In his report, Le Duan had stated pointedly, "Ideological work must enable everybody to recognize clearly, without the least confusion, that the direct and dangerous enemy of our nation is the Chinese expansionists and hegemonists."

In contrast to his pointed remarks against China, Le Duan reaffirmed Vietnam's friendship with the Soviet Union. Le Duan proclaimed, "Solidarity and cooperation in all fields with the Soviet Union; such is the cornerstone of the external policy of our party and our state."

While this orgy of self-recrimination and bureaucratic reorganization unfolded over several days, the leader of the Soviet delegation, a Political Bureau member named Mikhail Gorbachev, sat in a place of honor in the center of the dais, listening carefully. When he finally rose to address the congress, Gorbachev at first saluted the Vietnamese Communist party and cited it as "one of the most glorious fighting detachments of the international Com-

munist movement." To honor Vietnam's leaders, he then presented his country's highest award, the Order of Lenin, to Le Duan, Truong Chinh, and Pham Van Dong.

But the accomplishments of a fighting detachment differed greatly from those of peacetime economic managers, and Gorbachev went on in no uncertain terms to criticize Vietnam for its economic failings. Vietnam owed $2.3 billion to the Soviet Union and had no ability to repay. This, he made clear, was a matter of great concern to Moscow. While promising expanded programs of technical and economic aid and a doubling of trade by 1985, Gorbachev noted that the many joint projects between the two countries "oblige us to be constantly concerned with

Continuity and Change in the Vietnamese Political Bureau

Political Bureau in 1975	Political Bureau in 1976	Political Bureau in 1982
LE DUAN (1908)	LE DUAN	LE DUAN
TRUONG CHINH (1908)	TRUONG CHINH	TRUONG CHINH
PHAM VAN DONG (1906)	PHAM VAN DONG	PHAM VAN DONG
PHAM HUNG (1912)	PHAM HUNG	PHAM HUNG
Vo Nguyen Giap (1912)	LE DUC THO	LE DUC THO
LE DUC THO (1910)	Vo Nguyen Giap	VAN TIEN DUNG
Nguyen Duy Trinh (1910)	Nguyen Duy Trinh	Vo Chi Cong
Le Thanh Nghi (1911)	Le Thanh Nghi	Chu Huy Man
Hoang Van Hoan (1905)	Tran Quoc Hoan	To Huu
Tran Quoc Hoan (1910)	VAN TIEN DUNG	Vo Van Kiet
VAN TIEN DUNG (1917)	Le Van Luong (1910)	Do Muoi
	Nguyen Van Linh (1913)	Le Duc Anh*
	Vo Chi Cong (1912)	Nguyen Duc Tam (1920)
	Chu Huy Man (1920)	
	Alternate Members	**Alternate Members**
	To Huu (1920)	Nguyen Co Thach (1923)
	Vo Van Kiet (1923)	Dang Si Nguyen*
	Do Muoi (1910)	

(Birthdate of Political Bureau member in parentheses)
* Birthdate not available

A formal session of the 1982 Fifth Party Congress in Hanoi. Front row dignitaries include Le Duc Tho (third from left in glasses), Heng Samrin of Cambodia, Truong Chinh, Soviet delegate Mikhail Gorbachev, Le Duan, an unidentified Soviet general, Pham Van Dong, the Soviet ambassador, Pham Hung, and Generals Vo Nguyen Giap and Van Tien Dung.

increasing efficiency . . . and assuring 100 percent yield." Soviet participation in Vietnamese affairs was to deepen, and the presence of Soviet technical advisers was to become a fixture in the future of Vietnam. Such was the sober message from the relatively unknown Soviet official who three years hence was to become leader of the U.S.S.R.

Vietnam and the future

The Vietnamese Communists, no less than the country they ruled, were profoundly troubled as the first decade of independence drew near a close. North Vietnam had waged a long struggle to liberate the South and to reestablish its hegemony in Indochina. It had spent its national resources and treasure and hundreds of thousands of its people in pursuit of precious independence, but years after attaining its long-sought goals, reunified Vietnam was still far from enjoying the prosperity, or the peace, that victors long for as the fruits of victory. Defense spending consumed an estimated 50 to 60 percent of the national budget. Vietnam was alienated from its powerful neighbor China. It had soldiers fighting in Cambodia and tied down in Laos. Because of its occupation of Cambodia, Vietnam was shunned by most of its Asian neighbors as well.

After freeing part of Vietnam from its "neocolonialist" dependency on the United States, Vietnam found itself inextricably bound in a profound dependency on the Soviet Union. Although the party had made strides toward resolving its economic woes with a more realistic five-year plan that included some accommodation of capitalism, a stable economy that produced enough food for its people was still many years off. Measured against all relevant economic standards, Vietnam lay in the nether reaches of the Third World.

There was, in short, still no end in sight to what the Lao Dong party had set in motion in 1959, when, sparked by Le Duan's paper *The Path of the Revolution*, it went to war against the South. The Vietnamese Communist party had often said that the struggle of revolution might require a fifty-year war. If that prognosis held true, Vietnam's trials by the mid-1980s were over by only half.

Le Duan (right) and Pham Hung, two of Vietnam's aging leaders, arrive in Red Square, Moscow, in late 1982 for ceremonies marking the sixtieth anniversary of the forming of the Soviet Union.

A Restive Peace

In the decade since the end of the war, Vietnam struggled to build a nation ravaged physically and rent socially by a thirty-year conflict that touched every family. But the obstacles to progress were immense. A postwar baby boom produced more mouths to feed. Increases in food production were constant, yet never adequate. The largely socialist economy performed sluggishly, in part because the national budget continued to be drained by the cost of supporting a standing army of more than 1 million men and maintaining an occupation force in Cambodia. Adding to the difficulties, the Cambodian occupation robbed Vietnam of the international good will, loans, and aid it required to reinvigorate its economy and modernize its systems and cities. Although the spirit that allowed the Communists to prevail in the war seemed to persist, a decade after the fall of Saigon Vietnam remained one of the poorest of Asian nations.

An old French streetcar running through Hanoi picks up passengers in 1983. A 1985 visitor to Hanoi wrote that the French architecture gave the city "the look of a sleepy French provincial town. It is nothing like a capital."

At Long Binh, once U.S. Army headquarters in South Vietnam, workers recycle the steel from abandoned jeeps, tanks, planes, and trucks into reinforcing rods for use in concrete.

Weavers at the Hop Hoa carpet cooperative in Tay Ninh tie rugs for the small domestic market. Consumer goods remained scarce and overpriced in postwar Vietnam.

Right. A Soviet ship in Haiphong Harbor looms above a flotilla of fishing boats. Long into the 1980s, Soviet economic aid was one of the few factors keeping alive Vietnam's economy.

Soldiers of Vietnam's army, the world's fourth largest, line up for a "victory celebration" in Hanoi after battling Chinese invaders in Vietnam's northern provinces early in 1979.

PAVN tanks roll through Hue in 1985 in a parade recelebrating the capture of the Southern city a decade earlier.

Right. PAVN troops in postwar Vietnam performed a host of nonmilitary duties. Here, in 1985, members of the 317th Battalion work at widening Route 4 between Hanoi and Haiphong.

Relics and remains. While the Vietnamese Communists have enshrined the war effort in museums and memorials up and down the country, the people will perhaps never forget the pain inflicted by the decades of conflict. Left. One of the Vietcong's legendary feats was the construction of the vast tunnel network under Cu Chi, which the U.S. 25th Infantry Division called home between 1966 and 1970. After the war, some 100 kilometers of the underground complex became a tourist attraction. The curator of the museum, Vo Van Den, pictured here in 1985, entered the tunnels in 1945 as a member of the Vietminh and survived thirty years of war. Above. A young visitor pauses at the grave of a Communist soldier at the Truong Son Cemetery, the final resting place of more than 10,000 PAVN and PLAF dead near the former DMZ. Years after the war, estimates of Communist dead ranged from 400,000 to nearly 1 million.

Bibliography

I. Books and Articles

Addington, Dr. Larry H. "Antiaircraft Artillery Versus the Fighter-Bomber." *Army*, December 1973.

Aptheker, Herbert. *Mission to Hanoi*. International Publishers, 1966.

Ashmore, Harry S., and William C. Baggs. *Mission to Hanoi*. Putnam, 1968.

Bechir Yen Yahmed. "Hanoi's 'Business as Usual' Attitude to Bombing." *London Times*, April 17, 1967.

Berrigan, Fr. Daniel. "Fr. Daniel Berrigan on his Trip to Hanoi." *America*, March 9, 1968.

Blakey, Scott. *Prisoner at War: The Survival of Commander Richard A. Stratton*. Doubleday, 1978.

Bonds, Ray, ed. *The Vietnam War*. Crown, 1979.

Brown, John Pairman. "A Visit to the North Vietnamese." *The Christian Century*, January 3, 1968.

Brownlow, Cecil. "North Viet Air Threat Increases." *Aviation Week and Space Technology*, December 2, 1968.

Broyles, William, Jr. "The Road to Hill 10." *Atlantic Monthly*, April 1985.

Buehl, Lt. Col. Louis H. "Marxist Nation Building in the Democratic Republic of Vietnam." *Naval War College Review*, February 1970.

Burchett, Wilfred G. *Vietnam North*. International Publishers, 1967.

_____. "The Vietnam War: Past, Present, Future." *New World Review*, Spring 1968.

Burton, Lt. Col. Lance J. "North Vietnam's Military Logistics System: Its Contribution to the War, 1961–1969." Master's thesis, U.S. Command and General Staff College, 1977.

Buttinger, Joseph. *Vietnam: A Dragon Embattled*. Praeger, 1967.

Butz, J.S. "Those Bombings in North Vietnam." *Air Force*, April 1966.

Butz, Sam. "Our Pilots Call Hanoi 'Dodge City.'" *New York Times Magazine*, October 16, 1966.

Cameron, James. *Here Is Your Enemy*. Holt, Rinehart & Winston, 1966.

CBS News. "Honor, Duty and a War Called Vietnam." Broadcast April 25, 1985. Transcript.

Chaffard, Georges. "From Here to November." *Far Eastern Economic Review*, April 1, 1968.

_____. "Inside Vietcong Territory." *Viet-Report*, July 1965.

Chanda, Nayan. "A Last-Minute Rescue." *Far Eastern Economic Review*, February 27, 1981.

_____. "A Massive Shock for Vietnam." *Far Eastern Economic Review*, August 10, 1979.

_____. "No Peace Without Compromise." *Far Eastern Economic Review*, April 18, 1980.

_____. "Shake-up at the Bottom." *Far Eastern Economic Review*, April 16, 1982.

Chen, King C. "Hanoi vs. Peking: Policies and Relations—A Survey." *Asian Survey*, September 1972.

Colvin, John. "Hanoi in My Time." *The Washington Quarterly*, Spring 1981.

Conley, Michael. *The Communist Infrastructure in South Vietnam: A Study of Organization and Strategy*. American Univ. Pr., 1967.

Critchfield, Richard. "Hanoi's Peace Plan." *The New Leader*, December 30, 1968.

_____. "New Man in Hanoi." *The New Leader*, September 15, 1969.

Dawson, Alan. *55 Days*. Prentice-Hall, 1977.

Dellinger, Dave. "North Vietnam: Eyewitness Report." *Liberation*, December 1966.

_____. "The Prisoner of War Hoax." *Liberation*, December 1970.

Denton, Jeremiah A. *When Hell Was in Session*. Robert E. Hopper & Assoc., 1982.

Dommen, Arthur S. "The Future of North Vietnam." *Current History*, April 1970.

Doronila, Amando. "Hanoi Builds Supply Route Detours." *The Christian Science Monitor*, September 11, 1967.

Duiker, William J. *The Communist Road to Power in Vietnam*. Westview Pr., 1981.

Durr, John C. et al. *The North Vietnamese Regime: Institutions and Problems*. American Univ. Pr., 1969.

Elliott, David W. P. "NLF-DRV Strategy and the 1972 Spring Offensive." Interim Report #4, East Asia Project, Cornell Univ., January 1974.

_____. "North Vietnam Since Ho." *Problems of Communism*, July–August 1975.

Emmet, Christopher. "Russia's Role in Vietnam." *America*, July 29, 1967.

Fabian, Ferenc. "The Dugout Republic." *Far Eastern Economic Review*, May 11, 1967.

Face to Face with U.S. Armed Forces, I. Vietnamese Studies, No. 54, Foreign Languages Publishing House, 1979.

Face to Face with U.S. Armed Forces, II. Vietnamese Studies, No. 57, Foreign Languages Publishing House, 1980.

Fall, Bernard B. "Introduction." In *Primer for Revolt*, by Truong Chinh. Praeger, 1963.

_____. "North Vietnam: A Profile." *Problems of Communism*, July–August 1965.

_____. "Power and Pressure Groups in North Vietnam." In *North Vietnam Today*, edited by P. J. Honey. Praeger, 1962.

_____. "Report on North Vietnam: The Other Side of the 17th Parallel." *New York Times Magazine*, July 10, 1966.

_____. *The Two Vietnams*. Praeger, 1967.

_____. *Vietnam Witness, 1953–1966*. Praeger, 1966.

Feinberg, Rabbi Abraham I. *Hanoi Diary*. Longmans, 1967.

FitzGerald, Frances. *Fire in the Lake*. Vintage, 1972.

_____. "Journey to North Vietnam." *The New Yorker*, April 28, 1974.

Fonda, Jane. "Vietnam Journal: Rebirth of a Nation." *Rolling Stone*, July 4, 1974.

Friedman, Phoebe L. "Life Today in North Vietnam." *Nation*, December 10, 1973.

Gerassi, John. *North Vietnam: A Documentary*. Bobbs-Merrill, 1968.

_____. "Report From North Vietnam." *New Republic*, March 4, 1967.

Gervasi, Tom. *Arsenal of Democracy*. Grove Pr., 1981.

Glaubitz, Joachim. "Relations Between Communist China and Vietnam." In *Vietnam and the Sino-Soviet Dispute*, edited by Robert A. Rupen and Robert Farrell. Praeger, 1967.

Goodman, Allan E. *The Lost Peace*. Hoover Inst. Pr., 1978.

Goodstadt, Leo. "The Offensive Russians." *Far Eastern Economic Review*, October 9, 1971.

_____. "A War Between Lips and Teeth." *Far Eastern Economic Review*, January 8, 1973.

Gurtov, Melvin. "Hanoi on War and Peace." In *Vietnam and American Foreign Policy*, edited by John R. Boettinger. D. C. Heath, 1968.

Hai-Thu. *North Vietnam Against the U.S. Air Force*. Foreign Languages Publishing House, 1967.

Heneghan, George Martin. "Nationalism, Communism and the National Liberation Front: Dilemma for American Foreign Policy." Diss., 1970.

Hoang Son. "Re-education Camps and Human Rights in Vietnam: Which Human Rights?" *Vietnam Courier*, 1980.

Honey, P. J. *Communism in North Vietnam*. MIT Pr., 1963.

_____. *North Vietnam Quarterly, China News Analysis*. 1965–1982.

_____. "The Position of the DRV Leadership and the Succession to Ho Chi Minh." In *North Vietnam Today*, edited by P. J. Honey. Praeger, 1962.

In the Face of American Aggression, 1965–1967. Vietnamese Studies, No. 16, Foreign Languages Publishing House, 1968.

Joiner, Charles A. "Political Processes in the Two Vietnams." *Current History*, December 1970.

Jones, P. H. M. "As the North Sees It." *Far Eastern Economic Review*, March 18, 1965.

_____. "Hanoi's Options." *Far Eastern Economic Review*, February 2, 1969.

Julien, Claude. "Nous voulons réserver à Washington une issue honorable." *Le Monde*, May 18, 1972.

Kahin, George McTurnan, and John W. Lewis. *The United States in Vietnam*. Dell, 1967.

Karnow, Stanley. *Vietnam: A History*. Viking Pr., 1983.

Kelman, Steven. "'Viet Report' and the Lynd Mission." *The New Leader*, January 17, 1966.

Kissinger, Henry A. "The Viet Nam Negotiations." *Foreign Affairs*, January 1969.

_____. *The White House Years*. Little, Brown, 1979.

_____. *Years of Upheaval*. Little, Brown, 1982.

Knoebl, Kuno. *Victor Charlie: The Face of War in Vietnam*. Translated by Abe Farbstein. Praeger, 1967.

Kofsky, Frank. "Vietnam and Social Revolution." *Monthly Review*, March 1967.

Lacouture, Jean. *Ho Chi Minh*. Penguin Bks., 1968.

Lamont, Nicholas S. "On Communist Organization and Strategy in South Vietnam." *Public and International Affairs*, Spring 1965.

Latimer, Thomas Kennedy. "Hanoi's Leaders and their South Vietnam Policies: 1954–1968." Diss., 1972.

Le Duan. *On the Socialist Revolution in Vietnam*. 3 vols. Foreign Languages Publishing House, 1965.

_____. *Selected Writings*. Foreign Languages Publishing House, 1972.

Lewy, Guenter. *America in Vietnam*. Oxford Univ. Pr., 1978.

Livingston, David, Harold Gibbons, and Clifton Caldwell. "Labor Mission to Hanoi." *Nation*, April 24, 1972.

Lockwood, Lee. "North Vietnam Under Siege." *Life*, April 17, 1967.

_____. "Salisbury's Stake." *The New York Review of Books*, August 3, 1967.

London, Kurt. "Vietnam: A Sino-Soviet Dilemma." *Russian Review* 26(January 1967).

Loridan, Marceline. "Two Months on the Seventeenth Parallel." *L'Humanite Dimanche*. November 1967.

Lynd, Staughton, and Thomas Hayden. *The Other Side*. NAL, 1966.

McCarthy, Mary. "Hanoi: 1968." *The New York Review of Books*, May 23, 1968.

_____. "Hanoi II." *The New York Review of Books*, June 6, 1968.

_____. "North Vietnam: The Countryside." *The New York Review of Books*, June 20, 1968.

_____. *The Seventeenth Degree*. Harcourt Brace Jovanovich, 1974.

McGarvey, Patrick J. *Visions of Victory: Selected Vietnamese Communist Military Writings, 1964–1968*. Hoover Institution on War, Revolution and Peace, Stanford Univ., 1969.

Maneli, Mieczslaw. *War of the Vanquished*. Harper & Row, 1971.

Mau, Michael P. "The Training of Cadres in the Lao Dong Party of North Vietnam." *Asian Survey*, April 1972.

Mersky, Peter B., and Norman Polmar. *The Naval Air War in Vietnam*. The Nautical and Aviation Publishing Co., 1981.

Meyers, William. "November in Hanoi." *Nation*, December 8, 1969.

Moskin, J. Robert. "An Enemy Land at War." *Look*, July 25, 1967.

Mulligan, Capt. James A. *The Hanoi Commitment*. RIF Marketing, 1981.

Myozo, Mori. "The Logic and Psychology of North Vietnam." *The Japan Quarterly*, July–September 1967.

Niemoller, Martin. "Vietnam As I Saw It." *New Times*, March 1, 1967.

O'Ballance, Maj. Edgar. "The Ho Chi Minh Trail." *The Army Quarterly and Defense Journal* 94, no. 1(April 1967).

Oberdorfer, Don. *Tet*. Doubleday, 1971.

Ojha, Ishwer. "China and North Vietnam: The Limits of the Alliance." *Current History*, January 1968.

O'Neill, Robert J. *General Giap*. Praeger, 1969.

An Outline of Institutions of the DRVN. Foreign Languages Publishing House, 1974.

Papp, Daniel S. *Vietnam: The View from Moscow, Peking, Washington*. McFarland & Co., 1981.

Peterson, Iver. "The Bomber Pilots Like Their Work." *New York Times Magazine*, March 19, 1972.

Phan Thien Chau. "Leadership in the Viet Nam Workers Party: The Process of Transition." *Asian Survey*, September 1972.

Pike, Douglas. *History of Vietnamese Communism, 1925–1976*. Hoover Inst. Pr., 1978.

_____. "North Vietnam in 1971." *Asian Survey*, January 1972.

_____. "North Vietnam in the Year 1972." *Asian Survey*, January 1973.

————. *PAVN: People's Army of Vietnam.* Presidio Pr., 1986.

————. "Road to Victory." *War in Peace,* 60(1984).

————. "The Tet Offensive and the Escalation of the Vietnam War, 1965–1968: View from Hanoi." Paper, 1978.

————. *Viet Cong: The Organization and Technique of the National Liberation Front of South Vietnam.* MIT Pr., 1966.

————. *War, Peace, and the Vietcong.* MIT Pr., 1969.

————. "Years of Uncertainty." *War in Peace,* 48(1983).

Ping, Liu. "The Maoists and the North Vietnamese Communists." *Asian Outlook,* March 1971.

Porter, Gareth, ed. *Vietnam: The Definitive Documentation of Human Decisions.* 2 vols. Earl M. Coleman Enterprises, Inc., 1979.

Pratt, Lawrence. "North Vietnam and Sino-Soviet Tension." *Behind the Lines,* August 1967.

Race, Jeffrey. "The Origins of the Second Indochina War." *Asian Survey,* May 1970.

Raskin, Marcus G., and Bernard B. Fall, eds. *Viet-Nam Reader.* Random House, 1965.

Salisbury, Harrison E. *Behind the Lines: Hanoi.* Harper & Row, 1967.

Santoli, Al. *To Bear Any Burden.* E. P. Dutton, 1985.

Schoenbrun, David. "Journey to North Vietnam." *Saturday Evening Post,* December 16, 1967.

Shaplen, Robert. *The Lost Revolution.* Harper & Row, 1955.

————. *The Road From War: Vietnam 1965–1970.* Harper & Row, 1970.

Sharp, Adm. U.S.G. *Strategy for Defeat.* Presidio Pr., 1978.

Sheehan, Susan. *Ten Vietnamese.* Knopf, 1967.

Simler, Maj. Gen. George B. "North Vietnam's Air Defense System." *Air Force,* May 1967.

Smith, Melden E., Jr. "The Strategic Bombing Debate: World War II and Vietnam." *Journal of Contemporary History,* January 1977.

Snepp, Frank. *Decent Interval.* Random House, 1977.

Sontag, Susan. "Trip to Hanoi." *Esquire,* December 1969.

Spitz, Allan. "North Vietnamese Regime, Expansion vs. Consolidation." *Asian Studies,* January 1970.

Spragens, John, Jr. "Looking Ahead." *Southeast Asia Chronicle* 76(December 1980).

Stern, Kurt, and Jeanne Stern. *Ricefields, Battlefield: A Visit to North Vietnam.* Seven Seas Publishers, 1969.

Stockdale, Vice Adm. James B. *A Vietnam Experience.* Hoover Inst. Pr., 1984.

Stockdale, James B., and Sybil Stockdale. *In Love and War.* Harper & Row, 1984.

Tanham, George K. *Communist Revolutionary Warfare: From the Viet Minh to the Viet Cong.* Praeger, 1967.

Taylor, Telford. "Reports and Comments—North Vietnam." *Atlantic Monthly,* May 1973.

Thayer, Carlyle A. "Origin of the National Liberation Front: Debate on Unification within the Vietnam Workers' Party." *Vietnam Report,* Vietnam Council on Foreign Relations, July–August 1974.

Thompson, James Clay. *Rolling Thunder—Understanding Policy and Programming Failures.* Univ. of North Carolina Pr., 1980.

Ton That Thien. "Vietnam's New Economic Policy." *Pacific Affairs,* Winter 1983–1984.

Tran Van Tra. *Vietnam: History of the Bulwark B-2 Theater.* Vol. 5. GPO, 1983.

Trang Tran Nhu. "The Transformation of the Peasantry in North Vietnam." Diss., University of Pittsburgh, 1972.

Truong Chinh. *Forward Along the Path Charted by Karl Marx.* Foreign Languages Publishing House, 1969.

Truong Nhu Tang. *A Vietcong Memoir.* Harcourt Brace Jovanovich, 1985.

Turley, William S. "Army, Party and Society in the Democratic Republic of Vietnam." Diss., 1972.

————. "Civil-Military Relations in North Vietnam." *Asian Survey,* December 1969.

————. "The Democratic Republic of Vietnam and the Third Stage of the Revolution." *Asian Survey,* January 1974.

————. "Hanoi's Domestic Dilemmas." *Problems of Communism,* July–August 1980.

————. "Vietnam Since Reunification." *Problems of Communism,* March–April 1977.

————. "Women in the Communist Revolution in Vietnam." *Asian Survey,* September 1972.

Turner, Robert F. *Vietnamese Communism, Its Origins and Development.* Hoover Inst. Pr., 1975.

Van Dyke, Jon M. "The Bombing of Vietnam." *Center Magazine,* July–August 1970.

————. *North Vietnam's Strategy for Survival.* Pacific Bks., 1972.

Van Tien Dung. *Our Great Spring Victory.* Translated by Cora Weiss. Monthly Review Pr., 1977.

————. "People's War Against Air War of Destruction." *Vietnamese Studies,* No. 20, Foreign Languages Publishing House, 1968.

Vietnam: The Anti-U.S. Resistance War. People's Army Publishing House, 1982.

"Vietnam's Economy Entangled in Red Tape." *Business Review,* October 1984.

Vo Bam. "Opening the Trail." *Vietnam Courier,* May 1984.

Vo Nguyen Giap. *People's War Against the U.S.: Aero-Naval War.* Foreign Languages Publishing House, 1975.

————. *Selected Writings.* Foreign Languages Publishing House, 1977.

Vo Nhan Tri. "Wartime Economy of the DRV." *International Affairs,* February 1969.

Westmoreland, Gen. William C. *A Soldier Reports.* Dell, 1980.

Wohl, Paul. "Bomb Damage Minimized." *The Christian Science Monitor,* December 6, 1968.

Yamashita, Masao. "Glimpses of the Internal Situation in North Vietnam." *Pacific Community,* July 1971.

Zagoria, Donald. *Vietnam Triangle.* Pegasus, 1967.

Zasloff, Joseph J., and MacAlister Brown, eds. *Communism in Indochina.* Lexington Bks., 1975.

Zasloff, Joseph J., and Allan E. Goodman, eds. *Indochina in Conflict: A Political Assessment.* Lexington Bks., 1972.

II. Government and Government-Sponsored Publications

BDM Corporation. *A Study of Strategic Lessons Learned in Vietnam.* Vol. 1, The Enemy. National Technical Information Service, 1979.

Burbage, Maj. Paul et al. *The Battle for the Skies Over North Vietnam, 1964–1972.* Vol. 1, Monograph 2, USAF Southeast Asia Monograph Series, 1976.

Cao Van Vien. *The Final Collapse.* Indochina Monographs, U.S. Army Center of Military History, 1983.

Doglione, Col. John A. et al. *Airpower and the 1972 Spring Invasion.* Vol. 2, Monograph 3, USAF Southeast Asia Monograph Series, 1976.

Donnell, John C., and Melvin Gurtov. *North Vietnam: Left of Moscow, Right of Peking.* Rand Corporation, P-3794, February 1968.

Hoang Ngoc Lung. *Intelligence.* Indochina Monographs, U.S. Army Center of Military History, 1976.

————. *Strategy and Tactics.* Indochina Monographs, U.S. Army Center of Military History, 1978.

Hoeffding, Oleg. *Bombing North Vietnam: An Appraisal of Economic and Political Effects.* Rand Corporation, RM-5213-I-ISA, December 1966.

Jenkins, Brian. *Why the North Vietnamese Will Keep Fighting.* Rand Corporation, P-4395-1, March 1972.

Kellen, Konrad. *Conversations With Enemy Soldiers in Late 1968/Early 1969.* Rand Corporation, RM-6131-1, September 1970.

————. *A Profile of the PAVN Soldier in South Vietnam.* Rand Corporation, RM-5013-1-ISA/ARPA, June 1966.

LeGro, Col. William E. *Vietnam from Cease-Fire to Capitulation.* U.S. Army Center of Military History, 1981.

Momyer, Gen. William W. *Air Power in Three Wars (World War II, Korea, Vietnam).* USAF Southeast Asia Monograph Series, 1978.

————. *The Vietnamese Air Force, 1951–1975, An Analysis of Its Role in Combat.* Vol. 3, Monograph 4, USAF Southeast Asia Monograph Series, 1976.

Nguyen Duy Hinh. *Lam Son 719.* Indochina Monographs, U.S. Army Center of Military History, 1979.

Sharp, Adm. U.S.G. *Report on the War in Vietnam (As of 30 June 1968)—Section 1.* Washington, D.C., 1968.

Smith, Harvey et al. *Area Handbook for North Vietnam.* GPO, June 1966.

Soutchay Vongsavanh. *RLG Military Operations and Activities in the Laotian Panhandle.* Indochina Monographs, U.S. Army Center of Military History, 1981.

Sweetland, A. *Rallying Potential Among the North Vietnamese Armed Forces.* Rand Corporation, RM-6375-1, December 1970.

U.S. Congress. Senate. *Air War Against North Vietnam.* Hearings, 90th Cong., 1st sess., 1967.

————. Committee on Armed Services. *Air War Against North Vietnam.* Hearings before Preparedness Subcommittee, 90th Cong., 1st sess., 1967.

U.S. Department of Defense. *United States-Vietnam Relations 1945–1967.* GPO, 1971.

U.S. Department of State. *Aggression From the North: The Record of North Viet-Nam's Campaign To Conquer South Viet-Nam.* DOS Publication 7839, Far Eastern Series 130, 1965.

————. *Communist-Directed Forces in South Viet-Nam.* Viet-Nam Information Notes, Number 3. Office of Media Series, Bureau of Public Affairs, 1968.

————. *The Heart of the Problem. . . . Secretary Rusk, General Taylor Review Viet-Nam Policy in Senate Hearings,* Far Eastern Series 146, n.d.

————. *Southeast Asia Reports* (Various). Foreign Broadcast Information Service, 1965–1980.

————. *A Threat to the Peace: North Viet-Nam's Effort To Conquer South Viet-Nam.* Part 2. Far Eastern Series 110, 1961.

————. *Vietnam Documents and Research Notes.* GPO, n.d.

————. Office of the Historian. *Interrogation and Document Items, 89 and 103.* GPO, n.d.

Zasloff, J. J. *Political Motivation of the Viet Cong: The Vietminh Regroupees.* Rand Corporation RM-4703/2-ISA/ARPA, 1968.

III. Periodicals Consulted

The Christian Science Monitor, 1965–1973; *The Economist,* 1965–1985; *Far Eastern Economic Review,* 1965–1985; *The New York Times,* 1965–1985; *Newsweek,* 1965–1975; *Time,* 1965–1975; *U.S. News and World Reports,* 1965–1975; and *The Washington Post,* 1965–1985.

IV. Archives

Indochina Archive of the Institute of East Asian Studies, University of California, Berkeley The following sections of the archive were consulted by the authors:

Vietnam War
Assessment and Strategy
General
National Liberation Front
External Relations
North Vietnam and the Socialist Republic of Vietnam
Armed Forces
Social Movements and Mass Organizations
Foreign Relations
Cities
Culture
Security
Politics
Party
Government
Ideology
Communications and Propaganda
Emulation Movements
Economy
Asia/China/U.S.S.R./Japan/Southeast Asia
Biography

Chronology of Political and Military Events

August 1945	Ho Chi Minh proclaims independence of Democratic Republic of Vietnam.
September 1945–July 1954	French Indochina War.
February 1951	*Second Party Congress*. Lao Dong party formed.
July 22, 1954	Geneva accords establish provisional boundaries between Democratic Republic of Vietnam and new Republic of Vietnam.
July 1954	*Sixth Plenum*. Southern Vietminh ordered to support elections as means to unite North and South Vietnam.
April 1956	*Ninth Plenum*. Central Committee rejects Le Duan's appeal to initiate military action in South Vietnam.
January 1957	*Eleventh Plenum*. Central Committee approves Le Duan's *Path of Revolutionary Violence in the South*, advocating an aggressive policy against Diem.
January 1959	*Fifteenth Plenum*. Party endorses "all appropriate means" to bring about the downfall of the "American-Diem" regime.
September 1960	*Third Party Congress*. Party decides to carry out socialist revolution in the North and liberate the South through military force.
December 20, 1960	National Liberation Front formed.
November 1, 1963	Diem overthrown by ARVN generals.
December 1963	*Ninth Plenum*. Le Duan's political report elevates the war in the South to the party's highest priority.
August 7, 1964	U.S. Congress adopts Southeast Asia Resolution.
December 1964	Elements of 325th PAVN Division enter South Vietnam.
February 1965	Evacuation of North Vietnam cities begins.
March 1965	U.S. bombing campaign Rolling Thunder begins.
December 1965	*Twelfth Plenum*. Party calls for "decisive victory within a relatively short period of time."
December 1966–January 1967	*Thirteenth Plenum*. Party endorses diplomatic struggle and calls for "decisive victory . . . in the shortest time possible."
October–November 1967	Phase one of winter-spring offensive. Main force battles at Dak To, Loc Ninh, and Con Thien.
January–February 1968	Phase two of winter-spring offensive. Major PLAF onslaught against South Vietnamese cities and towns.
March 31, 1968	President Johnson announces end to the bombing of North Vietnam, U.S. desire for peace talks, and his retirement.
April 1968	Alliance of National Democratic and Peace Forces founded.
May 5, 1968	Phase three of winter-spring campaign. In Hanoi, Truong Chinh criticizes Le Duan and advocates a return to protracted guerrilla warfare.
November 1, 1968	U.S. halts bombing of North Vietnam.
April 1969	Party "Resolution C" outlines shift in strategy from main force offensives to limited military thrusts.
June 8, 1969	President Nixon announces the withdrawal of 25,000 American combat troops.
June 10, 1969	Provisional Revolutionary Government formed.
July 1, 1969	"Vietnamization" policy goes into effect in South Vietnam.
September 3, 1969	Death of Ho Chi Minh.
February 3, 1970	Le Duan, on the fortieth anniversary of Indochinese Communist party, reaffirms collective leadership and endorses technical modernization of PAVN.
April 30–June 30, 1970	U.S. incursion into Cambodia.
February 8–March 25, 1971	U.S. supports Lam Son 719—ARVN invasion into Laos.
July 15, 1971	President Nixon announces visit to China.
October 1971	Soviet President Podgorny visits Hanoi and promises more sophisticated arms to the DRV.
March 30, 1972	PAVN launches Easter offensive.
April 6, 1972	U.S. initiates Operation Linebacker.
May 8, 1972	Nixon announces mining of North Vietnam's harbors.
December 18–30, 1972	Christmas bombing of North Vietnam.
January 27, 1973	Agreement on Ending the War and Restoring Peace in Vietnam is signed.
October 1973	*Twenty-first Plenum*. Party decides "(T)he revolutionary path of the South is the path of revolutionary violence."
December 18, 1974–January 8, 1975	Two-year offensive against South Vietnam planned by Political Bureau and Central Military Committee.
April 30, 1975	Saigon occupied by PAVN troops.
July 1975	*Twenty-fourth Plenum*. Five-year plan drafted (1975–1980).
June 24, 1976	Unified National Assembly convenes. Country renamed Socialist Republic of Vietnam.
December 14–20, 1976	*Fourth Party Congress*. Lao Dong party renamed Communist party of Vietnam. Political Bureau membership expanded. Five-year plan officially approved.
March 1978	Party orders private trade ended.
June 29, 1978	Vietnam joins COMECON.
December 21, 1978	Vietnamese invasion of Cambodia.
February 17, 1979	Chinese invasion of Vietnam.
March 3, 1979	General mobilization of Vietnamese society.
July 1979	Former Political Bureau member Hoang Van Hoan defects to China.
September 1979	*Sixth Plenum*. Freer economic policies approved on a limited scale.
December 1980	*Ninth Plenum*. Sweeping directives liberalizing the economy signal rise of "pragmatists" in Political Bureau.
March 1982	*Fifth Party Congress*. New five-year plan (1980–1985) announced. Middle-level party purge and reorganization.

Photography Credits

Cover Photo
Nihon Denpa News, Ltd.

The Long Revolution
pp. 6–12, Ngo Vinh Long Collection.

The Brink of War
pp. 15–24, Vietnam News Agency. p. 25, Camera Press Ltd. p. 28, Eastfoto. p. 29, AP/Wide World. p. 33, Vietnam News Agency. p. 36, AP/Wide World.

A Race Against Time
p. 39, Alan Hutchinson Library. p. 41, Camera Press Ltd. p. 42, Vietnam News Agency. p. 47, top, Eastfoto; bottom, Vietnam News Agency. p. 49, James H. Pickerell Collection. p. 51, J. P. Moscardo—Black Star. p. 52, Jerry Rose—Courtesy Life Picture Service. p. 53, UPI/Bettmann Newsphotos. p. 57, Bunyo Ishikawa. p. 58, Ngo Vinh Long Collection. p. 60, Camera Press Ltd.

Ho Chi Minh Trail
p. 62, Ngo Vinh Long Collection. p. 64, Vietnam News Agency. p. 66, Nihon Denpa News, Ltd. p. 67, Vietnam News Agency.

Fortress North Vietnam
p. 69, Thomas Billhardt, GDR. p. 70, Black Star. p. 71, AP/Wide World. p. 73, Sovfoto. p. 75, AP/Wide World. pp. 76–77, Thomas Billhardt, GDR. p. 79, Lee Lockwood. p. 80, Lee Lockwood. p. 83, Vietnam News Agency. p. 84, AP/Wide World. p. 85, UPI/Bettmann Newsphotos. p. 87, Sovfoto. p. 88, Roger Pic. pp. 90–91, Sovfoto. p. 93, Marc Riboud—Magnum.

Mobilizing the Home Front
p. 95, Marc Riboud—Magnum. p. 97, Marc Riboud. p. 98, Lee Lockwood. p. 100, Nihon Denpa News, Ltd. p. 103, Marc Riboud—Magnum. p. 105, top, AP/Wide World; bottom left, Lee Lockwood—Black Star; bottom right, Marc Riboud. p. 108, Sovfoto. pp. 109–10, Marc Riboud. p. 113, top, Harrison Salisbury Collection; bottom, Gerard Guillaume—Magnum. p. 115, Marc Riboud. p. 117, Thomas Billhardt, GDR.

The North Takes Over
p. 119, Nihon Denpa News, Ltd. p. 120, Don McCullin—Magnum. p. 121, Ray Cranbourne—Black Star. p. 123, UPI/Bettmann Newsphotos. p. 125, © Larry Burrows Collection. p. 126, AP/Wide World. p. 129, Henri Bureau—SYGMA. p. 133, Marc Riboud. p. 134, Vietnam News Agency. p. 135, Agence France-Presse. p. 137, Photoreporters.

Easter Offensive
p. 138, Agence France-Presse. pp. 140–42, Vietnam News Agency. p. 144, Ngo Vinh Long Collection.

The Road to Saigon
p. 147, Vietnam News Agency—John Spragens, Jr., Collection. p. 149, © 1983 David Burnett—Contact Press Images. p. 152, Marc Riboud—Magnum. p. 153, Roger Pic. p. 154, Gamma-Liaison. p. 158, Vietnam News Agency. p. 159, Ngo Vinh Long Collection. p. 161, Agence Vietnamienne d'Information.

The Fruits of Victory
p. 163, Marc Riboud—Magnum. p. 165, Abbas—Magnum. p. 166, Marc Riboud—Magnum. p. 170, Jean-Claude Labbe/Gamma-Liaison. p. 171, Roger Pic. p. 173, Ngo Vinh Long Collection. p. 175, Nihon Denpa News, Ltd. p. 176, SYGMA.

A Restive Peace
p. 178, Eddie Adams—TIME Magazine. p. 180, top, Greg Davis; bottom, © 1976 Abbas—Contact Press Images. p. 181, © Tim Page. p. 182, top, © 1979 J. W. Lower—Contact Press Images; bottom, © Christopher Pillitz—The Picture Group, Inc. p. 183, © Tim Page. pp. 184–85, Dirck Halstead/Gamma-Liaison.

Maps on pp. 4–5 and chart and map on pp. 44–45 prepared by Diane McCaffery.

Acknowledgements

Boston Publishing Company would like to acknowledge the kind assistance of the following people: Dick Berry, Tokyo; Stephen Denney, Archivist, Indochina Archive, University of California, Berkeley; Do Hoi, Bureau Chief, Vietnam News Agency, New York; Elisabeth Kraemer-Singh, Time-Life Bureau, Bonn; Phan Manh Hung, Correspondent, Vietnam News Agency, New York; Douglas Pike, Director of the Indochina Archive, University of California, Berkeley.

Index

A

"Action Program," 131
A–4D aircraft, 77
Agence France Presse, 82
Air raids, 74, *76*, 77, *77*
AK47 assault rifle, 43, 46
Alliance of National, Democratic and Peace
    Forces, 122
Anderson, Ed, 108
An Loc, 138, *142, 143,* 148
Antiaircraft artillery, *58, 59, 83*
An Xuyen Province, 18
Aptheker, Herbert, 112
Armed Youth Assault Force, 170
ARVN, 53, 61, 126, 135, 136, 138, 156–58, 160
A Shau Valley, 134
Attentisme, 26
AT-3 "Sagger" rocket, 144

B

Bac Giang bridge, *83*
"Bach Dang Shipyard," *12–13*
Baggs, William, 82
Ban Me Thuot, 157, 158
Base Area 611, 46
Base Area 614, 46
Base Area 604, 46
Base Area 609, 46
Ben Cat, 160
Berrigan, Father Daniel, 112
B–57 light bomber, *52*
B–52 bomber, 77, 108, 148, 149, 151
Bien Hoa, *52, 159*
Binh Dinh Province, 57
Binh Tram, 32
Binh van, 50
"Boat people," 169
Boyd, Captain Charles, 116
Brezhnev, Leonid, 92
British Broadcasting Corporation, 112
Brown, John, 107
Bunker, Ellsworth, 128
Burchett, Wilfred, 73, 74
Burkov, Major N. P., *87*
Butterfield, Fox, 82
Butz, Sam, 84

C

Cabanes, B. J., 82
Cambodia, 136, 170, 171, *171,* 178
Cameron, James, 71, 72, 77, 88
"Campaign X," 135
Camp Carroll, 141, 148
Carmichael, Stokely, 108
Casualties, of Rolling Thunder, 82, 87; of Commu-
    nist offensive, 120, *122, 123;* of phase three, 124; of
    the North, 149, *149,* 150, 164, 185, *185*
Cat airfield, 84
Catbi, 86
Central Committee, orders Diem's downfall, 20;
    role in hierarchy, *45;* holds plenum, 51–53; de-
    centralizes, 94; plans offensive, 156; confronts
    debt, 165, 167, 172, 173; purges members, 174
Central Committee for Nam Bo, 16
Central Information Bureau, 106
Central Market, 116
Central Military Party Committee, 27, 44, *45,* 146,
    155, 156
Central Office for South Vietnam (COSVN), estab-
    lished, 16, *17,* 27; intelligence operations of, 26,
    28; calls for aggression, 35, 59; role in hierarchy,
    44, 45; cautions PLAF, 130
Central Research Agency (CRA), 26, 27
Central Reunification Committee, 44
Central Reunification Department, *44, 45*
China, gives less aid to the North, 34, 148, 169; dis-
    putes with Soviets, 40; trains AAA crews, 84; aids
    the North, 92, 93, *93,* 168; invades Vietnam, 171
Chingh–Nghia, 112
Cholon, 169
Chou En-lai, 148
Christmas bombings, 12, 150, 151
Chu Huy Man, Colonel General, 168, 174
Church-Case amendment, 136, 156
Chu Van Tan, General, 172
Colvin, John, 77
Combat Standing teams, 84
"Combat villages," 74
Combined Documents Exploitation Center, 30, 31
Committee for the Supervision of the South, 27
Common Sense Science, 74
Communists, use lacquer as propaganda, *6, 6, 7, 7,
    8, 185;* increase activity, 16, 18; collectivize all
    farmland, 19, *19;* on Ho Chi Minh Trail, *33;* infil-
    trate South, 38, *42, 43,* 46, 47, 52, 53, 155, 160;
    three-phase plan of, 58, 59, 61; mural, *110, 111;*
    soldiers, *119, 122, 123;* on peace, 146, 154; im-
    prove position, 156; troubled, 176
Conference of Communist and Workers' Parties,
    34
Con Thien, 59, 124
Contract systems, 172, 173
Convoy of Tears, 158, 159
Cooper-Church amendment, 136
COSVN (See Central Office for South Vietnam)
Criticism/self-criticism sessions, 48, 50
Cu Chi, *184*
Cultural Relations Ministry, 88
Cuu Long, 56

D

Dak To, 59, 124, 138, *144, 145*
Da Lat, 165
Da Nang, 159, *165*
Dan van, 50
Dau tranh, 50, 51, 53, 59, 61, 124, 126, 128, 130, 136
Decornoy, Jacques, 71
Dellinger, Dave, 82, 112
Democratic Republic of Vietnam (DRV), devel-
    opment of, *24,* 26, 28, 32; Four Points of, 56; in-
    creases antiaircraft artillery, 84, *84,* 85, 86; role of
    women in, 88, 99, 104; as a military society, *95,*
    101, 102, 104, *105,* 113, 115; black market in, 114,
    115, *115;* reconstruction of, 116
Deng Xiaoping, 171
Dich van, 50, 51, 124
Do Muoi, 168, 169, 174
Dong Hoi, *75, 84*
Don Luan, 157
Doronila, Amando, 78
Do Tien Hao, 82
DRV (See Democratic Republic of Vietnam)
DRV High Command, 44
Duc Phong, 157
Duong Vien, *10*

E

Easter offensive, 10, 138, *138, 140,* 141, *141,* 142, *142,*

143, 144, *144*, *145*, *149*
Evacuation, 72, 73, *73*, 74, 75, *75*, 76, *76*, 77, *77*, 78, 79, *79*
Evacuees, 74, 77, 78, 79, 113

F
Facts and Events, 112
Far Eastern Economic Review, 172, 173
F–4C Phantom jet, 68
Fifteenth Plenum, 19, 20, 29
Fifth Congress, 173, 174, 175, *175*, 176
57MM artillery, 92
Fighting Vietnam, 112
Fonda, Jane, 112, *113*
F–105 aircraft, 77
Ford, Gerald R., 157
Foreign Affairs, 124
"Four Point" plan, 55, 56
Fourth Party Congress, 167–69
FUNK (Front Uni National du Kampuchea) (See also Khmer Rouge), 135

G
Garwood, Robert, 31
General Logistics Directorate, 43
General Political Directorate, 102
General Staff, 43
General Training Directorate, 43
Geneva accords, 14, *15*, 16
Geneva Conference, 32
Gia Lam airfield, 84
Gorbachev, Mikhail, 175, *175*, 176
Greene, Felix, 82
Guerrilla warfare, 8, 56, 61

H
Ha Gia, 68
Hai Duong Province, 101, 104
Haiphong, 70, 72, 74, *77*, 82, 98, *99*, 149–51, 173, *180*, *181*, *182*, *183*
Hanoi, bombed, 68, 70, *70*, 71, *71*, *152*, *153*, *178*, *179*, *182*, *183*; evacuated, 71, 72, *73*, 79; air raids in, 77, *80*, *81*, 82, *83*; convoy in, 88, *89*; approaches Soviets, 92; disagrees with China, 93, 148, 172; cloth, *115*; smells victory, 146; demands on the South, 150; makes Tra head of PRG, 164; casualties of, 164
"Hanoi Hannah," 108
Hanoi Hilton, 108
Hanoi Moi, 114, 115
Hanoi Polytechnic University, 72, 116
Hanoi watchers, 30, 31
Harriman, W. Averell, 127
Hayden, Tom, 112
Hay Tay Province, 102
"Heart and the Gun, The," *8–9*
Heng Samrin, 175
Hersh, Seymour, 112
Highway, 13, *142*, *143*
Hoa, 168, 169
Hoa Binh Province, 74
Hoalia, 86
Hoang Minh Giam, 106, 107
Hoang Tung, 171
Hoang Van Hoan, 22, 132, 168, 172
Hoang Van Thai, Senior General, 54, 170
Ho Chi Minh, in 1950's, 16; as Northern–firster, 17–19, 56, 94, 99; as leader, 24, *24*, 25, *25*, 34, 92; likes three-phase plan, 59; meets with Soviets, *91*; poster of, *93*; honors civilians, 109; on bombing halt, 130; dies, 131
Ho Chi Minh Campaign, 160
Ho Chi Minh Trail, 29, 32, *33*, 46, *62*, *63*, *65*, *66*, *67*, 150, 155
Ho Chi Minh Youth Brigade, 168, 169
Hoc Tap, 24, 54, 106, 146
Honey, P. J., 101
Hop Hoa carpet cooperative, *180*

Hue, 16, *119*, 120, *120*, *122*, *123*, 159
Huynh Tan Phat, 122, 131
Huynh Van Gam, *8*

I
Independence Palace, 160, *160*, *161*
International Monetary Fund, 172
International War Crime Tribunal, 82

J
Johnson, Lyndon, 70, 112, 124, 128

K
Kep airfield, 84, 86
Khe Sanh, 61, 118, 120
Khmer Rouge, 135, 169, *170*, 171, *171*
Khoi Nghia, 50, 51, 120, 122
Khrushchev, Nikita, 18, 19, 34
Kien An airfield, 84, 86
Kien Hoa Province, 22
Kim Dong, 112
Kissinger, Henry, 127, *129*, 131, 148, 150, 151
Kontum, 138, 148
Kosygin, N. S. (Aleksei), 90, *90*, *91*, 92

L
Labor Youth Group, 101
Lacquer painting, *6–7*, *7–13*
Land reform, 19, *19*
Lao Cai, 171
Lao Dong party, establishes COSVN, 16; authorizes strategy, 19, *19*, 20, 22–24, 34, 51, 71; leaders, *22*, *23*; secures positions, 29; delegation to Moscow, 43, 91; structure, *44*, *45*, 48, *94*, *96*; self-criticism in, 101; propaganda of, 106, 107, 109, *109*, *110*, *111*; after Ho dies, 131, 132; on peace treaty, 154; wins, 162; confronts national debt, 165, 167
Laos, *62*, *63*, 136
Le Duan, life history of, 14, 16; wants Diem overthrown, 17, *17*; writes, 18; on missions for party, 19, 22, 24; wants war, 35, 37, 40, 43, *52*, 55, 56; meets with Soviets, *91*, 92, 175, *175*, 176, *176*, *177*; on China, 93; on economy, 114, 115, 165, 172, 174; challenged, 126; predicts U.S. departure, 156; permits tanks in battle, 157; cables Dung, 159
Le Duc Tho, as Political Bureau member, 16, *17*, 23, 27; on cadres, 99, 101; at peace talks, 128, *129*, 131, 150, 151, *154*, *155*; plans offensive, 155, 160; plans for economy, 165; reports on party, 174
Le Monde, 71
Le Quang Ba, General, 172
Le Quang Nghi, *23*, 132, 174
Lewis, Anthony, 112
Liberation, 112
Liberation Radio, 25, 108
Life, 78
Lin Piao, 93, 148
Loc Ninh, 59, 124, *142*, *143*, 148
Lockwood, Lee, 78
Lodge, Henry Cabot, 40
Long An Province, 22
Long Bien bridge, *83*
Long Binh, *180*
Long Live the People's War, 93
Lon Nol, 135
Look, 82
Loridan, Marceline, 84, 104
Luu Quy Ky, 88
Lynd, Staughton, 112

M
McCarthy, Mary, 112
Maclear, Michael, 116
McNamara, Robert, 87, 89
MACV, 53, 59, 61
Mai Van Hung, 46, 47
Malinovsky, Rodion, 93
Mao Tse-tung, *93*, 148

"Meeting," *10–11*
Mekong Delta, 41, 164
Miami News, 82
MiG–15, 84, 86
MiG–17, 84
MiG–16, 86
MiG–21, 84, 86
Military High Command, 43
Military Management Committee, 164
Military Region I, 159
Militia, 102, 104, *105*, 106
Minh Tranh, 35, 37
Ministry of Heavy Industry, 87
Ministry of National Defense, 43
Mission to Hanoi, 112
Momyer, General William, 84, 86
Mu Gia Pass, 32, 134
My Chanh River, 148

N
Nam Bo, 16
Nam Dinh, 70, 72, 74, 82, 104, *105*, 112
Nam Ha Province, 102
National Assembly, 167
National Council of National Reconciliation and Concord, 150
National Liberation Front (NLF), 8, 25, 27, 128
Nayan Chanda, 172, 173
Neorevolutionary warfare, 130, 135
Ne Pa Pass, 32
New Economic Zones, 168, 169
New York Times, 82, 87, 131
Nghe Tinh Province, 173
Ngo Dinh Diem, 16–18, 26, 37
Ngo Thi Tuyen, 109
Nguyen Chi Thanh, General, 18, 22, 35, 37, 53, 56
Nguyen Chon, 102
Nguyen Duy Trinh, *23*, 56, 59, 61, 131, 132, 174
Nguyen Hiem, *6*
Nguyen Khac Vien, 165
Nguyen Manh Thuan, 107
Nguyen Minh Ky, 120
Nguyen Thanh Le, 127
Nguyen Thiap Street, *80*, *81*
Nguyen Thi Binh, Madame, 131
Nguyen Thi Kim, 106
Nguyen Tuong Lai, 120
Nguyen Van Bay, 109
Nguyen Van Chu, *12*
Nguyen Van Thieu, 130, 142, 150, 151, 154, 155, 157, 158, 160
Nguyen Van Troi, 109
Nguyen Van Vinh, General, 27, 53, 59, 165, 168
Nhan Dan, 72, 77, 96, 99, 102, 104, 106, 114, 127, *132*, *133*, 146
Nhuc Ho cooperative, 107
"Night March," *6–7*
Ninh Thuan Province, 22
Ninth Plenum, 17, 37, 40, 43, 51, 52, 172
Nixon, Richard, 130, 136, 148–52, 156; Doctrine, 130
NLF (See National Liberation Front)
"Northern–firsters," 23, 35, 40, 55, 56, 61
North Vietnam (See also Democratic Republic of Vietnam), *58*, *59*, 150, *163*, 164, 165, *165*, 171
North Vietnamese, near Saigon, *36*, *37*; cope with wartime, 43, 45, 78, 79, 88, 89; political structure of, *44*, *45*; entertain, *51*; evacuate, 70–73, *73*, 74, *75*, *76*, 77, 78, *79*, *113*; practice civil defense, 74, 77–79, *103*, 104, *105*; women, 88, 99, 104, *105*; corruption among, 99, 101; veterans, 100, *100*; propaganda among, 106–8, *109*, *110*, *111*, 112, *113*; black market among, 114, 115, *115*; at peace talks, 128, *129*; resupply, 130; after Ho Chi Minh's death, 132, *133*; smell victory, 146, 151, *154*, *155*, *165*

O
100MM gun, 84, 135

175MM gun, 141, 148
130MM cannon, 148
130MM field gun, 138, 157
Operation Flaming Dart, 52
Operation Lam Son 719, 136, *137*, 148
Operation Linebacker, 149, 150, *152*, *153*
Operation Masher/White Wing, *57*
Operation Pierce Arrow, 70, 84
Operation Rolling Thunder, 52, 68, 70, 82, 84, 87, 107
Order of Lenin, 175
Ordinance Number 47, 17, 18
Other Side, The, 112

P
Paris peace talks, 127, 150, 151, 154, *154*, 155, *155*
Path of the Revolution in the South, The, 18, 176
PAVN (People's Army of Vietnam), improves equipment, 10, 34, *39*, *42*, *43*, 44, *64*, *65*; in training, 45–48, *66*, *67*, *87*; role in hierarchy, *45*, 48; modernizes, 54, 134, *134*, 135, *135*, 155, 170; attacks, 59, 120, 122, 135, 146, *147*, 148, *149*; during air raid, *69*; veterans, 100, *100*; as troops, 102, *103*, *138*, *139*, *142*, *143*, 144, *144*, *145*, *182*, *183*; starts phase three, 124; in the South, 150, 157, 160, 162, 169; at Ban Me Thuot, 158, *158*; at Hue, 159, *159*; fight Khmer Rouge, 171
Pentagon Papers, 16
People's Army, The, 107
People's Intelligence, 26
People's Liberation Armed Forces (PLAF) (See also Vietcong), 27, *28*, *29*, *41*, *45*, *47*, *60*, *61*, 118, 120, 130, 133, 164
People's Revolutionary Party (PRP), 27
People's War, People's Army, 50
Pham Hung, 16, 18, *23*, 24, 27, 56, 131, 136, 155–57, 160, 174, *175*, 176, *176*, *177*
Pham Van Dinh, Lieutenant Colonel, *140*, 141, *141*
Pham Van Dong, favors the South, 16–18; as leader, *22*, 24; plans, 40, 55, 56, 59, 165, 169, 172; wants negotiation, 61; on bombing, 88; meets with Soviets, *91*, 92, 175, *175*; honors civilians, 109, 131; on strategic thinking, 148; on ending war, 150; favors build-up, 154, 155, *155*, 156; tours, 171; continues contract system, 174
Phang Thang Toan, 116
Phan Van Binh, 114
Phat Diem, 82, *95*; Province, *152*
Phnom Penh, 171
Pho Nguyen Thiep Street, *113*
Phu Cam Cathedral, 120
Phuc Yen airfield, 84
Phu Ly, 82
Phuoc Binh, 157
Phuoc Long, 156, 157
Phu Quoc Island, 169
Phu Xa, 107
Pike, Douglas, 30, 31, 50, 162
PLAF (See People's Liberation Armed Forces)
Pleiku, 157
Podgorny, Nikolai V., 148
Political Bureau, forms, 16, 19; opens trail, 29; sees progress, 34, 35, 40, 51; role in hierarchy, *45*; evacuates cities, 70, 71; shelves industry, 72; influences government, 96; reorganizes, 116, 146, 156, 167, 168, 170; invades Cambodia, 171
Political Directorate, 42, 44
Pol Pot, 171
Poulo Condore, 16
Pravda, 70
Propaganda, 106, 107, 109, *109*, *110*, *111*, 112, 113
Provisional Revolutionary Government (PRG), 131, 154, 160, 162, 164

Q
Quan Doi Nhan Dan, 102, 106
Quang Binh, 79; Province, 107
Quang Ngai Province, 20, 21

Quang Tri City, *149*
Quang Tri Province, 44, *138*, *139*, *141*, *142*, 149, 150, 155, 156

R
Radio Free Asia, 112
Radio Hanoi, 34, 106, 108, *108*, 126, 165
Ramsey, Ronald, 108
Rand Corporation, 32
Red River, *88*, *89*
Red Square, *176*, *177*
Refugees, 169
Region V (Trung Bo), 44, *44*, *45*, 46
Regroupees, 14, *15*, 16, 28, 29, 32, 62
Resistance Will Win, The, 50
Resolution 9, 130
Revolutionary Youth League, 16
Route 4, *182*, *183*
Route 14, 157
Route 9, 46
Route 19, 157
Route 1, *147*, 159
Rusk, Dean, 89
Russell, Bertrand, 82

S
Saigon, *53*, *121*, 122, 124
Salisbury, Harrison, 74, 82, 87, 112, *113*
SAM-2 missile, 84
SA-2 missile, *69*
Schoenbrun, David, 82, 84, 106
Self-criticism, *98*, *99*
Senate Armed Services Committee, 89
Sharp, Admiral Ulysses S. Grant, 87, 89
Sihanouk, Prince Norodom, 135
Sihanouk Trail, 46
Sixth Plenum, 16, 172
Socialist Republic of Vietnam, 167, 169–72
Song Hao, Lieutenant General, 102, 116, 132
Sontag, Susan, 112
Son Tay, 29, 108
Sotan, 74
Southerners, 20, *20*, *21*, 28, *28*, 29
Southern-firsters, 35, 55, 58, 59
Southern Liberation Radio, 150
South Vietnamese, *51*, *125*, 156
Soviet Union, gives aid to the North, 34, 43, *180*, *181*; disputes with China, 40; trains AAA crews, 84, 86, *87*; welcomes North Vietnamese leaders, *91*, *176*, *177*; deepens involvement in the North, 168, 175, 176
Stern, Kurt, 104
Stockdale, Captain James B., 151
Surface-to-air missile (SAM), 84, *84*, *85*, 86, 151

T
Tan Son Nhut, *159*
Tay Ninh City, 157, *180*
Tay Ninh Province, 18, 22
Tchepone, 29
Tet Mau Than, 118, 124, 156
Tet offensive, *60*, *61*, *119*, 120, 124, *125*
T54 tank, *134*, 157, *160*, *161*
Thai Nguyen, 151, *166*, 167
Tham Trong Tao, 73
Thanh Hoa, 29, 70, 72, 78, 79, 100, *108*
Third Party Congress, 20, 22, 25, 28
Thirteenth Plenum, 55, 56
37MM artillery, 92
37MM cannon, 84
Three-man cell, 48
Three-phase plan, 58, 59
Thua Thien Province, *42*, *43*, 44, 134
Thu Huong ("Hanoi Hannah"), 108
Tien Hoan, *155*
Tien Phong, 102
Ton Duc Thang, 131
TOW (tube-launched, optically tracked, wire-

guided) missile, 144
Tran Dang Hoi, 82
Tran Do, General, 27, 122
Tran Duy Hung, 70
Tran Hung Dao Street, *110*, *111*
Tran Nam Trung, 31, *136*
Tran Quoc Hoan, 116
Tran Thi Ve, 109
Tran Van Tra, Lieutenant General, 27, 120, 156, 157, 160, 164, 174
Tri-Thien-Hue (TTH), 44, *44*, *45*, 46, 120
Trung Bo, 17
Truong Chinh, as leader, 18, *22*, 24, 131, 132; on PAVN, 35, 40, 54; agrees with Giap, 59; meets with Soviets, *91*, 175, *175*; on economy, 114, 115, 165, 167; criticizes war, 124, 126, 127, *127*; on offensive, 154, 155, *155*, 156, 157; argues with Giap, 169, 170; retains party seat, 174
Truong Nhu Tang, 26, 27, 122, 131, 136, 156, 164
Truong Son Cemetery, *185*
Truong Son Mountains, *62*, *63*
T34 tank, *134*, *135*
Twelfth Plenum, 53, 55
12.7MM machine gun, *60*, *61*, 84
23MM cannon, 84

U
United States, observes Geneva settlement, 32; commits to the South, 35; soldiers, *57*, *116*, 124; attacks Hanoi, 68, 70, *70*; bombs the North, *64*, *65*, 78, 79, *80*, *81*, 82, *83*, 84, *84*; policy, 130, 131; in Cambodia, 136; disengages, 146, 150
University of Hanoi, 73

V
Van Dien, 68
Van Tien Dung, General, 44, 70, 120, 132, 156, 159, 169, 174, *175*
Varnenska, Monica, 86
Vietcong, 22, 48, *49*, 50, *53*, *121*
Vietminh, 14, *15*, 18
Vietnam, 12, 178
Vietnam Communist party, 168
Vietnamese, *166*, *167*, *170*
Vietnamese Studies, 112
"Vietnamization," 130
Viet Tri, 70, 72
Vinh, 70, *163*
Vinh Linh, 79
Vinh Phuong, Lieutenant Colonel, *140*, 141, *141*
Voice of America, 112
Voice of Vietnam, 112
Vo Nguyen Giap, General, as Northern-firster, *23*, 24, 169; plans strategy, 40, 43, 53, 55, 58, 59, 61, 104, 124; on PAVN, 54; on guerrillas, 56; meets with Soviets, *91*; after Ho Chi Minh's death, 131, 132, 155, *155*, 174, *175*
Vo Thung, 79
Vo Van Den, *184*
Vo Van Kiet, 164, 165, 168, 172, 174
Vu Trong Kinh, 89

W
Walker, Gerald, 108
War Powers Act, 136, 156
Weiss, Cora, 108
Western Highlands Front Command (B-3 Front), 44, *44*, *45*
Westmoreland, General William, 53, 55, 61, 124

XYZ
Xuan Loc, 160
Xuan Mai, 29
Xuan Thuy, 127
Yen Cho farm cooperative, *90*
Yen Vien, 68
Youth Shock Brigade, 106
Zinn, Howard, 112

Names, Acronyms, Terms

AAA—antiaircraft artillery.

ANDPF—Alliance of National, Democratic and Peace Forces. A front organization used to mobilize support among the urban masses. In June 1969, the alliance and the NLF merged to establish the PRG.

ARVN—Army of the Republic of (South) Vietnam.

Binh Tram—PAVN logistical unit responsible for defense and maintenance for a section of the Ho Chi Minh Trail.

Bo doi—uniformed PAVN soldier.

cadre—a full member of the ruling Lao Dong party in North Vietnam, often given supervisory or bureaucratic responsibilities within the party and/or government.

Central Military Party Committee—a subcommittee of the Lao Dong Central Committee that exerted party control over the DRV Ministry of Defense.

CINCPAC—Commander in Chief, Pacific. Commander of American forces in the Pacific, including Southeast Asia.

COMECON—Council for Mutual Economic Assistance; the Soviet bloc joined by Vietnam in 1978.

COSVN—Central Office for South Vietnam. Communist military and political headquarters for southern South Vietnam.

dau tranh—the Communist philosophy and strategy of the "struggle movement," encompassing both struggle against the enemy and with oneself to be a perfect revolutionary. Assumes two forms: *tranh vu trang* (armed struggle) and *dau tranh chinh tri* (political struggle).

DMZ—demilitarized zone. Established by the Geneva accords of 1954, provisionally dividing North Vietnam from South Vietnam along the seventeenth parallel.

Flaming Dart—code name for U.S. and South Vietnamese air strikes against North Vietnam on February 7–8, 1965, in reprisal for VC attacks.

FUNK—Front Uni National du Kampuchea (National United Front of Kampuchea). Popular front established in 1970 and nominally headed by Prince Norodom Sihanouk, dedicated to the overthrow of the Lon Nol government in Phnom Penh. Also known as the Khmer Rouge.

Geneva accords—signed by the French and Vietminh in 1954 ending the French Indochina War, they established a provisional boundary between the Democratic Republic of Vietnam (DRV) and the new Republic of Vietnam.

Hoa—ethnic Chinese population of Vietnam.

Ho Chi Minh Trail—a network of roads and pathways through the jungles and mountains of Laos and Cambodia that served as the principal PAVN infiltration route of men and materiel into South Vietnam.

ICP—Indochinese Communist party. Founded by Ho Chi Minh in 1930. Replaced the Vietnam Communist party.

Khmer Rouge—originally members of the Pracheachon, the Cambodian leftist party. Named "Khmers Rouges" by Sihanouk to distinguish them from the right-wing "blues."

Khoi Nghia—"General Uprising," the theoretical climax of *dau tranh*. Predicts the final liberation of the cities through an uprising of the population.

Lao Dong party—Vietnam Workers' party (Marxist-Leninist party of North Vietnam), founded by Ho Chi Minh in May 1951. Absorbed the Vietminh and was the ruling party of the DRV.

Linebacker I—code name for U.S. bombing of North Vietnam resumed in April 1972 in response to the Easter offensive.

Linebacker II—code name for the so-called Christmas bombing of North Vietnam in December 1972.

MAAG—Military Assistance Advisory Group. U.S. military advisory program to South Vietnam beginning in 1955.

MACV—Military Assistance Command (South), Vietnam. U.S. command over all U.S. military activities in Vietnam, originated in 1962.

MiG—Soviet-designed fighter aircraft developed by Mikoyan and Gurevich.

Military Management Committee—military-political supervisory group established by Hanoi after the victory in 1975 to take charge of the Saigon region.

Military Region (MR)—the Communist geographic division of Vietnam. MRs 1–4 lay entirely in the DRV. MR Tri-Thien-Hue (TTH) included the two northernmost provinces of the GVN. The B-3 Front contained the western highlands, while MR 5 encompassed several coastal provinces. COSVN commanded the entire southern region of South Vietnam.

NCNRC—National Council of National Reconciliation and Concord. Charged by the Paris peace accords to organize general and local elections for a new South Vietnamese government. Composed of the two combatants and a mutually agreeable "third force."

NEZs—New Economic Zones. Agricultural areas and jungle lands that Vietnam hoped after 1975 to recover and cultivate.

NLF—National Liberation Front. Officially the National Front for the Liberation of the South. Formed on December 20, 1960, it aimed to overthrow South Vietnam's government and reunite North and South Vietnam. The NLF included Communists and non-Communists.

NVA—U.S. designation for North Vietnamese Army. Officially PAVN (People's Army of Vietnam).

Paris agreement—Agreement on Ending the War and Restoring Peace in Vietnam, signed in Paris on January 27, 1973.

Party Congress—officially the highest authority in the Lao Dong party in which delegates decide the basic party line and doctrine. In practice the decision-making powers reside in the Central Committee and its Political Bureau.

Pathet Lao—Laotian Communist forces under the leadership of Prince Souphanouvang.

PAVN—People's Army of Vietnam. Originally the armed forces of the DRV, later of the SRV.

piaster—South Vietnamese unit of currency.

Pierce Arrow—code name for U.S. air strikes against North Vietnam in August 1964 in retaliation for alleged attacks on U.S. vessels in the Gulf of Tonkin.

PLAF—People's Liberation Armed Forces. The military arm of the NLF. Also known as "VC."

plenum—meeting of the Lao Dong party's Central Committee. Numbered consecutively, starting over with each party Congress.

Political Bureau (Politburo)—executive committee of the Central Committee and hence the ruling body of the Communist party.

PRG—Provisional Revolutionary Government. The government established by the NLF in June 1969.

PRP—People's Revolutionary party. Communist party that dominated the NLF. Founded on January 15, 1962, it was the nominally independent southern branch of the Lao Dong party in South Vietnam.

regroupees—the approximately 87,000 Vietminh soldiers who went from South to North Vietnam in 1954, as mandated by the Geneva accords.

Revolutionary Youth League—first Communist organization in Vietnam, founded in June 1925 by Ho Chi Minh.

Rolling Thunder—code name for U.S. air campaign against North Vietnam conducted from March 2, 1965, to October 31, 1968.

RVNAF—Republic of (South) Vietnam Armed Forces.

SAM—surface-to-air missile.

sapper—PAVN/PLAF commando who penetrated allied defenses.

SRV—Socialist Republic of Vietnam. Name given to reunified Vietnam by the National Assembly in 1976.

van—the "action program" of *dau tranh chinh tri* (political struggle): *dan van* (action among the people), *binh van* (action among the military), and *dich van* (action among the enemy).

VC—Vietcong. Originally derogatory slang for the NLF; a contraction of Vietnam Cong San (Vietnamese Communist).

VCP—Vietnamese Communist party. Founded by Ho Chi Minh in 1930. The Fourth Party Congress in 1976 adopted the name as a tribute to Ho Chi Minh.

Vietminh—coalition founded by Ho Chi Minh in 1941. Absorbed by the Lao Dong party in 1951.